T0146634

BLUE BLOODS

The Missing Twins (Race Relations during the Depression)

(This story is about what racism was like during the depression years.)

FANNIE ADAMS; ROLLAND TAYLOR

authorHOUSE®

AuthorHouse™
1663 Liberty Drive
Bloomington, IN 47403
www.authorhouse.com
Phone: 1 (800) 839-8640

Published by AuthorHouse 08/28/2017

ISBN: 978-1-5462-0517-3 (sc)
ISBN: 978-1-5462-0516-6 (hc)
ISBN: 978-1-5462-0515-9 (e)

Library of Congress Control Number: 2017912881

Print information available on the last page.

CHAPTER I

World War I was over and it was Armistice Day and the town hall of Novenger was ablaze with color and was alive with music. The community had gathered to honor its heroes of World War I.

Lieutenant John Barke had arrived home from France the night before. He was tall, dark, lean, handsome, and very distinguished looking, so thought the women. As he entered the hall every female eye there focused upon him in open admiration. That is, all except one very interesting pair of eyes.

The efforts of the ladies were lost on him. Lieutenant Blake saw only the girl swinging the baton. Turning eagerly to his parents he asked in an undertone, "Who is she?" Can't seem to place her. The army boasts of its band leaders but that kid beats them a mile."

"Kid!" snorted his father. "She gave her age as twenty in the application."

John's mother hastened to say, "That's our new high school teacher, Lucy Travis."

"From down in Alabama," added his father laconically.

"Son, you should hear her play the piano," explained his mother. "Everybody wants to take lessons, particularly the young men."

Lucy Travis did make a delightful picture in her blue-and-gold band suit, with her tiny cap perched saucily over her golden curls. Her violet blue eyes dance and her cheeks were pink with excitement. Actually she made everybody there think of a fairy queen as her lithe body swayed to the rhythm of the baton.

John Barke's brown eyes scarcely left the teacher' face, but Miss Travis was too absorbed in her music to notice his attention. Neither did she seem aware of the adoring eyes of the scores of other young men. She was more interested in music than men. However, the young office did maneuver to meet her before the evening was over.

Even the high school boys noticed John's attention to their teacher, for must of the older ones were secretly in love with her themselves. "Look at John Barke, old J.B.'son!" said one of the boys.

"Yeah, he's fallin' hard for Miss Lucy. Can't keep his eye offin her," said another. "He's so tall and big, she barely comes to his shoulders," he added enviously. "Wonder if she knows his dad owns this town?"

Late that night after Lucy Travis returned from her evening with John Barke to her room with Miss Troop, the old fashioned English teacher. Miss Troop said with a smile, "Lucy, you look as if you have seen visions of the celestial world."

The girl blushed prettily and asked, "Mary, is it wicked to be so happy?"

"No darling. John Barke is charming enough to turn any girl's head. Such a figure! And that head of wavy black hair is enough to drive any woman crazy. . . and let me tell you, few soldiers have such a record for bravery as he. And last, but not least, his dad is the richest man in the state; but let me warn you, old J.B. Barke is the meanest. However until tonight, no girl has ever succeeded in getting a second look from John, although plenty have tried their best."

It was a whirlwind courtship. John took Lucy to school each morning in his new Cadillac. Every afternoon his car was waiting in front of the high school, no matter if she were ready to leave at four or at six. Then they often took long drives into the country.

Although Lucy had gone through college her heart remained untouched.

This was her first love. Strange to say, not one person in the community much as hinted that she might be attracted by the Barke millions. They knew she was not that kind of girl.

Then one day John walked into his father's bank, determination stamped on his face. The Citizens' Bank of Novinger was actually owned and operated by J. B. Barke, for he not only owned the controlling interest but most of the stock.

Without hesitation or preliminaries John began, "Dad, Lucy Travis and I love each other and plan to be married Christmas Day. I wanted you to be the first to know."

The old banker looked like a keg of gunpowder ready to explode as he demanded, his face a florid red, "John Lieuelen Barke, have you gone start mad? You never so much as heard of this Travis woman until six weeks ago. What to you know about her background? You don' know one thing about her family or who they may be."

John squared his broad shoulders. "I know that Lucy is the sweetest girl ever created. True I do not know her family but I'm marrying her, not her family. This I do know, her family could be only the very best old Alabama could produce."

The tiny muscle on the banker's left jaw stood out like a cord. "John," he thundered, "to my knowledge you have scarcely looked twice at the same girl in all you twenty-five years. I don't believe you even had your adolescent puppy loves. Now after five years of distinguished service for Uncle Sam, you let an unknown chit of a girl bowel you over."

John strove for self-control, speaking calmly but with decision. "Father, I'm no longer a child. I know what I want. It would grieve me deeply should you and mother not consent to our marriage. I'd hoped to have you accept and love Lucy as a daughter. But remember this, no power on earth can prevent me from marrying her."

When he sank into his chair a smile played bout his fully, sensuous lips, lips that could be so hard and cruel. "My dear son," he began in a tone John had never remembered hearing from him before, "please wait until next June to marry, Lucy Travis is a lovely girl and it is not difficult to understand why you became infatuated with her.

"But can't you see the school needs her services? Teachers are very difficult to secure these days, especially instructors with her musical abilities. Without doubt you never would consent to your wife teaching. John, for my sake won't you wait until school closes? Remember I am president of the school board."

John as an officer was used to reading faces. He looked curiously at his father, his own countenance showing no indication of relenting. He studied his father's dark eyes so much like his, yet very, very different, trying to read the face that suddenly became gentle. Why should his father oppose his marriage? Surely he had waited long enough to choose a mate. Why should he suspicion Lucy Travis?

3

The bank president was fighting for time, feeling sure that his son would tire of his craze to this new girl. So he said, "Visit the girl and her parents at the holidays, in her Alabama home if you like. Maybe her family will measure to the blue bloods of our family. Remember, the Barnes are French and can trace their lineage back for two-hundred years.

The young lieutenant sat in defiant silence. He had heard this boast of family blood all his life; it meant so little. In the trenches peasant and nobleman died alike. "No use talking, dad. My mind is made up."

"John, if you rush into this marriage without taking time to give it due consideration, you shall reap the consequences!" blustered the banker, his large course features livid with rage.

"Cut me off! Disinherit me! Kick me out! Do what you will, I have two strong hands. Nothing can prevent me from marrying Lucy Travis."

J. B. Barke had brains, otherwise he never could have become a millionaire and a ruler of a small town. Seeing he could not bully his son he said, "John, you know it would break your mother's heart if you left home. Be reasonable for her sake. Go visit Lucy and her family as I suggested, and," he knew his son's possible vulnerable spot, "upon your return the first of January, you may come into the bank as cashier."

His father had played his trump and no one knew it better than the man himself. From childhood John's one dream had been to become cashier of the Citizens Bank. Since he could remember he had played bank, always he was the cashier. Only his father could make this possible. He was a dictator in his own rights.

This hit John right between the eyes, just as his father aimed it should. Now it was the young man's turn to stalk up and down the room, his handsome face set. His hands clinched. Finally with reluctance he managed to say, his voice hoarse with suppressed emotion, "You win, Dad."

A few days before Christmas, John and Lucy, and the old fashioned English teacher, Mary Troop, were on their way to sunny Alabama in John's Cadillac. The plain little teacher, Mary Troop, had been taken along to prevent the merry tongues from wagging.

Since the Barkes had moved to Novinger and J. B. had taken over the bank as president, the village of Novinger lived and moved and had its being at the crack of the whip of the burly banker. Secretly the people of the small town had dubbed him the Czar. He dominated village Council meetings, indicating who or who should not serve or do this or that. He practically appointed the Mayor, the school teachers, and dictated to the church pastor.

One time a certain man lifted a voice in protest against such blatant tyranny. In less that no time foreclosure proceedings were started on his farm for the bank held the mortgage. That was the first year the Barkes lived in Novinger. The town learned its lesson. Ever after that the community fawned upon the man who owned them and their bank and bowed to his slightest wish. Their town was in a depression and many depended upon bank notes.

The bankers wife was a drab, timid little creature, realizing her soul was not her own. The villagers loved and pitied her, yet seldom did any one have the courage to cross the threshold of her door for fear of meeting her lord and master.

John was her only living child, the one bright spot in her unhappy life. She admired Lucy Travis and believed her son was making a wise choice. Since her husband never took her into his confidence or discussed family affairs with her she was ignorant of the conversation that had taken place in the bank between her two men.

After John left the bank its president pondered the question of his son's marriage to the music teach from down South. "No telling what this slip of a girl may do to upset the well-regulated life of the Barke family," he growled to himself. "Who knows who or what her folks may be. Plenty of poor white trash down there. But by June John should have come to his senses. Should he not, I'll think of something to prevent this marriage."

On Christmas Day Lucy became Mrs. John Barke. It was a pretty wedding, held only in the humble cottage of her parents at Creston, Alabama. Just Mary Troop and the parents witnessed the ceremony. Lucy had reminded her handsome lover of his promise to his father.

But he only answered gaily, "I know, darling. You see I had no power to do otherwise. Why should we wait until June? Haven't I waited for you all my life? It used to worry me because girls never interested me; guess that is what spoiled dad. Maybe he thought I never would marry. But the night I walked into that hall and saw you twirling that baton, I knew why. You and you alone were the one for me."

Jacob and Mrs. Travis were too overcome by the elegance of the Cadillac and the dignity of the tall lieutenant to whisper even one word of protest against their daughter's hasty marriage. However, it would have done little good had they done so, John was determined and Lucy had no will of her own in this case.

John was in high spirits saying, "Now that we are married dad is sure to give in. Until he refused to consent to our marriage never in all my life has he denied me anything." He lost no time in sending his parents a telegram as soon as the ceremony was over. Then they started on their honeymoon.

Mary Troop boarded the train for the North, promising to find a teacher to fill Lucy's place in the Novinger school and if necessary to beard the lion in his den in their behalf. But she warned them, "John you better give you dad time to cool off. Maybe before long he will answer your wire and invite you home."

After their honeymoon a week later, John was not really surprised or worried because his father had not answered. "Dad is sure to let me sweat awhile," he said laughingly.

A month passed and no word came. Getting uneasy, John wrote Mary Troop who replied, "Your father did everything but thrown me out of this office the minute I mentioned your name. He seems to imagine I was in the plot. I dare not contact your mother."

On the honeymoon John's roll of bills had vanished like hoarfrost in a noon-day sun. Neither had he and Jacob Travis been successful in trying to land any kind of work for him. In the past he had written checks on his father' account at will, for this had been a family understanding. He dare not use this privilege now in his great need.

Lucy begged to shoulder her share of this burden. "John music instructors are needed everywhere," she urged. "I would be performing a patriotic duty to help out in this national emergency. And surely, darling, it is our emergency as well. I need not teach except for the remainder of this year-"

"Never!" John declared hotly. "No wife of mine will support me."

When the second month dragged to an end they had nearly despaired of ever hearing from John's father. Then to their great relief and joy a telegram arrived from his mother. Of course the old Czar would not humble himself to send it. "Come home your father has forgiven you."

CHAPTER II

One blissful year passed with Mr. and Mrs. John Barke heading the social life at the small community. Because everybody feared and hated J. B. Barke, the town had formed the habit of leaving the family entirely alone as much as they dared. But now since Lucy was loved by everyone, for her sake the villagers welcomed John to their inner circle.

Lucy and her musical talent were sought for on all occasions. She not only played at church services, but school programs still included her. She was invited everywhere for her own charming self, as well as for her music.

John was not unaware of the feeling against his father and that he and his mother were both avoided as well as the banker. Being of an independent nature, this had not bothered him too much. But now it made him very happy and proud that his lovely wife was a favorite in the community and that he was accepted for her sake. Mother Blake loved Lucy like a daughter, while the old man treated just as gruffly as he did his own wife and the rest of the world. No one was sure whether he loved or hated his son's wife.

Since John was her idol Mrs. Barke looked forward to the expected heir with great pride. She talked about it to all her friends and wrote to her neighbors in James town where they had lived before moving to Novinger. The approaching event was ever in her mind and conversation.

Dainty garments began to arrive from her many friends, both in the village and from Jamestown. Lucy's friends and relatives from Alabama sent their gifts as well. The pretty cottage that J. B. Barke had given them upon their return from the South was overflowing with baby things.

It seems to be the nature of some folks never to like to see other folks happy. Old J.B. Barke was one of those, so now he just couldn't stand it to see so much joy spread around his home. "Mother," he roared, "from the way you carry on one might think this is the first child ever to be born. You mind me of a fussy old hen with but one chick."

Still he could not completely squelch her, for she replied, "Father, it still grieves me for our little Jerry, even if I never did get to see his baby face." She dried her eyes on the corner of her white apron. "Lucy's child shall take the place of my lost baby. If it is a boy, can't we name him Jerry?"

The man's face went white and his hand shook. "Don't say such a thing! Of course I never could bear to give another child that name, and you know it." Mrs. Barke had not realized her husband's grief had been so deep.

Jerry had been born two years after John's birth. Mrs. Barke had been too ill at the time to know or see her little son. All she knew was the small mound in the Barke lot in the Jamestown cemetery. A small slab marked the place. All it said was "Jerry." It had seemed so strange that her husband had never wanted to talk about his death and objected when she mentioned his name. But that had been so long ago, twenty-four years ago.

But in some ways the old banker showed a kind spirit, like he told them all that his new grandchild must be born at his mansion, not in a public hospital. Folks called it queer ideas when they heard it. "Too many risks in maternity hospitals," he insisted. "Could lose your baby, nurses are careless and could exchange children."

For proof he displayed a number of newspaper clippings. Both Jerry and John had been born under the paternal roof. "All my grandchildren are to be born in my home. Doc and mother can look after everything." This did not prove a hardship on either the patient or the physician and nurse, since his mansion was well equipped for just such care.

Neither John nor Lucy objected, for perhaps every young couple have a lurking fear that their child might be exchanged for one not their own if they went to the hospital. They would surely rest easier if they had such an efficient doctor as did the Barkes to look after their family. Of course the neighbors merely chuckled saying, "High folks can have all the strange ideas they like, even if the rest of us can't," and they did admit the Barkes might have a point anyway.

The day approached and Lucy was moved to the big house on the hill. Dr. Cunningham and his two nurses were to fly in to the Barke house at the first tinkle of the telephone. Dr. Cunningham still lived and practiced in Jamestown where the Barkes had formerly lived. However, the Barke family were still his prime interest.

He had been the family physician since before J. B. married. He knew the family with all its virtues and failings. He was as much the family advisor as he was the family doctor; although he would have scorned the idea that he was even a distant cousin to a psychiatrist.

While the villagers had smiled at the banker's queer ideas and trembled at his viciousness, they fluttered with excitement and awe when they saw the doctor's private plane zoom overhead and purr to a landing upon the Barke premises.

The women of the small town gathered in small groups and waited. To be sure, not one of the neighbors was invited to assist at this great event. No indeed!

John anxious and fearful, sat huddled in his chair in the living room. As time passed, he paced the floor up and down the hall, his face ashen gray. Old J. B. Barke growled and stalked about like a huge polar bear.

Who would have thought the gruff, hard-headed old banker would have been so concerned about the approach of his first grandson? Was he reliving the birth and loss of his own little Jerry of so man years before? Men have strange ways of showing grief, it is said.

Mother Barke fluttered here and there trying to be everywhere at once much to the disgust of Rose Garner, the smug professional in white uniform who was substituting for the doctor's regular nurse that had married and left him not long before.

Lulu Simpson, his faithful office nurse, had been with him for many years. So after long waiting, she opened the bedroom door wide enough to put her head out and announced with an important air, "It's a girl," and disappeared.

John walking the hall rushed to the door, only to see it close firmly in his face. "Miss Simpson, Lulu wait!" he called when he found the door wouldn't open. "Tell me, Lulu, is Lucy all right?" He pushed with all his might to open the door.

He did succeed in pushing it open a little, but a white uniform blocked his way. "No, no, Mr. Barke, you can't come in now," said Rose Garner officiously.

John thrust aside the insolent nurse and hurried to his wife's side, dropping down on his knees beside the bed. Lucy's eyes were closed, her face bloodless. "Darling, speak to me" he said softly. He took her delicate hand in his and pressed his cheek against the cold fingers.

Rushing to the side of the physician he whispered hoarsely, "Doc, can't you do something? Is she dead?"

"John, be a man," commanded the doctor sternly. "Lucy is not dead, but she is a very sick girl. We are doing all in human power to help her."

"Want to see your little daughter, Mr. Barke?" asked Miss Garner, holding up the child for his inspection. "The very image of her mother-see those golden ringlets, Mr. Barke?"

Almost by force, Dr. Cunningham and the banker led John from his wife's room. After the door was closed on the men, Rose Garner whispered to Lulu Simpson, "Wouldn't life be worth living to have the love of such a man as John Barke? He simply worships his wife."

"Any man would worship Lucy," replied the older nurse. "Doesn't she look just like a beautiful angel lying there so still and white?"

Hours passed. The morning sun peered in through the closed shutters. John waked the floor or sat in mute silence, suffering as only a new father can. When the maid called breakfast neither her nor the doctor tasted a bite of food, while mother Barke lay huddled on the couch a bottle of smelling salts in her hand, declaring the thought of food made her ill.

Strange to say, the bank did not open for neither John nor his father wanted to leave the house where Lucy still lay so near death's door. After their return from Alabama, John was very happy to go into the bank with his father, not as cashier as he once anticipated but as teller.

Time passed, every minute, each ticking of the great clock on the wall, sounding to John like the tolling of the death knell of his beloved wife.

At noon, Miss Simpson cautiously signaled J. B. Barke who followed her to the dining room. John sprang to his feet, but she motioned him back. The doctor went to the dining room and the door closed. Mother bark began to cry while John forced the door open.

"What is this?" he demanded indignantly. "Lucy is my wife-I will not be left in the dark! Is she dead?" Meeting only a startled silence he rushed to Lucy's room. Rose Garner barred the door but John seized her wrists and savagely pushed her out of the door.

He failed to see the scornful smile that wreathed the carmine lips of the young nurse. His eyes sought only his suffering wife who lay staring at him from a face so stricken he scarcely recognized it.

"Lucy," he groaned kneeling beside the bed, "don't you know me? I'm John, your husband. Whisper my name dear." He smothered with kisses the white hand that lay on the bed, while she only stared with wide eyes.

Rose Garner fluttered over the kneeling man. "Mr. Barke," she whispered in honeyed tones, "don't you want to see your other twin?" She indicated the far side of the bed where she turned back the covers.

John got to his feet and glanced at the two bundles. With a thud he fell back against the closet door. Lucy gave a weak despairing cry, while Rose rushed out for help.

Again John was led from the room. He and Doctor Cunningham followed J. B. to his private office and the key was turned in the door. The banker's white faced matched that of his son's.

John was the the first to speak. "Father, Doc, what does it mean? Am I under some delusion, having a horrible dream?"

Dr. Cunningham averted his eyes. The bank president sat with his chin dropped on his chest.

"Answer me!" thundered young Barke. "Why this silence, this mystery?" he demanded, looking from one to the other.

The graying doctor groaned aloud. "John, I wish it were only a dream!"

He stopped, unable to go on. Finally he spoke in a hoarse whisper, it was just as if he had been rehearsing his words. "Son, I brought you into this world and have looked after you ever since. You are like my very own." He cleared his throat, then stopped.

Indignantly John said, "Doc, stop avoiding the question. What is the reason for all this?"

With a great effort the physician spoke. "John, your wife has twins. One is white-and-the-other-is-a-mulatto."

"But how can this be?" asked the horrified man.

"You are no doubt assured of your wife's chastity but do you know her family, her background? In the South as well as in the North, the races do mix-"

"Can't you see that it is impossible, for Lucy is a perfect blond-a type of a true Caucasian. True her parents are brunette, still they are no darker skinned than dad and me-"

Old J. B. Barke interrupted. "John, you know the Barkes are French," he spoke in terse clipped tones. "I warned you against your hasty marriage. I begged, I implored you to take time to learn her background. Now you see? It is never safe to jump into marriage with just any one."

"Yes, father, I know. Yet how can Lucy have tainted blood-such a beautiful girl!" His words ended with a sob.

The doctor was quick to explain. "Many people carry Negro blood and are unaware of it. Some may know that they have tainted blood, are part Negro, but keep it secret, hoping and often succeeding, in passing themselves off as white. Their secret may die with them, unless it shows up in their descendants." He stopped and stared at the young man before him.

The doctor continued, "John, in appearance, the little daughter, like Lucy is a perfect Caucasian, yet her child may show Negro traits. On the other hand should you son marry a white girl, their children might have little of the characteristics of the colored race. However, it is a common saying that because the Negro is a dominant race it can show traits down toe the fortieth generation."

Angrily the old Czar interrupted with, "Doc, stop this falderal and get down to business!"

The physician cleared his throat meekly and asked, "John, the question is not why your wife had colored blood but what are you going to do about it?" John jumped from his chair and began pacing the floor. "I don't know. I can't think. Let me out of here. I must escape this house of horrors!"

The great white house with its closed shutters was shrouded in mystery. The village waited and watched. While there was neither sight nor sign of the doctor and his nurses, yet his plane rested conspicuously on the Barke estate.

Folks sat up with a start as the young officer drove down the street and madly down the river road. Many hours later he came tearing back. He entered the home of his father with its closed shutters and silence and bolted the door.

"John is taking it hard," murmured Lulu Simpson softly, filled with pity for both him and Lucy. "But the problem may solve itself soon, for with him never coming near her she may fade out of the picture just any time."

Rose Garner giggled heartlessly and replied, "Well, if Lucy does succumb to the shock, I'm ready and willing to console the heart-broken husband."

Lulu Simpson, the doctor's faithful nurse, shot her a look she hoped might kill her dead.

After giving mother Barke one peep at her new granddaughter, Dr. Cunningham ordered the woman to bed saying, Mrs. Bark, you have worried yourself sick. You must now get some sleep." Then Miss Simpson gave her a shot in the arm to relax her nerves, she told her.

"She must not know of Lucy's other twin now," said old J.B. It might the said of him that if he had one soft spot in his hard old heart it was his wife. "The disgrace would send her to her grave."

The third day arrived. The bank had been closed all this time, while the mansion was still shrouded in mystery. Finally John came down stairs looking as if he had just escaped from a concentration camp in Germany. He ate for the first time, but only to gulp a cup of black coffee and a tiny roll.

Again the three men were closeted behind bolted doors. John managed to ask, "How is she? Will-will she live? And-and the other twin is he going to survive?" His voice was hoarse, scarcely above a whisper.

The family physician replied, "The twins are husky, particularly the boy. Lucy is doing as well as can be expected under this mental strain. John, unless it is ended soon it may break her."

"Has she-" John cleared his throat. "Does- does she ask for, that is, has she called for me?"

Answered the doctor, "No. She just lies there. She says nothing, merely lies there and waits and listens. Eats almost nothing and sleeps only under a powerful sedative. I fear two things-"

"Meaning?" John asked fearfully. For once in his life the old Czar sank in the background and for the moment was seemingly forgotten.

"Suicide or the loss of reason. She can't endure this strain much longer. It's up to you my boy. Face the issue like a soldier."

"What can I do?"

Old man Bark sat staring at his son while the doctor replied. "Go on living with Lucy and bring up a family, part white, part black-"

His father dropped his head on the massive oak desk and gave a suppressed groan.

Dr. Cunningham sat looking at the banker and continued. "Neither your father nor your mother could survive the shock of such a disgrace. You could give Lucy and the boy a large sum of money which your father would willingly provide and dispose of her by divorce."

Here the banker interrupted to say, "Still the world would know our disgrace-this your mother could never, never endure. It would kill her outright, son."

"Another solution," continued the doctor in a slow even tone, "is to report that Lucy died in childbirth." He refused to see the horror in the young man's face, but went on grimly to say, "Endow her magnificently and send her and the other twin to her parents in Alabama."

John buried his head in his hands, while great sobs shook his stalwart frame. The doctor continued. "Only the nurses know the facts, besides us. Nurses are sworn to secrecy by the nurses' oath. Lulu would never tell anyway. Rose is different, but even she should not break her oath or violate the sacred nurses' code. Too bad she had to be on this case."

The dark shutters of the white house on the hill remained closed. Crepe hung on the door of the bank as well as the doors of the two Barke houses. The citizens of Novinger not only grieved, they felt cheated-they adored any and every funeral. A Barke funeral would have been an event to talk about for years to come.

"Maybe it is natural for services to be held in Jamestown," they complained, "but why a private service? We could all have gone to Jamestown. We loved Lucy. Such stuck-up ideas of rich folks."

What disgusted them most was that a notice in the Novinger newspaper requested there be no floral offerings. "Why did the old Czar have to be so mean?" they said.

The village watched and mourned as the Jamestown's big gray hearse drove solemnly out of the banker's broad driveway. The Barke's lovely limousine slowly followed down the road, clothed in mourning, shrouded in mystery.

What the town did not know was that ten days after the birth of the twins, a plane left their community at midnight. It carried Lucy and the other twin, the boy they had never seen nor heard of. Dr. Cunningham had been commissioned to fly to the South-land to take John's wife and the other child to her parents. Lulu Simpson had bent sent back to Jamestown to care for the office, while Rose remained at the Barke home to care for baby Jeanette.

Immediately after the funeral, John had moved his personal belongings from the bungalow where he and Lucy had spent their few blissful days. He was positive he never wanted to step inside the house again, although he left everything just as it had been when he had moved Lucy to his father' home. He closed the shutters and turned the key in the door.

Mother Barke was delighted to have her son with her, and especially to have Jeanette. To her, the baby girl was her long-lost Jerry, for who she still shed tears.

The villagers eyed the old banker in surprise. It seemed strange to see him grief stricken, deciding maybe the old Czar had a heart after all. Yet he returned to the bank gruffer than ever.

John was a mere shadow of his former self. Except in the bank he spoke to no one, not seeming to see the person he met on the street face to face. Instead he stared straight before him as if in a trance.

He was in a constant debate with himself. Wondering if he had done the right thing in permitting his father to send Lucy and the other twin away. This question beat upon his brain night and day.

"She was but the victim of circumstances; maybe some racial fanatic had married a Negro merely to prove his theory." He was positive she did not know she carried Negro blood. His great worry was because he had sent her away without even one comforting word. He wondered how he could have been so cruel, so heartless.

He slept little. When he did, he was tormented by hideous dreams. Once he awoke wet with perspiration, thinking Lucy was by his side but she was a Negress. The dream was so real he snapped on the light to assure himself. Yet he simply couldn't escape the horrible feeling.

"Of course she is a Negro, even if she does not show it," he whispered to himself. "No, no, I never could have gone on living with her. Her very touch would have repelled me. When I saw that other twin, I actually recoiled from Lucy."

CHAPTER III

And how were Lucy and the other Twin faring? J. B. Barke had ordered Dr. Cunningham to take them direct to her parents at Creston, Alabama and he took it for granted his instruction had been carried out.

Up to this time Lucy had been very docile, permitting folks to push her around as they saw fit. But she was becoming physically stronger every day and able to think more clearly, gradually recovering from the shock the events had put upon her.

En-route to Alabama she said to the doctor, "I will not go home now. Mother and father have not been told of the birth of the Twins nor of our coming. The shock of such news would be beyond endurance, so drop me off at Lawton, Alabama, it is only a hundred miles from home. From there I can write my parents and prepare them for our coming."

Against his better judgment, the doctor complied with her request. Lucy registered in a plain, but seemingly respectable little hotel in Lawton. She told the doctor it would be less conspicuous to choose an insignificant place.

In her room, his voice husky, he had said, "My girl, don't blame me too much for this trouble. You must understand I'm acting under orders for the Barke family, who feel that they are doing what seems best for all concerned."

Laying the infant on the bed she replied hastily, "Yes, yes, I know."

"Lucy, you understand you understand your part of this plan, don't you?"

"Yes," she replied with a firm voice, "I'm to assume the name of Anna Travis. You saw me register that way downstairs. Lucy Barke is peacefully lying in her casket in the Jamestown cemetery. In six months John goes to some distant state and obtains a divorce from me on desertion grounds-just in case his wife decides not to stay in her burial place-so you tell me. But my honest belief is he wants the divorce to he can marry again."

"It would surprise me if John every seeks another wife, yet that is beside the question now. But the money, you still refuse to accept it?" he asked, a frown of worry between his beastly brows. "Child, you will need that money to raise your child."

"Money can never cover my disgrace nor give me back my self respect. Money can never repay the heart aches, neither can it give me back my little Jeanette nor my husband's love. Keep your money!"

"Lucy, you are not strong enough to work, and your parents-they-are-not-rich-"

She finally agreed to take only sufficient money to keep her until she was strong enough to work again. Then he drew from his brief case some very official-looking documents. "But-but you will sign the papers?" he asked.

Without a moment's hesitation Lucy signed away all claims to the John Barke estate of millions of dollars. Also, a statement that she would never again use her real name nor divulge the secret pact, neither would she willingly cross her husband's path or in any way lay claim to her daughter.

The doctor put the document back in his case and arose to leave. Lucy, it tears my heart to seem to be deserting you in your great need. I would feel so much better if you were safe with your parents, and I would not think of leaving you now but I'm already late to an important medical convention in Boston. This convention means much to me.

The old doctor bade the girl goodbye and pointed his plane toward New England. Upon his arrival at his destination he sent a short report of his Alabama trip to J. B. Barke. He did not, however, see the necessity of mentioning the fact that Lucy had not gone directly to the home of her parents. He did state that she had refused the money, except a pittance.

The great president of the Citizen's Bank of Novinger drew a check in five figures to Anna Travis and mailed it to her home at Creston, Alabama. He wanted the disagreeable matter settled once and for all time. He imagined that money was the panacea for all human ills.

His generous check did not settle the case, for before many days the letter came back marked, "Unclaimed. No such name in the directory ever heard of."

Strange to say, by the very same mail came a letter for John from Mrs. Travis. As usual old J. B. was the first to see the incoming mail. So he ripped open the envelope, saying to himself that it was no use to upset his son more than he already was. The letter read, "John why don't you write. I've written and written but no answer. Has the baby arrived? Is Lucy all right? Please answer by return mail. We are very worried."

The banker returned the letter to the envelope and placed it with its companions in the secret drawer of his desk and turned the key. Immediately he sent for the doctor, who lost no time obeying the summons, wondering just what the trouble might be, yet fearing the matters had gone wrong with Lucy and the baby.

J. B. Barke never minced words. So now he roared, "Doc, what in under the light of the moon have you done with Lucy and her kid?" Although he handed him the letter addressed to John and the one returned to him he gave not time to read them. "Did you make way with them? Although that's exactly what I'd like to do, it is entirely too dangerous."

"Of course I wouldn't do such a wicked thing!" began the doctor.

The banker's course lips curled in scorn. "Then you took them to Boston with you-just like your soft heart to let her wheedle you into permitting her to lose herself in that city in order to hide her disgrace."

The doctor had to give the facts. "I left Lucy and the infant in Lawton, Alabama, only a hundred miles from home at Creston. She simply refused to go on until she had first written them she was on the way. She insisted the shock would be too much for them if she went home without writing first. I didn't want to leave her in Lawton, but never dreamed she wouldn't go on in a few days."

"Fool! You said yourself the girl was sick with grief and not capable of being left alone, that you feared insanity or suicide. It's not that I care what happens to her and the brat but what they can do to us, the Barkes and you!"

"I'm indeed sorry, J. B. Yet you need not fear that Jacob Travis will make trouble. From John's report, they are just kind, simple, sort of back-woodsy, country folks."

"Yeah, yeah, I know. But, Doc, where can they be?"

"No doubt she is trying to work, probably still right in the small town, where I dropped her. It won't be difficult to find her in such a place. I'll fly there at once and compel her to go home to her parents."

John had not been surprised to see their family physician, supposing he had come to check his mother's heart or look over little Jeanette again. Every since he could remember, Dr. Cunningham had come and gone in the Barke family like one of its members. However, this visit did bring up all the pain and suffering to his mind of Lucy trouble and her midnight flight.

At the present time the one bright spot in John's dreary life was his golden-haired daughter. He was finally becoming used to her nurse, for she seemed very thoughtful. Every time he came into the house she hurried to bring him the baby.

He didn't deny he had loathed the nurse at first but she had changed this opinion by showing such devotion and fondness for the child. He couldn't help from appreciating her kind, gentle method of handling the infant. And the more he saw Jeanette, the oftener he though of Lucy, for the child was the very image of her mother.

Now just to ally suspicion, Dr. Cunningham made a pretense of examine the baby. To John's delight, he pronounced her in perfect condition. Then the old man hopped to his place and headed it for Alabama. Soon it zoomed down on Lawton and he hurried into the tiny hotel where he left Lucy, now known at Anna Travis.

A dull-looking man slouched behind the desk, pulling on an old cob pipe. In response to the doctor's inquiry he asked without moving in his chair, "Amy Travis? Hain't no such a gal here. Niver heard tell of her."

As the doctor looked him up and down he muttered to himself, "This is the very creature who registered the girl." He wondered how to get information from him. "May I see your register?"

"Hep yourself."

There it was. Anna Travis, room 49. "Please think hard," pleaded Doc. "It is of the utmost importance that we find the girl and her child. When did she check out?"

The man scratched his bush head. "Can't recollect nothin' about her. What'd she look like?"

"Be so good as to call the proprietor," demanded the physician. His patience was fast ebbing.

"I'm him. And I'm thinkin' as hard as the law allows, I reckon."

Dr. Cunningham called at the police station and a private detective was put on the job to locate Anna Travis who had disappeared with her infant son three weeks before.

The detective and the doctor returned to the hotel. A colored maid said she remembered bringing milk for a baby to Room 49. She remembered for a generous tip. Upon questioning she told them the young woman had been crying when she took the milk to her room.

Returning to the desk the two men tried to get the clerk to talk, for the doctor thought he might look a bit brighter now. "Yeah, I do recollect somethin' about a gal with a youngin bein' here.

He shifted the cud of tobacco to the other cheek. "Yes, sir, that gal did pull out of here the same day. You had paid for several days but she never ask for her dough back again or said a word to no biddy as to where she was goin'."

"How could she leave?! Asked Doc. "She was too weak to carry the baby and baggage."

"Well, she took the kid all bundled up in a blanket. Then after a spell, a Nigger boy come in asking kin he get the stuff outen Room 49."

The detective wanted to know where the boy took the luggage. "Where did he go? Who was with him? What did the boy look like?"

Then the doctor asked, "How old was the colored boy and how was he dressed?"

"Your questions be too fast for me," said the hotel man, taking time out to squirt a mouthful of tobacco in the direction of the spittoon that grace the opposite side of the room. "The boy mighten be fourteen, mebby more, mebby less. I didn't see nobody with him-, 'taint my business to see too much in a thrivin' business like this hotel."

Neither questioning nor offers of money seem to have any power to awaken the man's dull brain. So Dr. Cunningham left with the detective, telling him it was up to him to find the missing girl and her child. Then pointing the nose of his plane toward Creston, Alabama, he went to interview the Travis Family.

He did find the Travis's plain folks. But to a Southerner no insult is more deadly than to intimate he or his family carries Negro blood. "My Lucy have Nigger blood?" shouted Jacob Travis, his usually meek eyes carrying fire.

Mrs. Travis asked, "Pa, what's the man sayin' about Lucy? That she has a Nigger baby and run away to hide her shame? Pa, make him find her. Maybe the poor child went and killed herself." She walked the floor and wrung her hands.

"Where's John, the sneak? Demanded Jacob Travis. "Why didn't he come along? Ma, if I can borrow the money for carfare, I'll go all the way to Iowa and clean up the Barke clan. Plenty of neighbors would be glad to help me do it too- saying my girl had Nigger blood!"

Dr. Cunningham was a born diplomat or he never would have managed J. B. Barkes' affairs for almost thirty ears. Yet this Travis case was different. Their daughter had been willfully pronounced dead and buried, after being charged with tainted blood. Now that she had disappeared, a murder charge could be filed against the Barkes, unless she could be located.

Yes, the Travis Family would have to be appeased and at once. The doctor used the Barke formula-money. He did not know these fine people of the South. Jacob as furious and ready to strike the doctor.

"Money? Money, you pay money for the life of my innocent daughter? Screamed Mrs. Travis, "Dog! Leave my house before I spit in your face."

"Mrs. Travis," began the physician in his very best tone, "without doubt your daughter doesn't want to be found. She must be alive but wants to hide her disgrace from you and her father. Unless we move wisely, she will prevent us from ever locating her. Please let me try to find her-I have the Barke millions at my disposal. Your indiscretions could force her to commit some rash act."

Finally both Mr. and Mrs. Travis did give their consent and the doctor put on the greatest man-hunt the state of Alabama ever witnessed. During the first few months the search was carried on in secret, for Lucy's disappearance must not come to the notice of her husband, John Barke.

After these efforts failed, Jacob Travis demanded that a notice be published in the newspaper. No picture was given, only the obscure name of Anna Travis, a name which meant nothing to to world.

But that notice did catch the eye of John and he demanded, "Father what does this mean?" as he passed to paper to him. The banker was then forced to tell him what had happened.

"O Dad, I have killed my beautiful wife! I have caused her to take her own life."

"Son, I don't believe she is dead. Every foot of ground for miles around Lawton has been combed. The rivers and lakes have been dragged. Lucy and her son are alive. She does not want to be found but her hiding place cannot remain secret much longer."

"John," his father lowered his voice, "I'm leaving no stone upturned. Why I even put detectives on the trail of Doc's trip to Boston. To be sure I still have the utmost confidence in him but Lucy's disappearance was such a mystery, I was taking no chances, figuring she could have induced him to take her to the city where she might lose herself. Once we thought we had made a discovery-"

"What, Dad? I demand to know everything. If I can find her never again shall she be sent away no matter what you may say or do to me. Did the detectives find her in Boston and where is she now? Tell me!"

"Of course they did not find her. It was a false clue. Doc had been seen with a young woman carrying an infant. They were entering a large city hospital of Boston, but it was proved conclusively to be some one else, not Lucy."

"Then who was the woman? You have deceived me more than once, you shall not this time."

"Oh, it was just some patient and her child that the Medical Convention had used for their experimentation. A human guinea pig, Doc called her."

"Detectives are fools! I'm going to Alabama and Boston and I know I can and will find her. My poor, darling wife." He rushed from the room, too proud to let his father see his tears.

It took all of Dr. Cunningham's tact, ingenuity, and diplomacy to persuade John Barke to give up his wild idea. "You will only place a noose around your own neck besides involving you and your father," he insisted.

The deeper the young husband's grief became the oftener he sought solace in Jeanette's dimpled face. For she was by this time old enough to coo and play with him. For an hour at a time he sat romping with her. She resembled her mother so much he almost imagined he were in the presence of his beloved Lucy.

Rose Garner was the soul of devotion to the child. She taught the baby to pull her father's crisp curls and tweak his big ears. Day by the attractive but heartless nurse wormed her way into the heart of John Barke. Because he worshiped his child and Rose was always with her, he thought of them together.

One day J. B. Barke called John into his office at the bank. "Sit down, son. I have something to say to you. It has been six months since Lucy left you."

John turned a deadly pallor. "Yes?"

"The divorce? Have you forgotten the plan agreed upon?"

Angrily came the reply, "We have committed enough crimes in the name of that plan. Do not expect me to seek any divorce, for I shall never marry again."

The banker's face began to turn red in anger. "John, you promised fair and square to go away in six months for your divorce."

"You have driven me already to do what my soul loathes. You shall not force me to do this thing," he stalked out of the office without a backward glance.

The Czar was not easily beaten in battle. Morning, noon, and night he pressed the subject on his heart-broken son. Finally when the search for Lucy looked hopeless, to silence his father, he gave in. As had been agreed upon, he obtained a divorce upon desertion in a state so far away no one in Novenger heard about it.

That is but Rose, Doc, and J.B. Barke. She was gleeful and doubled her efforts, scheming a thousand ways to win the handsome man. But he didn't see her except as his child's nurse and companion.

Whenever possible, upon any small pretext, she enticed John to Jeanette's nursery, maybe to adjust a window, or perhaps ask his advice about something for the child's room. Often she hinted the baby needed fresh air, and since she was tired herself, a ride in the Cadillac might be beneficial to them both. It's often said men do not understand women. It surely is true they are entirely too easily taken by the duplicity of cunning women.

Almost every night found her and Jeanette sitting under the big cedar on the front lawn, and of course always dressed with special care to attract masculine eyes. Besides, she was sure to provide cold drinks or something of the sort to tempt a tired man. Her eye was on his millions!

One day a letter came for John and for once the Czar failed to prevent it from reaching its intended destination. It was from Jacob Travis and told of the death of his wife. "John, the doctor pronounced it heart failure but you and I know her death was caused by heart-break. You are now responsible for the death of three persons in my family."

The pompous bank president sent Mr. Travis a fat check and an elegant floral piece. Both the check and the flowers were refused with the bitterest scorn. Again Mr. Barke had misjudged the Travis sense of honor.

Finally another letter came from the detectives to the doctor saying, "We have given up the hunt for Anna Travis and her child and have closed the case, so far as we are concerned, for we can do no more." It was just as if the earth had opened and swallowed the mother and her infant.

"I have murdered my angel wife," groaned John to himself. "I'm nothing but a sneaking coward."

"Good riddance," muttered the banker through his teeth. Naturally he felt more secure with Lucy out of the way. He no longer feared Jacob Travis or his friends. The man had proved himself harmless. The Czar knew Jacob Travis might grieve for his lost daughter and her child but he would never take measures to punish the culprits responsible for her disappearance and probable death.

Mother Barke had mourned all these months for her sweet daughter-in-law whom she supposed lay in her grave in the Jamestown cemetery. She faithfully carried flowers for her grave along with those for little Jerry's small mound.

Rose Garner, like John's father felt more secure with Lucy resting peacefully under the sod or in some watery grave. Her ghost might haunt them some dark night but it could never prevent either she or the Czar from carrying out their evil schemes.

Dr. Cunningham refused to believe that Lucy was dead. "Neither will I stop my search for her. She is only hiding and sooner or later I will find her. I shall go to my grave seeking her hiding place." But no one else shared his optimism, not even John.

CHAPTER IV

Were Lucy and her child dead? Dr. Cunningham had left Lucy, now christened Anna Travis by the Barkes, at the Lawton Hotel early in the afternoon. She did not unpack, but at once called for a maid to bring her some milk for the baby. After feeding him she tucked him in bed, then hurried to the telephone.

Her hands shook with palsy. Supposing her friend was out of town? Or perhaps she was no longer a member of the Parkhurst College faculty, for Lucy had not heard from her since she married John Barke.

How relieved she was she she heard the familiar voice and she said, "Miss Harriet, this is Belle. You know who I am." She used her college nickname, not daring to use her own, and she spoke in a low guarded tone. "Can you meet me immediately at Lucas and South streets?"

Harriet Kieth gave no sign of surprise, asked no questions, knowing she was needed. And in an unbelievable short time Lucy sat beside the youngish gray-hair woman in her closed car.

Without hesitation or preliminaries Lucy said, "Please drive to the city park. With the throng of merry-makers about us we will be less conspicuous." In less time that it takes to relate it, the teacher had the tragic story.

Miss Kieth asked indignantly, "How could those low-bred Northerners make such an unfounded charge? You with Negro blood in your veins! They merely wanted to discard you. Yet John Barke did appear like a prince of a man when I saw him after your wedding. May I see the baby? I adore babies."

Slowly and hesitatingly Lucy uncovered the child's face. With a cry of horror the teacher drew back. Neither woman spoke. In all her four years in class under Harriet Kieth, Lucy had never seen her lose he composure once.

However, the woman quickly regained her poise and said, "Lucy, you have asked my advice. You have a serious situation that requires immediate action. You may consider my plan extreme but I am sure it is for the best."

"Please, dear Harriet, I will try to accept whatever you advise."

A colored boy was found, one who appeared bright and intelligent. To him the teacher said, "Here is a dollar. Go to Room 49 of the Lawton Hotel and bring back all the baggage. Ask no questions, answer none. Do as you are told and you shall have another half-dollar upon your return. Get a move on you."

"Lucy, my advice is for you to disappear. First we will place your child in a colored orphanage." The woman pretended not to hear the girl's cry of horror. "Assume a new name, and go away. Regain your broken health. Get a new outlook on life, and begin life anew."

"How can I forget my babies? John and papa and mama?"

"Forget them! I will place your son in the orphanage as your protege."

"Why a Negro orphanage?"

"That way you are less likely to be traced, besides he will be better off to grow up with his own kind and to think he has no parents. He will ever be near enough for me to look after. Try to forget him and everything about your marriage. Live for the future."

Between sobs the girl asked, "How can I forget?"

"We must face facts. Facts can be hard. John let them bury you. So far as he is concerned you are to dead to him and little Jeanette. You son will be far happier if he does not know he has white blood or white parents."

"But father and mother?"

"Either way they are bound to suffer. Should you take your mulatto child home, think of their grief and disgrace. True they will worry if you disappear but your first concern is yourself and your child and your safety. No telling what that old banker might do next, should he find you. He's a man you would not like to meet alone some dark night."

The Negro youth brought the grips and placed them in the car. Lucy was silent, thinking hard. Could she desert this small piece of humanity? He was so tiny, so helpless, and not to blame for having Negro blood.

Finally, she decided Miss Kieth was right. There just is no place in society for a colored child with white parents. He would be taunted by both white and Negro associates. Even his friends would subject him to cruel questioning. He would be happier never to know he had parents.

They drove immediately to the teacher's mountain cabin. "Lucy, have no fear here, for no one will come near you. There are ample provisions in the cupboard, for I have been spending week-ends here part of the time. Make yourself right at home."

"If I hurry I have just time to get into the orphanage this afternoon. Tomorrow after classes, I should be able to make final arrangements. Since I happen to be a faculty member of the college much red tape is sure to be dispensed with. Good-bye, Lucy. Keep up your courage, child."

It was all so rapid the girl in the log cabin was dazed. As she watched her seemingly only friend in the world drive down the winding mountain trail, she dropped exhausted into a low rocker. She gazed out across the evergreen trees that covered the mountain side and hid the tiny hut and shivered with fear.

She gazed long and tenderly at the infant in her arms. Jerry Randall, she had named him, since talking with Harriet Kieth. For a child must have a name to be registered at the orphanage. Jerry and Jeanette were pretty names for twins. At the thought of her little daughter she had lost forever, a great lump lodged in her throat.

Lucy had told Miss Kieth about that other Jerry, John Barke's brother who had died in infancy. Had he lived, he would now be a grown man. And her son's uncle.

The following day Jerry Randall left his mothers arms to be be placed in the King's Orphanage in Mobile, just across the line in Tennessee. The teacher had insisted it better for the mother not to go along. Not only for safety reasons did she advise it but because no mother could endure the ordeal of placing her child among those woolly heads. Neither could she survive the fire of official questioning of the bigoted female at the desk.

The third day Miss Kieth drove Lucy across the mountains in her closed car. The girl wore a new tailored traveling suit and hat and was heavily veiled Even the shrewd eyes of Dr. Cunningham would not have recognized the smartly dressed young lady who boarded the crowded tourist train headed for Palm Beach, Florida.

As she bade her good-bye Harriet said, "Keep your head high and a stiff upper lip. Just tell Auntie Maude that I sent you as a sort of traveling companion, for she is very lonely. She will ask no questions and pay you handsomely. Her droll humor will be a real tonic for your shattered nerves."

"Harriet, I cannot thank you enough. You will-will visit Jerry?"

"Of course. Elsie-better become accustomed to your new name. Remember Lucy Barke lies in the Jamestown cemetery. Anna Travis was lost in the mountains near Lawton, Alabama. You are Elsie Hamilton, just out of college and have overworked and need the invigorating air of the ocean. That is why you have sought employment with the heiress, Miss Maude Hardesty."

"If only the Barkes and detectives won't follow me."

"There isn't a chance. Soon my vacation will start and I will be with you. Keep saying to yourself, 'There's no proof that I carry Negro blood. I will forget the charge.' Your bridges are burned. Begin life from here."

As the girl boarded the train she felt forlorn, forsaken. She was without home, name, parents, husband, children, friends, except Harriet, and starting on an uncharted course. A long life lay before her who had known only love, shelter and a protected home.

Elsie still wondered if she had done the right thing in putting her child in an orphanage, especially a Negro orphanage. Harriet had reasoned he would thus avoid embarrassing explanations when he grew up. His mind would not be torn between mental anguish and conflicts to believe he was a Negro instead of mixed blood, mongrel, she called it. She insisted each race should be proud not ashamed of its own.

Then the thought came that while Jerry now looked much like the colored race, he might change later in life. No one is sure what an infant will look like when it grows up.

Harriet had said on their way to the station, "Elsie the mixture of Negro blood brings only shame and hatred to both races. Negro blood in white veins seems to act as a poison, causing that person to despise the white man for not accepting him as a member of his race and he hates his own Negro blood more than the white man despises him. It is the mixing of blood that causes all the racial strife; in other words it is the mixed breed who are the racial fighters."

Elsie wondered if this were true. Maybe so, for such a person is neither white nor black; he is both. He hates his parents for crossing blood; he hates himself for not having pure blood, and he hates both the black and the white man.

Miss Maude Hardesty, the spinster heiress, was delighted with her niece's latest find. When she saw the girl she knew Elsie Hamilton was exactly what she had been waiting for. "Harriet is a real psychiatrist. She knows exactly what I need to ensure happiness," Elsie said to herself.

Yes, Harriet knew that her aunt Maude Hardesty would mother Elsie back to health. Maybe now Lucy could think of herself as Elsie, somebody else, and forget herself and her family troubles.

The heiress was used to receiving surprises from her niece. This time she had received but a short telegram saying, "Elsie Hamilton is coming as your companion. Meet her at the six o'clock evening Flier on Tuesday. Harriet." That was all the explanation, that and nothing more.

But this was not the first such message received from Harriet. During the years she had sent more than one of her girls to be loved back to normal living. Miss Hardesty always paid the girls magnificently for this privilege. That was part of the game.

The woman had loved Elsie the moment she laid eyes on her wan face and tragic eyes as she alighted from the train. She realized some great sorrow was gnawing at the girls' heart but not one personal question did she ask. She treated her just as if she were any normal girl who was weary from four years of strenuous study in college.

The two women ate, slept, or did nothing but lie on the beach and bask in the longer sun. Sometimes they rowed on the bay or ventured out in Miss Hardesty's yacht. Although they talked little, the silence was not embarrassing, only soothing, understanding. They entertained when it suited their fancy but they were not slave to society. The woman was law unto herself.

But it worried Elsie because she had no duties. One day she could endure it no longer, but asked, "Miss Hardesty, shall I read to you?" They lay under a large striped beach umbrella. Elsie wasn't used to being so idle. "Just what is a paid companion supposed to do?"

"Don't worry, child. I guess I am queer. You see I am all alone in life. Merely to have someone near me or with me is all I require. You can't imagine how lonely I was before you came, Elsie. Now life is worth living."

To a lonely love-starved soul, appreciation is like water to a famished traveler in the desert. To be wanted and to be needed was exactly what the girl needed most. Miss Hardesty was a wise woman as well as a kind one.

When Harriet Kieth arrived for her vacation she was delighted to see the change in her protege. "Elsie, you are a new person. Aunt Maude and the beach have worked miracles. A few more months and you will begin to look like yourself again."

It was good to have Harriet, for Elsie wanted ask about Jerry and she wondered if the Barkes had been looking for her. Then too, she needed help to plan her future.

"Jerry is actually growing like a weed, you wouldn't know him." Harriet told her.

Miss Kieth had been told of the manhunt for Anna Travis, and she heard it from everyone all over Lawton. The story had been in every mouth there. She had not written this to Elsie, knowing she had troubles enough. She remembered that neither Elsie nor her aunt read the newspaper as a rule.

In terror the girl cried, "Then they are sure to follow me here!"

"No, the trail is growing cold. That stupid hotel proprietor where you stopped could tell the detectives little. Girl, we did a magnificent job covering you tracks. Some day I may thank that hotel man for his part."

The summer passed and the vacation for Miss Kieth ended. Although she did her best to persuade Elsie to remain with her aunt, the girl knew she was not earning her fat pay-check; besides she was restless. She wanted work.

As Harriet took her train for Parkhurst College, Lawton, Alabama, Elsie Hamilton boarded the crowded bus for Ardmore, New York. She had accepted a teaching position as head of the music department of the high school there.

Once there she worked hard, for she had not only the music in senior high but in junior high as well. She was glad to be busy. It gave her less time to think. Soon she became quite popular with the students and might have made many friends.

Elsie's mind was too troubled to make any friends. One day Georgia Regan, the Latin teacher remarked, "Isn't Miss Hamilton a mysterious girl. I think I know her, then she withdraws herself into her sweet dignity and then I'm shut out."

"Such a wistfully sad person," was the way Ellen Maxwell characterized Elsie. "I really would like to know her better.

"Me too," put in Jack Billings, the math teacher of senior high. "I'd like the privilege of bringing out the dimple in her left cheek. Once I saw it when she smiled at Lilly Page, the crippled girl in the freshman class."

Several of the younger female teachers wished Jack would become interested in them, for he was a very eligible bachelor and the only unmarried member of the faculty. Yet the girls were not jealous of Elsie Hamilton for she noticed neither Jack nor any other man.

Maude Hardesty and Harriet Kieth wrote regularly to Elsie. Jerry was well and growing. Harriet didn't believe in writing details about the baby. The day she had driven Elsie to the mountain cabin she had advised, "My dear, try to kill your maternal instincts."

In one of her letters she had repeated this admonition. "Try to forget. You will never be permitted to see your daughter. You should not try to visit your son. For your own peace of mind forget you ever had children."

Harriet wrote that the papers were full of the account of the disappearance of Anna Travis. Elsie was glad that her picture did not appear, wondering what her school would say should they learn who she was. Finally she read a short account in the New Your Times.

For once she was glad for the Barke millions. Knowing that old J. B. would buy out every newspaper in the land before he would permit the name or picture of Lucy Barke of Novinger, wife of John Barke, be given. The name of Anna Travis meant nothing to the reading public.

Then the letter came from Harriet that was almost the last straw to Elsie's sorrow. "Elsie I learned today that your mother died suddenly last night-found dead in bed. The doctor pronounced it heart failure. Remember I told you last summer about her heart ailment. Please, dear, do not go home or try to contact your father. It will be difficult not to do so, but you cannot afford to be found now.

Elsie knew it was grief that had hastened her mother's death, grief for her. Maybe if she had gone home she could have prevented that death. Too late for that now, she would follow Harriet's advice.

Christmas came with its joys for most of the world. Georgie Ragan begged Elsie to join her in their house party. Jack Billings invited her to accompany him to New York to the foot ball game, but she declined both invitations. She longed to be alone with her grief.

To her Christmas brought more sorrow for it was the second wedding anniversary. No bride had been so madly in love as she; she felt sure. Was it only two years? It seemed like a hundred.

In her room she relieved the past, thinking of how she had loved John and still loved him. But worst of all, she couldn't forget the look of horror on his face when he saw little Jerry. She covered her face in humiliation as she remembered how he recoiled from her as if she might have been some vile reptile.

She threw herself across the bed and experienced too much anguish to shed a tear. It was impossible to forget the night the doctor had almost forced her to board his plane for Alabama, while old J. B. Barke stood by bullying her into submission. How she had hoped against hope that John would come and demand that they stop persecuting her and force her to remain with him, no matter what anyone said, whether his father or the doctor.

Instead, John had not so much as told her and his little son good-bye. In fact, he had not spoken one word to her or come near her since the day he learned she had given birth to twins, one a mulatto child.

"Oh, John, how could you have been so cruel?" she cried in anguish.

She pictured the time when Jeanette would grow up in the Barke home to become a fine lady. She wondered if she would visit the mound in Jamestown cemetery where she supposed her mother lay buried. Would she sometime drop a tear for her?

Elsie realized that by now the Twins would be old enough to be creeping and lisping their first words, the age mother love most. Oh, to hear them say, "Mama." She wondered how she could go on living with seemingly everything she loved most gone from her forever.

Far into the night she lay moaning and whispering to herself. "Neither Jerry nor Jeanette will ever know the meaning of the word, mother." Then she stopped and gasped. "No, no, John must not marry again! I never could see another woman take my place in his heart, or be a mother to my little daughter."

Quickly she pulled on her silk-lined fur coat, tied a dark scarf about her head and stepped stealthily out of her room, down the hall, and out into the frosty, stillness of the the night. Oh, how cold it was!

Elsie Hamilton began walking, not knowing nor caring where her feet led her. Her teeth chattered and her fingers tingled with the biting cold, but she scarcely felt the sting. She only knew that she must somehow walk off this horror that hung over her like a pall.

"Why should I go on living? What have I to live for," she asked herself as her heels clicked on the icy walk. Like a lone shadow she continued down the street toward the mighty river.

Elsie stood on the bridge and stared down into the dark, swiftly-moving waters, too cold to freeze over. She thought of the many other sorrow-crazed persons who might have stood on this bridge and contemplated what was now in her mind. As the city clock tolled off the hour of three o'clock she shuddered.

"Mother is gone," Elsie said to herself. "Soon father must follow her. So far as I am concerned, John and the Twins are dead. Never, never again can I expect to see them. I have not in all my life wronged anyone as far as I know. I am branded! Even Harriet may think I am part Negro.

"Only Harriet Kieth and Miss Hardesty would know who I am or would mourn for me. It would give the high school something to talk and wonder about for ages to come. Yes, the mysterious music teacher who had some secret sorrow she was unable to carry came to the bridge one Christmas night-"

All alone she stood. All alone and no one understood. She clinched her fists and cried, "I can't go on! Oh, I can't! I can't!"

CHAPTER V

At Novinger, Iowa, the green shutters are open wide and the house and grounds are gay with festive light. For it is Christmas Eve and a decorated tree hangs with gorgeously wrapped packages and is resplendent with brightly colored lights that gleam from the parlor windows.

The spruce and cedar trees that surround the lovely white house are covered with snow that glistens in the bright moonlight like myriads of diamonds. In the circular driveway in front of the house stands John Barke's Cadillac fresh from the factory. On the grounds back of the house sits Dr. Cunningham's familiar plane.

A caterer and a buxom cook from the city bustle about the kitchen. Two waitresses in black uniforms with white cuffs flit importantly to and from the dining room. The table is laid with the costliest linen, china, cut glass, silver, flowers and all that goes to display a man's wealth and social position.

A wedding is to take place in the grand old parlor with its velvet tapestries, rich carpets, and lovely old furniture. Rose Garner had at last coiled herself around the poor bleeding heart of John Barke. Exactly two years after his marriage to the talented Lucy Travis, Rose Garner becomes the second Mrs. John Barke.

The bride had insisted the wedding be done up in a style befitting the Barke's station in life. Rose was well aware she did not want her wedding at the ranshackled house with its poverty and filth that she called home.

John had insisted it be a quiet, unostentatious ceremony Rose. Invited most of the town folk and scores of her own relatives and friends from her home in Ohio.

But she also wanted a new car. A compromise ensued. John bought a new car, although his car had been so new his friends scarcely recognized the change. Rose sent to her home for the minister to perform the ceremony. She arranged an elaborate dinner, although the only guests were Lulu Simpson, Dr. Cunningham's faithful nurse, and Dr. Cunningham. In fact, the doctor could scarcely be counted a guest. He was more like the family. Mother Barke refused to have any thing to do with the dinner or the wedding.

During the ceremony the old Banker looked like he were witnessing an execution, while his wife wept all during the entire ordeal. The doctor sat stern and grim, not once focusing his eyes on the bejeweled bride.

The groom stood pale and dazed beside the overdressed girl in her white satin and diamonds and pearls. The very expression on her face was enough to warn any man to beware. Her defiant smile, really a smirk, said plainly, "Aha, you see I've done it! The reins are in my hands, watch out!"

Only little Jeanette seemed to enjoy herself, for she sat on the lap of Miss Simpson and chattered and gurgled with delight. Poor child, it was almost the last time she would really be happy. She knew not what was before her. Lulu Simpson had not been at the home of the Barkes since the fatal birth of the Twins, but that scene was burned into her consciousness as if with a hot iron.

Lulu hugged the golden-haired, blue-eyed baby to her and thought, "She is the image of her mother." She had loved Lucy with a passionate love. Now she recalled the words of the woman standing beside the groom, those words, "If Lucy succumbs to the shock of the birth of the other child, I'm ready and willing to console the heart-broken husband." Now she smugly smiled and smirked beside that same husband.

"How could John have been such a fool, such an idiot?" Lulu thought, staring at his tragic face. She marveled at the stupidity of men as John went through the farce of taking that viper-girl to his heart for a wife. A vile viper who would not only poison him with her sting, but his beloved daughter as well.

As John had taken his place beside this gaudily-dressed woman for the ceremony he tried to remember just how he happened to propose marriage to her. "Or did I propose?" he wondered dully. "I'm sure I never told her I loved her. My heart is dead and buried with Lucy, where her body lies."

After the wedding dinner was ended, John and his new bride started in his car on a short honeymoon trip to visit the home of her parents in

Columbus, Ohio. He had not wanted to go there but she insisted, for she wanted to show off her handsome millionaire husband.

That Garner family was indeed a shock to him. While Lucy Travis had come from a home of simplicity, yes, from a humble home, it had been a place of culture and refinement. This Garner family were not only dirty, filthy, and poverty stricken. They were loud, cheap and coarse. Their very speech and tone of voice betrayed their station in life.

Upon their return from Ohio, John and Rose, and Jeanette moved into his pretty bungalow that had been closed since he had moved Lucy to his father's home for the birth of the Twins. His half-healed wounds were rudely torn open. Gentle, little Lucy's face met him from every nook and corner of the house.

There was the dressing table where she had arranged her unruly curls. Here sat the piano where her gifted fingers brought forth sweet, soothing strains of music. There was her special chair where she loved to sit and read or mend.

Rose closed doors with a harsh bang. Her high heels clicked spitefully-for to John this was hallowed ground and all harsh sounds seemed a desecration. The loud jazz she picked out with two fingers on the piano grated viciously on his sensitive ears.

Rose spoke to Jeanette in a high coarse voice, often harshly. He wondered why he had never noticed this uncouthness in the woman before. Yet what disturbed him most was the change in his little daughter, for the child clung to him, seemingly in fear of her former nurse.

Before a month had elapsed Rose said, "John, darling, this house is so old-fashioned! I'd actually be ashamed to bring my friends or relatives here to visit us!"

The man's mouth dropped open. He wondered if he could have heard aright. He remembered distinctly the picture of the Garner house in the unrestricted section of Columbus. It was like comparing his modern new house to a pig sty.

He demanded indignantly, "Rose, pray tell me what is the matter with this house? It is the prettiest, most charming, up-to-date house in our town."

"You poor ignorant lamb!" she scoffed patronizingly. "What does this town know about architecture compared my great city. I wish papa could send us one of the best architects from his city. He would soon show you what is the matter with this dump!"

John was not only angry, more angry than he ever remembered being, but he was hurt more than words can express. He wondered how his wife could have the gall to speak such brazen lies. Why her people were ignorant trash! Well, she could just calm down. He never would make changes in his lovely house, for my woman, much less for a shrew who had not only come from the wrong side of the railroad tracks but from the heart of the slum district.

But when women like Rose Garner Barke sets her head, by hook or crook, she gets her way. The underlying reason for Rose asking to model the house was to obliterate every trace of Lucy's presence. She was no fool, being smart enough to realize she did not hold her husband's affections. Lucy, not she, held his love and respect. Then like too many women, she liked to wield her authority.

Rose was well aware that old J. B. Barke hated her, and that Mother Barke feared and despised her as much as the gentle woman was capable of disliking any human being. Neither was she blind to the fact that the town looked down on her with disdain for her coarseness and for grabbing John so soon after the supposed death of their beloved Lucy whom they had looked up to and adored.

So this malicious woman found satisfaction in taking out her spite on the Barke family, and flouting her newly-acquired riches in the face of the gasping villagers. Sadistic pleasure was the only kind of happiness Rose had ever known, or was capable of experiencing.

Although John Barke had stoutly declared he never would change the structure of his house, before a month had gone by, the Ohio architect was on the ground. And as it was to be expected, it was to his advantage to suggest radical changes. He needed money and the Barke millions were too great a temptation to him to speak honestly. He and Rose wrangled a contract out of John and soon the bungalow began to have the appearance of the woman living inside, showy and gaudy.

Finally the house remodeling was completed. The architect received a fat check, and the gloatingly happy Mrs. Barke bade him good-bye and he returned from where he had come from. Still Rose was not satisfied, in fact, she had merely begun her program of spending the Barke money.

She used the woman's customary weapon, that is, she employed the weapon of the unscrupulous woman. Sitting on the arm of her husband's chair she wheedled, "John darling, can't we have some pretty furniture for our new house? This old stuff gets on my nerves. Honey, you know we must furnish our house to set off its beauty. Please, let's get rid of every stick of this old-fashioned stuff. I can't stand that piano! It reminds me too much of the mother and of your other Twin!"

John's face became lived, his fists clinched. "Rose, don't you dare make such a remark again in my presence," he said, seising her by the shoulders, "Think what you will but never utter a slurring remark against the mother of my daughter. You are not worthy so speak her name."

Rose flew into hysterics. "I knew you never loved me, marrying me merely to care for your child."

To end the miserable scene, he promised to dispose of all of the furnishings, except the rosewood piano, declaring that the piano must be saved for Jeanette.

Still John's troubles did not end here, for with a woman like Rose, the more she gets, the more she demands, and the oftener she wins in battle the more she will fight.

Now she clamored for gaudy clothes and loud parties to show off her new house and new furnishings-anything to spend and squander money. Ignorant and greedy folks never know what they really want, their mind is too small to realize the big things of life. For the first time Rose had money. At home it had been a scramble to find enough to satisfy their appetites for their large shiftless family.

The people Rose invited from the city to her parties were all just like her, and John considered them a disgrace to his home and the community. When he protested she only laughed scornfully in his face. "Darling, you are behind the times-you are so very old-fashioned."

Hotly he replied, "Maybe I am behind the times and old-fashioned but I'm not accustomed to associating with such trash, such common, cheap people. Don't you realize, Rose, that people are talking about us all over town? We are not in the habit of seeing women smoke and become intoxicated in our community. Please, quit smoking and drinking for Jeanette's sake. I know you love her just as much as I do and want her to grow up into a refined and cultured lady."

"Yes, sweetheart," she said coyly. "I will try to set a good example for Lucy's child." Always since marrying John, Rose had spoken of Jeanette as Lucy's child, trying to drive the dart deeper into his heart.

As Rose made her promise there was a glint in her deep-set eyes that boded no good for her innocent step-child, for she hated Jeannette with a hatred as strong as that for her mother. She was jealous of both.

John did not see the look in his wife's eyes and he believed that while Rose had her faults, she did love his child. How gullible can a husband be?

But from this time on the woman became more and more subtle in all her schemes, especially when they concerned Jeanette.

CHAPTER VI

Ten eventful years have slid by since the somber wedding of John Barke and Rose Garner, his baby's nurse. These years have been filled to overflowing in the lives of many persons.

John Travis still sits alone in his small cottage down in Creston, Alabama. Although old and broken in health, the fires that burn in his faded brown eyes indicate his spirit is not entirely broken. No longer does he look the once, meek, man once seen.

His years have been spent in brooding and grieving for his wife and missing daughter. Mr. Travis is convinced in his own mind that Lucy and her child have been the victim of the Barke malice, that they have been cruelly murdered. The man has neither money nor influence, nor the desire for revenge. He well know that revenge could not bring back his daughter and her son. Neither would it return his faithful wife.

Jerry Randall, Lucy's other twin, is still in the King's Orphanage. While he has grown to be quite a big boy, he is smaller than many of the woolly headed lads of his age in the institution, for he is forced to work extremely hard, entirely too hard for his age. He is the carrier of wood and water for this institution.

Listen in for a moment to what goes on at the orphanage. "Whar is you, Jerry Randall?" screams the big fat black cook. "Bring you water from the spring this very minute, you ole poor white trash! Here, you lazy brat, take your two buckets. An' if you spill one single drop, I'll skin the hide right offn your dirty back. Git along wit you."

Sad to say, it seems to be the nature of man to persecute one another. Much is said about the cruelty of the white man against the black slave but if and when the black race is in power, the same persecution is shown, as in Jerry's case. Particularly is this true of both races against the mixed offspring. There is a racial antagonism, one that cannot be excused, and whichever has the power, it is sure to be displayed.

Harriet Kieth knew what was going on at the orphanage, some of it at least, and she did attempt a protest. "Madam," she said once to the stiffly starched superintendent, "the Kings Orphanage has the reputation of being kind to ists inmate-"

"Yes'm, Mis Kieth. This is the kindest orphanage in the whole world," she declared, rolling her eyes in an impressive manner, holding her two-hundred pounds proudly.

"Then why do you permit the cruel treatment of Jerry Randall?" asked the teacher. "He is a guest here. His benefactor pays double the price paid for other children-"

"No Mis, no!" interrupted the woman. "That's a great bit falsehood and an altogether misrepresentation of our magnificent and highly reputed institution."

"Madam, do you wish me to prove it?" demanded Miss Kieth indignantly. "Little Jerry is a guest here and unless he chooses to work, need do no manual labor. You would not care to have this report reach the ears of the authorities."

The woman at the desk promised to make a thorough investigation. Yet there is more than one method of persecution. Like at the school table, Jerry's manners of eating were mimicked, for he had inherited a refinement, the less favored lacked.

"Putin' on airs like white folks," jeered the children, pretending to eat like he did. Even his virtues became vices in the institution.

Although he had inherited some of his grandfather Barkes fighting ability, the odds were always against him, for the other children ganged up on him, then tattled, making him the aggressor. Thus he always bore the punishment, when he merely had been trying to defend himself, but there was no one in the institution who cared whether Jerry had justice or fair play or not. In fact, the adults were as guilty as the children.

On the playground he was slighted, seldom being permitted to participate in the games. Even the schoolroom was a place of torture. Being of better parentage, he was naturally quicker at his lessons than his classmates.

Of course, his colored instructors resented this, since he showed strongly his white blood. Often the teachers might say something like this, "Now, children, Mister Randall will elucidate on the subject," then she would join the children in uproarious laughter. Jerry was so bewildered and unhappy.

One day he found a cracked mirror and stole away and studied his face, trying to find out why the children called him "white-washed face." "Huh, my face does look different, not really black, just sort of yellow-like. Hey, who ever heard of a white Nigger?"

He looked some more and puzzled. "Same lips, same flat nose. Hair kinda curly but not a bit kinky. Yes, sir, I'm a white nigger. Bet that is why the kids don't like me and the very reason my nice Miss Kieth does think a lot of me, for my face is more like hers."

The discovery seemed to comfort him and help him face the taunts of the children and the unkindness of this teachers and supervisors. He surely needed something to help him endure the persecution, for every waking hour they made faces at him, winked, pinched him, pounded him, did something to hurt him. The sneers of the adults were what discouraged him most.

Human beings ae so very much like the lower creations. Watch a yard of chickens. Should the flock be composed of all white, the black fowl placed in their pen causes trouble, for chickens are not color blind. Right away all the white flock jumps on the black one and may peck it to death. Reverse the color and the same experience takes place. If and when the pen is full of black fowls, a white chicken placed with them is sure to be jumped on and may be killed.

The Chinaman does not like the white man, feeling superior to the Caucasian race. He admires his yellow skin and almond eyes, confident he is more handsome and wise than his white brother. The Hindu wants to become a white man.

Each race should be proud of its own and envy no other. Each should have its own sphere in which to live and rule. Intermingling of races, to the point of intermarriage, brings only strife and heartache. Poor little Jerry was a victim of just such an integration of the races and he must suffer for the indiscretions of his forefathers the rest of his life, a suffering that could have been prevented.

Jerry could not understand why he had no colored visitors like the other children. One day a maid at the orphanage opened his eyes when she ran him out of the kitchen screaming, "You, Jerry, get out of here. You-you never had no daddy. You is jist some pore white gal's brat. We is respectable colored folks, we is!

Night after night Jerry cried himself to sleep. Why didn't he have a daddy? That was his worry night after night. When Miss Kieth visited him he asked, "Wasn't my daddy killed in the war? Isn't that what you told me-that he died in the trenches in France? I know you told me that."

"Yes, yes, child. Why so you ask?" she felt that deception was surely justifiable in his case.

His next question stggered her. "What is a brat? Am I some pore white gal's black brat?"

When Miss Kieth asked to take Jerry for a week's vacation, eyebrows were lifted superciliously. Children rolled their eyes as only Negro children know how.

Although Jerry was no tattle-tale, by skillful questioning Harriet was able to get the picture of his life at the orphanage. For Lucy's sake as well as the boy's she must do something immediately. Besides, Jerry should be where there was a children's choir; for he had inherited some of his mother's musical talent.

Miss Kieth place him in a white orphanage in Illinois, for she had heard that Northerners were kinder to colored folks than were Southerners. She was determined to find the truth of the matter, being a Southerner herself.

A month later she visited the institution and took Jerry for a ride in her car. Surely he had gained weight and he appeared improved physically. "Well, how goes it? Which place do you like best, son?"

She was surprised at the answer she received, "I don't know, Miss Kieth," he replied hesitatingly. "Better food here, teachers are good enough, and the kids seem to like me, but they laugh at everything I do and say, I don't believe they are making fun of me, but-"

"Go on, Jerry."

"Really, they make me feel kinda like a trained puppy or monkey or something. They tease me an awful lot. Say what is a coon?" The woman shuddered.

The boy continued, not waiting for an answer to his question. "Sometimes they get me in a circle and sing a silly song like this, "Coon, Coon, Coon, I wish my color would fade. Wish I was a white men instead of a Coon, Coon, Coon."

"Now Miss Kieth, why should I want to be a white man? Isn't a black man just as good as a white man, except maybe a white man has more money?"

The questions were coming too fast and too thick for this wise college teacher and she had no answer for them.

"And say," persisted the child, "I overheard a girl talking about me and she said, 'Poor kid. He is neither white nor black.' Why, Miss Kieth? And who is the lady who gives you money for my keep? She never comes to see me-other kids have folks visit them, white folks, that is."

"The nice lady who pays for your care, Jerry, lives a long way off-hundreds and hundreds of miles- but she is very kind. She is interested in boys like you."

"Say Miss Keith, do you think it is right for kids to call me Nigger?"

"Well, I-"

"And sometimes the boys won't let me have my turn at the bat. They say 'H's just a Nigger, he won't mind." I got feelings same as a white boy. Then sometimes they treat me better than they do the white kids. Anyway, they aren't half as mean as in that Nigger orphanage." The teacher had to smile, here was the boy who had just complained because he was dubbed 'Nigger' using the same term on others. "Oh to see ourselves as others see us."

Miss Kieth left Jerry in the white orphanage. At least he was getting good food and he is in the children's choir, she reasoned. It was several months before she again visited him. Then she observed him at play, in the schoolroom, and with the adults.

She was shocked. "He is being ruined. His one aim in life is to show off." When he rolled his eyes, "Negro fashion, even the teachers burst into gales of laughter. She wondered what she should do, this was something impossible to stop or prevent.

She put it up to the boy himself. "Jerry, how would you like to return to the King's Orphanage in Tennessee?"

"Oh, Miss Kieth, please don't make me go back there! He cried frantically, his eyes full of terror. "I'll run away first. I never could again live with those dirty Niggers."

Here it was again, Jerry using the very terms he had so bitterly protested against. Or perhaps he no longer considered himself a Negro. Anyway, he never would consent to be returned to the colored orphanage, that is certain. All she could do was to let the matter ride for the time being.

Ten years have passed since Elsie Hamilton stood on that New York bridge at three o'clock in the morning on a dismal Christmas Eve and stared down at the dark icy waters, wondering what to do with her life. The emptiness and cruelty of life for her seemed more than she could bear, harder than the pangs of death.

Her one cry was that she had no one who cared whether she lived or died. She know she had no real claim on either Harriet or Miss Hardesty. They merely felt sorry for her. She long to see Jerry and Jeanette, but most of all she wanted to look once more into John's eyes. The she remembered her pledge never to try to see them again.

The biting, cruel wind whipped her coat about her. The dark waters far below the bridge where she stood surged and writhed like slithering, slimy snakes ready to devour her body the moment she struck their surface.

"One! Two! Three! Four!" clanged the town clock. Elsie Hamilton clutched the railing of the bridge for support. Was the clock tolling her knell?

Then she wondered what right had she to take the life God had given her. She decided it was just as wicked to take her own life as it was to take the life of another. Besides, it was cowardly to run away from trouble. "Only a sniveling coward commits suicide. He considers himself brave but that is not, true, for it takes far more courage to face life as it is than to end it all by death."

She bowed her head in humility and prayed for courage to go on living. In her prayer she asked that she might be given a purpose in life to live for. The the answer came. "Devote your life to helping others. Help those less fortunate than you." Yes, she would serve humanity and try to forget her own heartaches.

That was ten years ago. Those ten years have been kind to Elsie in one way, she has changed little in appearancees except to lose her unhappy, dejected look. A sweet, patient air settled down on her. She is charming, beautiful, if possible more than when John Barke fell in love with her that Armistice Day years before.

After teaching in Ardore High, in New York, for some time she reentered college to further develop her musical talent. Now she became the youngest member of the faculty of the Boston Girl's exclusive seminary. She looked like one of the older girls than the head of the conservatory of music.

But back in Novinger, Iowa, John Barke is showing gray at the temples, although he is still very handsome, if a most unhappy man. Sad lines show about his eyes and mouth, and he is often found brooding with a far-away look in his dark eyes. Although he had at last become cashier of the Citizens's Bank, it did not bring happiness to him.

Old J. B. Barke is more of the Czar than ever, for he practically owns the souls of the men far and wide, as well as their farms and other possessions. For while the world may be suffering from a depression, but not this old money bag. Although hated and feared by all who know him, many, many are forced to bow to him and his power. Only he has the wherewith to hand out the money needed.

Young Jeanette Barke is the picture of her mother Lucy. Yet she is a sad sweet girl, worshiped by her meek little grandmother, despised by Rose, her step-mother, because she is beautiful and talented, and idolized by her father.

Lucile is the child of John and Rose and she is the image of her father with the soul of her mother. Now at the age of nine she is the leader of the children of her age in the community, and a tyrant at home. While she is bold, even brazen, and aggressive, Jeanette is shy and timid.

Rose Garner Barke's daughter has jet-black hair that hangs in natural curls. He cherry-red lips and jet-black eyes contrast sharply with her sister' golden curls, deep-blue eyes, and milk-white skin.

Lucy's daughter might also have been the darling of little-girl society in Novinger excet for her sister and step-mother. Rose had nourished her daughter's growing jealousy for her talented sister. All of her life Jeannette had been made to feel their envy and malice.

Even when Lucile was a baby if Jeannette so much as picked up one of her toys to examine, she was reprimanded. Her step-mother usually snatched it from her and screamed, "Shame on you! A great big girl like you snitching baby's playthings!" Jeannette was less than two years older than her sister and small for her age.

Yet in the presence of the Barkes, Rose made an extravagant display of affect and solicitude for her step-daughter. In this she was successful she deceived both John and the grandmother. Jeanette would never tattle on her sister or mother no matter what they might do to her and they knew this.

Perhaps the meanest act of Rose was to deny Jeanette most of the privileges due her. Once when a party was being given for the smaller girls at school, Rose announced just as she saw John coming home for supper, Jeannette darling, moma is sorry that her little girl cannot attend the party tonight. Too bad to have to be so ill."

Jeanette looked up in astonishment and asked, "Mother, what makes you think I am sick? I never felt better in all my life. Mama, do let me to to this party-you did not let me attend the last three times when Lucile went." Tears rolled down the child's cheeks and her lips trembled.

Putting her arms around Jeanette she said, "Papa, the poor little dear told me when she came home from school how sick she felt. Now she has heard about the party at Peggy Twining's and she wants to pretend she is feeling fine." Adding playfully but sweetly, "You sly little puss."

Innocently Lucile looked up at her father's puzzled face through her long curling eye-lashes and said, "Daddy, sister told me on the way home from school she felt so sick she did not want supper and was going straight to bed."

John stared at his blue-eyed daughter with her quivering lips and knew in his heart she had never deceived anybody in her life, neither was capable of doing so. He was bewildered, not realizing this was a customary practice of the wife to prevent Jeanette from living a normal life, from enjoying the childhood pleasures that meant so much to a little girl her age.

Regardless of where she went with Jeanette became the object of Lucile's slights, jibes, and sarcasm. Often she would say, "Come, girls, we don't want her, she is too big to play with us." Like sheep, children follow the leader without thinking.

It was Lucile's delight to get her sister in a group of children and whisper, eyeing Jeanette and snickering. This spiteful little girl loved to turn her sister's friends against her by tale-bearing and starting some false report.

Why were John and grandma so extremely blind as to what was taking place before their eyes. The villagers knew and discussed it among themselves quite freely.

The minister's wife said one day, "Isn't it too bad the way the second Mrs. Barke and her daughter treat Lucy's child?"

Replied Miss Cook, the high school principle, "Jeanette is a very talented girl in music, playing the piano beautifully. Unusual for a young child. Miss Connock, her music teacher from Jamestown, told me she never saw so talented a child of her age, inherited her mother's musical ability-you know she is really a genius. At the piano, that is. No wonder they hate Jeanette."

Lowering her voice the minister's wife said, "Miss Cook, please don't repeat this, but Miss Connock told me confidently that she can hardly bear to give lessons to Lucile. For no matter what the girl attempts to play, whether hymns or strictly classical selections she turns them into tin-pan jazz."

No wonder that Rose and her daughter were jealous of Jeanette.

Dr. Cunningham still looked after the welfare of the Barkes, and he saw what was taking place; what was being done to Lucy's child and wondered what could do to stop it. Talking to his office nurse he asked, "Should I speak to John about it?"

Lulu Simpson advised him to wait. "Rose has John tied hand and foot. What could any man do with a woman like her, especially since she knows the great secret of his life and would not hesitate to use it against him it if suited her evil purpose.

CHAPTER VII

"Ben, what would I do without you?" asked Jeanette Barke one afternoon as she stepped out of the high school. The tall handsome dark-eyed boy had been waiting as usual to escort her home and away from the taunts and jeers and insinuations of her schoolmates. He took her books and bent his head to look into her lovely face.

Benjamin Hooper was one grade beyond Jeanette in school but had been her protector and champion since she had entered first grade. The Hoopers rated next to the Barkes in wealth, culture, and social standing in Novinger. The boy was an only child, yet popular with both students and teachers. But for his protection and understanding, Jeanette would have had a much harder time in life.

The increasing jealousy of Rose had led her to overstep herself. For she had broken her nurses' pledge and revealed a patient's secret but as we know she was a person who had little regard for honor of any kind. In her rage she had told her daughter much of the story of her sister's birth.

To be sure she had cautioned secrecy, yet well-knowing and not caring that no twelve-year-old girl is going to keep such an exciting a story about a rival whom she hates, and especially not a girl of Lucile's character, for she is just like her mother. She stoops at nothing if it furthers her own plans. So she lost no time spreading the fascinating tale.

Like her mother she pretended to be very discreet as she said, "Now girls, don't you dare tell! How important she felt. "If you tell a living soul, see what my Grandpa Barke will do to you. Mama says he would fill the jails with your papas and would take your homes right out from under you." The girls tingled with excitement and terror.

Surely a deep mystery surrounded John Barke's elder daughter and she became the object of curiosity and gossip. Often she was included in various invitations in the village merely to let the crowd stare at her and speculated about her story.

"Nigger blood, you say?" whispered a tall girl of the gang in awe-stricken tones at one of those gatherings.

"Then how could she be so sweet and beautiful?" asked Ben Hooper indignantly.

"Of course you can think no ill of your lady fair!" jeered Lucile.

Ben bowed low in mock humility and replied, "My dear Miss Lucile Barke your hair is as black as the midnight and is exquisitely curly. Your eyes are a velvety black, while your complexion is a lovely dusky-white. Now my dear, your charming sister is as fair as an angel!"

With a cat-like spring Lucile slapped him hard on the jaw, leaving a long red mark. "Old smarty, take that!" she screamed. "And if you say another word, I'll brand the other cheek as well."

The talk of the younger set reached their parents and in alarm they tried to silence them realizing that if the scandal reached the ears of Jeanette's grandfather the very Old Nick would be to pay.

But the neighbors slyly whispered among themselves. Could the story really be true? Then they recalled the strange funeral of John's wife Lucy. "Not one soul of us saw Lucy after she was reported to be dead. The casket was never opened at Jamestown. I heard that straight," reported one woman.

"Now they say," answered the butcher's wife, "that coffin was empty. Imagine that! But you can trust old man Barke to think up more meanesss than all the world put together. You heard, of course, that the foxy old doctor took Lucy away off someplace and she killed herself."

"Yes, I did hear that," said the depot agent's wife. "Still no one seems to know what became of the black baby boy. Maybe she killed him too when she took her own life."

Ben Hooper and her music were all that prevented Jeanette from quitting school and becoming a recluse. To be sure she did not know what was being said about her, but she did realize something unkind was being told and that was shunned and slighted by most of the young people. Save Ben, she really had no friends. She knew something was seriously wrong.

The mystery was maddening. Often she came suddenly upon some group, adults as well as the youth, who would be taking in undertones. When they saw her, they gave quick startled stares and scattered quietly.

She was too proud to ask her father, and her grandmother would not know. She didn't like to ask Ben, feeling sure it must be something about her family of a private nature. Of one thing she was positive, and her sister and step-mother were at the bottom of the trouble. But what was it? Why should a young girl like her be the subject of gossip? What had she done?

Finally Dr. Cunningham got the story that was being circulated all over the community, a story that was in everybody's mouth, young and old. He realized that the stories being told came from the mother and daughter. He listened and watched, making a call at the school upon the pretense of some medical inspection, and after hearing what was being gossiped about he wrangled an invitation for dinner at John's home. He must see the family together.

He listened to the family, he was appalled at the cunning and duplicity of Rose and her pretty but hateful daughter in the way that they treated Jeanette. He was staggered at John's blindness. Why couldn't he see through the woman's mask? Her devotion to her step-daughter was enough to arouse suspicion even had he not been on her trail. The young banker seemed entirely unaware of what was being done to his family daughter.

As the Doctor thought about it, he decided that he needed to encourage John to get Jeanette away from the mother and daughter.

The following day Doc went to the bank and stalked directly to John's private office. "Well, I guess you feel mighty proud of yourself, becoming vice-president of the bank." After a few more inconsequential remarks he turn to the subject nearest to his heart. "John, you have a very fine daughter-"

Quickly he was interrupted, for the young banker had been well-trained by his wife. "I have two fine daughters, Doc."

"Yeah, sure. But Jeanette is almost a young lady. What are your plans for her, John?"

"The fact is, I have been too busy looking after business to think much about it. However, Ben Hooper seems to have taken over the responsibility of looking after her. There is a fine boy and will make just as fine a man."

"Jeanette is highly gifted in music, I hear. Had you considered sending her East to study music? You do plan on sending her to college, don't you? Every girl should have college, these days, especially those who can well afford it."

John started, then turned pale. "Doc, I'm probably a selfish beast but how could I give her up for even a few years?"

As has been shown Dr. Cunningham was a born diplomat, a real artist at handling men and influencing people. Here was a real problem that needed to be solved and he planned to do just that. So before he left that bank office, John had promised to send his eldest daughter East to study music. She would graduate from high the following May and was to enter a girls' school in September. Of course Boston was considered the only proper place for girls like Jeanette.

That evening John broke the news to his wife and youngest daughter. "Are you crazy, John Barke?" she screamed at the top of her voice. "How can you think of sending that child half way across the nation to school when we have plenty of excellent colleges just as good not far from home? I supposed you loved her and wanted her home."

He reminded her that Jeanette would be seventeen in only a weak and that Miss Comstock, her music teacher from Jamestown, had warned them a year ago that she could teach her no more piano but should have more advanced instructor.

"Lucy's girl is all you can ever think of! Poor little Lucile is always neglected." Although his wife raved and stormed, John was becoming weary of her mad fits, realising how humiliating it must be to Jeanette. He didn't know just why but was convinced his favorite daughter was very unhappy. This was the real reason he had consented to send her East, hoping a change might help her.

For weeks Rose nagged and fussed. At first John avoided home as much as possible, but finally realise he was being a coward and leaving Jeannette to face the trouble alone. Also about this time he became suspicious of his wife's daughter, deciding she was only putting on an act.

Then Mother Barke was told of the plans for Jeanette and she was most pleased, knowing that the girl was most unhappy. She did not know exactly why but feared Rose might be two-faced, for she realized the woman was capable of any meanness.

Ben Hooper did not like to think of Jeanette going so far away. Although he had completed high school the previous year, his plans were to remain on the farm, working with his father on the shares, so of course he hoped to have the girl near him. Eventually he hoped to have her with him permanently, although they were too young to talk of their plans yet.

Now he plead, "Jeannette, please give up your plans-you can't leave me!"

"Ben, you know I can't endure this torture longer. I must escape. You must visit me in Boston, men are allowed to call on girls in such schools. Say, why don't you go East and attend college or the university? Oh, Ben, that would be wonderful if you would."

Try as she would, Rose could not prevent John from sending Jeanette away to college. For once he set down his foot. She was somewhat mollified by his promise to send Lucile away to boarding school to study music when she completed high school in two more years.

Dr. Cunningham asked Lulu Simpson if she wouldn't take Jeanette to the city and help her buy clothes for college. Let her have every beautiful and fussy thing any girl could wish. John will be only to glad to foot the bill."

Miss Simpson replied, "Doc, I'll do it. Won't that old step-mother pop her eyes when she sees our purchases? I detested Rose in our training days, now I hate her for what she has done to Lucy's daughter."

So the prim, gray-haired Miss Simpson took the girl to Chicago. "Now, child, we must use great care to buy only the latest styles, for you are going to one of the most exclusive woman's colleges in the East." Lulu not only wanted Jeannette to have the loveliest clothes for college, she wanted to tease and tantalize her step-mother.

The two shoppers spent a fully week in the city, attending the most expensive theaters and living at the swankiest hotels. The listened to the best in music which sent the girl into ecstasies of delight. Besides the game of tantalizing Rose, Lulu hope to build up Jeanette's morale before leaving for college. So they visited parks, window shopped, just for the fun of it, and did everything a small town girl would enjoy doing on her first trip to a city.

John had handed his daughter his checkbook and told her not to skimp on herself, and she followed his example. Lulu was surprised at the good taste Jeannette used in selecting her clothes. Now she possessed a wardrobe that might be the envy of any princess and when Rose and Lucile saw it, they were almost beside themselves with jealously.

Jeanette cried herself to sleep almost every night, consoled only by the knowlede that soon, she would be away from it all. Both her father and Ben had promised to visit her in Boston.

Then Ben decided he really did need a university education, even if he did plan only to become a farmer. Where could he find such a good place to study agriculture as in Boston University? Of course the one great reason for his newly acquired thirst for knowledge was his longing to be near Jeanette, not simply to be able to see her oftener but to protect her from the wolves that prowl around girls' colleges. And unless he became a college man how could he compete?

"Won't you be the queen of the ball in Boston?" sneered Lucile. "If folks only knew the truth about you! Some day the world will know. I wish I dare tell now!" Insinuations often can hurt more than open charges.

Lucile's black eyes snapped fire and her cherry-lips curled in disdain as she said, "You imagine your mother was a saint. Just wait till you hear the truth about that woman." She kept up her vigilance to the very last minute.

To hear her mother's name slandered hurt worse than all the rest. These charges caused Jeanette to wonder why her father never mentioned her mother, for it was plain to see he still loved her dearly, much better than his second wife. Then she decided it must be because of Rose's jealousy that he dare not speak of her.

Then she wondered why there were no pictures of her mother, not even a snapshot. Surely there must have been a wedding picture. Because folks often remarked that she looked exactly like her mother made her more curious to see a picture. Dare she ask her grandmother if she had any pictures of her mother? For years she had eagerly scrutinized every family photograph hoping to be told that some of them were of her mother.

Often she accompanied her grandmother to the Jamestown cemetery to place flowers on the graves of her mother and uncle Jerry. But she found little here except the inscription on the slab, "Lucy, wife of John Barke." Just that and no more, like the one of little Jerry whose grave was beside her. This bit of information and the slurring remarks of Lucile and Rose were all the information she could glean from all sources. She wished she might talk about her to Ben.

While Lucile was making vicious thrusts at her sister, she was delighted at the prospects of going to Boston in two years, only it seemed too long off.

"Mom, Jeanette will be having all the fun while I'm stuck here in this poky old school for two years."

Rose had no intentions of making her daughter wait so long. During Jeanette's Chicago trip, a be-speckled youth was installed in the Barke home to act as a tutor to Lucile. But this did not suit the girl any better. "Mama, do you mean to make me study summer?"

"My pet, don't worry your pretty head. You need not study. This man is paid well to get you a diploma in a hurry. Baby, you are to go to Boston next year, not two years from now as you father plans. If your dad were not so old-fashioned and behind the times you would not have to have a diploma." She smiled cunningly and maliciously.

Had John Barke really understood the method being used by his wife and daughter to obtain that important document, the diploma, he no doubt would have protested loudly. But it perhaps would have done him little good, for Rose was determined, and when she set her head to a task, she usually rode down all opposition.

Rose Garner Barke did have a good brain if only she would use it for a good cause, something worth while instead of for selfish and vicious purposes. Too often her energies were put forth to injure somebody and bring gain to herself and her daughter.

CHAPTER VIII

The Boston Seminary, exclusive school for young ladies, opened with a quiet flourish. Rich and cultured girls from all over the land were in attendance. The glamour of it all nearly overwhelmed the shy girl from the small town of Novinger. Jeanette Barke was one of the youngest and most strikingly beautiful girls to pass through the lines of the student-faculty reception.

Elsie Hamilton, with her slender figure and youthful face, stood in the receiving line with the other faculty and board members. She loved to meet the girls, even if she had gone through this formality for a number of years.

In imagination, each girl she met was always her own long-lost daughter. On this particular night she was thinking more than ever of her children. "Maybe my sweet bright-haired daughter died in infancy," she said to herself. "If alive, she may be married. In small communities, girls marry very-young."

This attractive teacher with the few threads of gray among the golden strands of hair was also wondering about her mulatto son. "Where is Jerry tonight?" Miss Kieth had written that he had run away from the white farmer who had taken him from the orphanage in Illinois the year before to give him a home. Not even Harriet knew where the boy was.

Although he had written Miss Kieth, all of his letters had been mailed on the train, giving no identifying postmarks. Else recalled one quotation from Harriet's letter that greatly disturbed her. "Miss Kieth, I'm sorry to seem ungrateful to you and the farmer who gave me the home, but I'm seeing the world. Don't worry, I know how to take care of myself."

As Miss Hamilton continued to meet the new girls, her mind was far away. She recalled another quotation from Harriet's letter. "For one thing," Jerry had said, "I'm determined to find out who I am. Too many taunts about my parents. Maybe I'm not a Nigger after all." If he were only happy and contented, it would be easier for her.

Suddenly Miss Hamilton brought herself back to her present environment. She thought to herself, "What a pretty girl is coming."

"Miss Hamilton, Miss Barke of Novinger, Iowa." The blood drained from the woman's face. She swayed and would have fallen but for the protecting arm of Lang Smith, a handsome board member of the seminary.

The girl had been too self-conscious to give the swooning woman more than her finger tips and passed on the next person in line. She did not realize that anything unusual was taking place.

"Lang," whispered Elsie meekly, I'm better now. So sorry to have made a scene."

"Elsie, you did not make a scene. Only a very few persons noticed that you left the line. This room is too warm and you have over-worked."

Lang Smith, socialite and prominent member of the board of directors of the college, had been Miss Hamilton's devoted slave for a long time. She had tried to convince the wealthy, distinguished looking man she had no intentions of ever marrying.

"Lang, I've loved and lost. I cannot love another," she told him. But he had been content to be a friend, if he could be no more.

Now the white-faced woman at the reception said, "Please, Lang, take me back. I'm quite all right now, I must not miss any more of the girls." Although he protested, she insisted, saying to herself, "I must get one more glimpse of her dear face."

As Jeanette passed on down the line Elsie noted every graceful movement. She wondered who had trained her in such good taste in dress. With pride swelling her mother's heart she saw the warm reception the girl was getting from both faculty and students.

"If only I could see her eyes and their expression," she thought. But when she did see them, so much like her own, her heart sank, for the sweet, pathetic haunted look in her eyes told her some tragedy lay back of them.

Miss Hamilton was prevented from getting near her daughter again that evening. She long to find out so many things. She spent the night trying to devise ways of meeting and becoming acquainted with this lovely creature, this child whom she had never expected to see again. Was she only dreaming and would she suddenly awaken.

As the students began to register next day Elsie's one thought was to get another glimpse of her own daughter. When at last she saw her approaching her desk and learned the girl was to major in music, the woman felt the need of Lang Smith's strong arm again, but she managed to keep her composure.

To think that Jeanette was to specialize in the study of piano when Miss Hamilton would be her teacher was too good to be true. Elsie knew she would be seeing her several times each week. Surely that was a miracle.

A few days after this Jeanette remarked to Margaret, her roommate, who had spent two years at the seminary, "I just love my piano teacher. Every time I see her I feel like squeezing her. Now isn't that the silliest thing you ever heard of when I have known her less than a week? Wouldn't she be shocked to hear that? She would know that I am only a lonesome country kid."

"Miss Hamilton is the most loved teacher in the college. Her students all worship her," said Margaret Sonne enthusiastically . "Don't hesitate to show her affection. It is rumored that she has had a great tragedy in her life. Lang Smith, one of the most eligible bachelors in Boston, has tried for years to lead her to the altar."

With a dreamy expression in her eyes Jeanette said, "I hope that when I reach her age I may be half as sweet as she is."

Margaret drew in her breath with a quick start. "Jeanette Barke, you will think me crazy, but it seems to me this minute that you look enough like Miss Hamilton to be her kid sister."

Jeanette laughed at the idea but she often thought of it, knowing she would love to have her for her mother. Of course she was not old enough for that, she said to herself. "I wonder if mother did look like her? If only I had a picture of her." Then she remembered she didn't so much as know the maiden name of her mother.

Miss Hamilton encouraged the girl's confidence, and she soon learned that John Barke had married Rose Garner.

"Why did it have to be that girl? She cried to herself. "No wonder Jeanette is unhappy. What has that spiteful woman done to her?" Elsie remembered the scene at her bedside when the twins were born, how mean and scornful this nurse had been, so different from Lulu Simpson.

Jeanette mentioned her sister Lucile, but to Elsie Hamilton, she seemed reluctant to do so. The woman's mother heart read between the lines, and wondered what Rose and her daughter might not have done to this newly-found daughter of hers.

The attractive girl from the Midwest had more than one admirer before too long, but Ben Hooper stood first in her estimation. Elsie liked the many youth with his frank open countenance. His stalwart figure and sparkling dark eyes reminded her of John Barke as she remembered him.

Far into the night Miss Hamilton lay awake and thought about her daughter and her home life. A floods of memories filled her brain. She wondered if John were gray and middle-aged appearing. While the teacher's hair was flecked with silver, her cheek was as smooth and velvety as a girls.

Under the warmth of love and friendship Jeanette lost her dejected expression. Her wistful smile bloomed into buoyant laughter of normal girlhood.

One day Miss Sonne remarked to Miss Hamilton, "Jeanette can perhaps count more friends than any new girl here." Because she has been snubbed and suffered so much the girl is always kind and considerate to all she met, never willingly slighting anyone. To be sure this brought its fruits. Besides, it was soon learned that the Barkes were very rich people.

Another thing that made Jeanette popular was that both students and faculty began to notice that she was a favorite of her teacher, Miss Hamilton. But it did not turn the girl's head to be liked by students and teachers; she had been too unhappy all her life to become vain now.

Elsie hoped to discourage her daughter from accepting too much attention from the young swains about the seminar. For with her beauty and reputed riches, she was literally deluged with invitations. He mother long to keep her sweet and unspoiled.

It is a well-known fact that some people who have been snubbed all their lives and are suddenly plunged into popularity may be utterly ruined. But Miss Hamilton need not have feared for Jeanette, for the girl had a wise little head, proving she could manage the situation.

One day in late winter the girl came bounding into the studio. "Oh, Miss Hamilton, daddy may visit me at Easter time! Here is a letter I just received. I have the nicest father in the world and you are my very dearest teacher. I can hardly wait for daddy to meet you."

Elsie Hamilton clutched the sides of the piano and sank down heavily on the bench.

"You are ill." The girl flew to the window and pushed it up. Elsie's face was livid and great drops of sweat stood out on her forehead. "Shall I call the school doctor, Miss Hamilton?" asked the girl anxiously.

"No, dear. I will be all right in a moment. Please help me to the lounge in the next room." There were no more lessons in the teacher's studio that day.

Jeannet came early the next morning. "Miss Hamilton you look absolutely sick. Do you think you should work today?"

"I am feeling better, Jeanette. It was kind of you to come, dear." Elsie had slept little that night, trying to decide what she should do, knowing she never could afford to let the Barkes find her now. Neither could she run away just as she had found her beloved daughter.

She kept worrying about the subject when one day just before Easter Jeanette walked into the studio looking very unhappy and said, "Daddy can't come after all. Moma took sick the very night he was going to start. He called the family doctor but couldn't fine one thing wrong with her, still mother insisted she had appendicitis. She is a graduate nurse. Doc told father to go anyway, but of course he wouldn't do that."

Miss Hamilton drew a sigh of relief. It was easy to understand that Rose was up to her usual tricks, yet for once she was glad the woman had prevented John from making his trip to Boston. Yet, she did not feel secure, knowing that sooner or later she must face the issue again.

Jeanette pulled the letter from her pocket and smiled in spite of her disappointment. "Miss Hamilton, do listen to this. "Daughter, you have written so much about your piano instructor, I am eager to meet her.'"

Elsie hoped her daughter could not hear the beating of her heart. To her it sounded like the beating of an anvil. After Jeanette left the woman sat staring out of the window, but she did not see the bright sprinng grass and leaves nor the song of the birds. She thought only of the prooblem that confronted her.

She tried to still her shaking hands. "Why can't I learn self-control? It is childish of a woman of my age and experience to show emotion." she scolded. "Surely a kind Providence guided me to my daughter, it will not let me lose her again, but will show me how to meet my husband."

Then she smiled to herself. "How vain of me to fear. Am I not a middle-aged woman? It is almost twenty years since Dr. Cunningham took me to Alabama in his plane. If I keep my poise, John never would recognize for surely I have changed decidedly.

"Besides, he thinks me dead. Jeanette told me her mother died at her birth, and without doubt when the Barkes could not find me after I ran away from that Lawton Hotel they think I was lost or committed suicide.

"Anyway, John Barke never would expect to find me in this old established New England college. He would be thinking of me as I looked when he let his old father kick me out of his house. He must think of me as the crushed, forsaken wife he discarded so long ago, believing I would not be able to rise above the disgrace. No, my husband never would know me if he met me face to face on the street. I have nothing to fear."

CHAPTER IX

Miss Hamilton was not only a very busy teacher, for several years she had carried on various humanitarian activities in the cities. Besides two orphanages she visited regularly, she looked after a slum family.

Charley Hoke and his family lived down in the Negro section of Boston, the dirtiest and lowest of the slum areas. Mr. Hoke was not a full-blooded Negro, but his wife and children, save one, were as black as midnight.

Miriam, his ten-year-old daughter, looked more like an angel than a child. Her big blue eyes stared out of a pale pinched face from a halo of soft yellow curls. Her skin was soft and delicate.

For several years Elsie Hamilton had practically kept this family from starvation. There were ten children in all. Mr. Hoke was one of Boston's garbage haulers, but his small check would not feed twelve mouths.

All of his children showed symptoms of the dread and crippling malady of rickets. They also showed they were suffering from malnutrition. Two were crippled from rickets; one wearing braces on both legs, the other too crippled to take a step.

The Salvation Army and the city welfare helped care for the family, while Miss Hamilton gave them clothing as well as food and money. Charley's aged uncle in Nova Scotia sent him small checks at regular intervals.

Some of the faculty members of the Boston Girls' Seminary knew a little about Elsie's charities, but the girls knew nothing of those activities. Lang Smith sometimes accompanied her on her visits and did his bit.

One day Jeanette said, "Miss Hamilton, excuse me, but I saw you yesterday. I-I don't want to seem impertinent, but you were riding with such a-"

"So you saw me with Miriam. She is my little protege."

"Your what? She was such a beautiful child, yet she looked queer."

"Miriam, as well as all of her brothers and sisters suffer from rickets. Yesterday I was taking her to the city clinic for treatments." Then she gave a brief sketch of the Hoke family.

"How interesting! And such a noble work. May I go with you when you visit them next time?"

Miss Hamilton hesitated. Surely it could do not harm to take her along. She had too much spending money anyway, it would do her good to use some of it for the family, they needed it so desperately. Elsie's check would only go so far.

These visits to the colored family in the Boston slums were another tie that bound the hearts of these two lonely women. But had Elsie only known all of the facts about Jeanette's persecution at home, she would never have permitted her to visit the Negro family.

The girl's kind heart went out to the Hokes, especially to the pretty little Miriam. Much of her allowance after that went to help the family. She enjoyed buying pretty clothes for Miriam, and sometimes she and the teacher made over garments for her from their own clothes.

As the school year neared its close Jeanette knew it had been the happiest days of her life; in fact the first time she had ever really been happy and contented. She had made many close friends, and to her knowledge not one enemy. Best of all, she had found Miss Hamilton. Being so happy, she almost forgot how miserable her home could be with her sister and step-mother.

One day not long before school was to close Jeanette came dancing into the studio, waving a telegram. "Oh, Miss Hamilton, daddy is coming for commencement. The message just came. Tomorrow you shall meet my father, the nicest daddy any girl ever had." Then a cloud flitted over her face. "Lucile is coming too. You will want to meet my sister."

At last Elsie must face the issue. After the girl left she said to herself, "I dare not meet John yet, and I do not want to meet his other daughter, Rose Garner's girl."

She managed to drag through her school duties, then she hurried to her apartment and turned the key in the door. Throwing herself across the bed she hoped the earth would open and hide her. She realized she dare not run away.

"Tomorrow I must face him, the father of my children, yet he is tied to another woman." She realized she loved him as much as the day he sent her away. Try as hard as she could, it was impossible for her to hate him, for discarding her and letting her father send her away.

It was no use for her to argue to herself that John would not recognize her after almost twenty years. Around and around went her thoughts. Should she run away? That would arouse suspicion. And what would Jeanette think?

Without attempting to eat a bite she made ready for bed, but not to sleep. Chiding herself for being childish about the matter, she attempted to read to calm her mind, but it was no use. All night long she wrangled with her question. Daylight found her still awake, still wondering what to do.

But nature settled the question, for when she attempted to rise, she fell half-fainting back on the pillow, neither could she sit up in bed. Maggie, the maid who came in to help every morning insisted she call a doctor. Miss Hamilton refused, but by noon she was glad to do so.

The school physician came and after carefully checking Miss Hamilton's condition said briskly, "Nothing very serious, my dear. Overwork. Too much strain on that heart. Remember this is not the first time it has acted up. Remain quietly in bed for a few days. Now Maggie, you are the maid, allow no callers.

Jeanette sent flowers and a loving note saying, "We are staying until tomorrow to show Lucile the city. Dear Miss Hamilton, how can I leave without seeing you once more?"

Elsie reached into her desk for stationery and penned a note. "Jeanette, this afternoon at five o'clock Maggie will be away on an errand. Could you come at that time?"

As long as she lived Elsie Hamiltdon knew she would cherish those few moments spent with her daughter. Both women seemed to sense a bond deeper than that of teacher and student. At parting Miss Hamilton sobbed outright, while Jeanette cried as if her heart would break, remembering the home she must soon face.

The girl had not told her teacher the latest trouble that confronted her. As soon as Lucile arrived she announced, "Jeanette, I am picking out our room right now, for I am coming back with you in September. Yes,

September. Don't stare like a moron, for I have my diploma. Finished high in three years! Don't you wish you had brains like your sister?"

How Jeanette hated to give up her good roommate, Margaret Some, but dared not refuse to room with her sister, realizing it would cause unkind comment, besides Lucile would be just that much meaner. It was of those things she was thinking of when she and Miss Hamilton bade goodbye.

On the long drive to Novinger, Iowa, Lucile insisted on riding in the back seat with Ben Hooper. The dark scowl on his face amused Jeanette, and she was delighted to have the privilege of this intimate ride in the front seat with her father.

He said, "Daughter, what have you done to yourself? You do not look like the same girl who left us last fall. Darling, you are too sweet for words!" With his free arm John Barke pressed her to him and kissed her pink cheek. Lucile saw the love and adoration in her father's eyes and clinched her small fists and swore vengeance. Ben too saw the expression in John's face; neither did the wicked look in the face of the girl beside him escape his eyes, and he vowed to protect and shield Jeanette with his own life, if need be.

The first evening after her arrival home her father said, "Jeanette, play for us. Rose come and listen to our little lady play the piano."

The second-Mrs. Barke's small gray eyes became points of steel, but with a guileless smile upon her thin lips she came into the room. Her claws were carefully sheathed for future use.

After Jeanette had finished the woman said, "That is swell music, my dear. But, John, darling, don't you notice what time the child has? Honey, mother must help you with your time."

Mrs. Barke could ply "Three Blind Mice," "Beautiful Katy," and "Chew, Chew Her Gum" with two fingers by ear. That, and that only, was the present extent of her musical ability. She possessed as much ear for music and its time as a white owl.

But again she spoke up. "Papa, now let Jeanette listen to Lucile play the piano. The child never neglects her music. It is her very life. That is why I'm so eager for her to go East. If that Miss Hamilton isn't far enough advanced to teach her, we must find a private instructor in the city of Boston. Some day, Lucile, darling, you shall study abroad."

With an important swish of skirts and a toss of her raven curls she settled herself on the bench. Then with many flourishes of her white jeweled hands and much ungainly motion of her elbows, she flew over the keys.

Her mother sat on the edge of her chair, bending forward, her eyes gleaming, her lips parted to drink in the divine notes that came from her daughter's fingers. With an audible sigh of satisfaction when the noise ended she said, "Now that is classical music with some pep to it!"

Even John appeared embarrassed, while Jeanette sat with downcast eyes, which Rose mistook for jealousy and envy for her sister's marvelous talent. Jeanette's cheeks burned with with shame and mortification. She said to herself, "Bach would surely turn over in his grave if he could hear that racket called one of his compositions." Her heart cried out against such blatant ignorance. "What will Miss Hamilton say!"

CHAPTER X

The summer of persecution with her sister and step-mother in Novinger finally came to an end for Jeanette Barke. But for her father and Ben Hooper she felt she would have died. She marvelled at the blindness of her father. Why couldn't he see what Rose and Lucile were doing to her?

As she thought of returning to the seminary and again being with her music instructor, she was filled with delightful anticipations. Yet she looked forward to the new situation with her sister in school also with grave apprehension. Still she realized she had many friends at the college, surely Lucile could not influence them against her.

When they arrived at the seminary and met Elsie, Lucile was as brazen as usual and said, "Miss Hamilton," haughtily extending the tips of her fingers to merely touch the friendly extended hand. "I have heard so much about you, I feel I already know you."

Elsie was struck by the girl's dark, sparkling beauty, so much like her father, yet she was Rose Garner herself, except in appearance. Miss Hamilton was shocked at the hard mouth with its bold, red lips, and the attractive, though sly and cunning, dark eyes.

The teacher said to herself, "Will Boston's exclusive and cultured college be able to tame or refine this hateful, ill-bred girl?"

Yet strange as it may seem Lucile took by storm the young men who frequented the college circle. Yet, men are unpredictable in affairs of the heart.

Although reputed to be the stronger sex they often display the wisdom of children when dealing with women of beauty. This girl was not only beautiful but rich as well. She had not been slow in letting the fact be known that she was heir to the Barke millions.

She loved to display her expensive clothes with their gaudy colors. Jeanette's wardrobe of modest colors was the object of her scorn. "We are young but once. Why dress to look like some prim school-marm? Now my clothes-color, beautiful rich, gorgeous color. See these jewels. Dad tried to tell mom that I was too young to wear this lovely pearl neckless.

"But what do men know about women's dress? Daddy has spent all of his life in a hick town, except when in the army long ago. Beside, the army didn't tell him anything about the dress of women. Now mama, she came from the city, and she keeps up with the times."

With her loud manners, gay colors, and display of jewels Lucile did abash the young men. To them she was exciting, intoxicating. Had she not been an heiress would they have been blind to her garish manners?

However, she did not succeed so well with the women of the college. Most of the girls of the better families accepted her with reservations, recognizing her only because they loved and admired her sister. A certain number of the freshmen girls said she was fun and welcomed her to their circle.

Miss Hamilton watched with interest this drama of every day life, speculating on what Lucile might do to make her daughter unhappy. But suddenly Elsie's interest was diverted into another channel. Miss Kieth had written a letter, enclosing one from Jerry, but his letter had given no identifying postmark.

"I am busting broncos on a real ranch, lots of fun," said the letter. "By now I'm almost convinced there is no Negro blood in my family, at least I refuse to think so. If cornered, I merely brush it off by saying there might be a little Greek or Spanish blood in my ancestors."

"No honest Negro parent wants his son to bring home a white wife. More than one colored father has slammed the door in the face of his son who tries this. Yes, Harriet Kieth was right, intermarriage between the races brings sorrow to both races. How will the lives of my two precious children end? And who is to blame for this? How could I have Negro blood?"

At the holiday season Miss Hamilton felt a sinister influence creeping about her daughter. Jeanette had lost her vivaciousness, she had not been happy all year, not since Lucile had come on the scene. Yet something more serious was now in the atmosphere.

Her popularity was gone. Young men no longer rushed her for engagements; in fact few of them even asked to take her out. They were too enamored with the enchanting Lucile to notice her quieter sister. Only Ben Hooper remained faithful among the men. Elsie compared his devotion width that of Lang Smith to her.

Jeanette grew thin and her music lost much of its charm. More and more she spent her leisure time with her music teacher, seemingly dreading to go to her room. She avoided her former friends except Margaret her former roommate and Ben Hooper.

Weeks and months rolled on. Elsie was not able to get at the bottom of the trouble, yet it was plain to see that Lucile was the reason for all of her sister's unhappiness. Still there was nothing that she could put her finger on.

The school year was nearing its close. Jeanette looked more troubled than ever. Elsie said to herself, "Dare I invite her to spend her vacation with me? We would go to the beautiful Canadian woods, from her envious sister and spiteful step-mother.

Only Jeanette knew what she had endured all year from Lucile. Taunts and sneers about her mother were heapd on her. The dark insinuations were driving her mad.

She protested, she pleaded with her sister, but to no avail. "Why do you make slurring remarks before my friends, Lucile, dear. Can't you see that you are driving away every friend I possess?"

This was the very aim of the malicious girl, and she had succeeded beyond her fondest hopes. Upon her arrival at the seminary in September, Jeannette was one of the most popular girls on the campus. Now she was shunned, ignored, and made the object of cruel gossip.

"Mama," wrote Lucile, "you should see my angel sister these days. She acts as if she had lost her last friend, and that is almost the truth. Last year she really was a popular girl-that was before I came. I have put her just where she belongs, in the same social status she occupied in Novinger."

"She stays in our room but little, for which I am most thankful. No one ever visits her but Margaret, her former roommate. She moans and groans and even cries in her sleep-when she sleeps. Now me, I sleep like a baby."

"Why shouldn't I sleep and be happy?" continued the letter. "I have had ten proposals of marriage since I came, but I doubt if Jeanette has had even one, unless it is from Ben Hooper. He is still silly about her."

"The boys who want to marry me are mostly from the university. The girls here at the seminary warn me against all of them because they are from poor families. My friends call them poor scraps who are after my money. All they are are gold diggers."

"But, Oh mom, I have my eyes on a certain man, well, I haven't seen him yet, but he is the most eligible bachelor in Boston. Now maybe Lang Smith is really is just as big a catch, but Miss Hamilton seems to have her net around him, besides he is too old for me.

"As I started to say, this Howard Everett is hard to trap. No girl has ever succeeded in interesting him in the least so far. The Everets belong to one of New England's oldest families.

"Wait until he hears about our family. Grandpa says the Barkes can trace their family back for five-hundred years, or is it thousand? I tell everybody we are French, and maybe we came from a royal family, that I am not too sure. That is enough to keep them interested. Besides, I brag about you coming from the city and that your family belong to-I forget what I say. So wait until Howard learns about me."

For once Lucile did tell the truth, and she did not exaggerate when she said the Everetts were one of the oldest, most aristocratic families in old Boston. Besides, they had wealth, culture and brains. Many young ladies had indeed tried to catch Howard. Would Lucile succeed where others had failed?

When Elsie Hamilton invited Jeanette to accompany her on her vacation the girl was delighted and immediately sent her father a letter. "Please, daddy, may I go? Nothing would please me so much as to spend a summer with my teacher. Say that I may go."

By return mail came a long letter from her step-mother saying, "You ungrateful selfish girl. After all your sister has done for you all you life, you would now run away off to Canada and leave her to spend the summer alone in this hick town. Think what she has had to put up from you all year in school. You should hide you head in shame. Of course your father is not letting you traipse off to Canada with a strange woman, even if she is your teacher."

Although Rose stormed and nagged she could not prevent John from consenting to her request. He set his lips in a straight line and said, "Jeanette needs a real vacation, for she has worked extremely hard in school. Ben says she looks thin and pale, The trip should do her good and fit her for school next fall."

Ben had dropped a few poignant remarks to John a to the state of affairs with his two daughters when he went home at Christmas time. It was a shock to the father, but he promised to keep his eyes open in the future.

Just before commencement, Miss Hamilton and Jeanette made a final call at the Hoke home. A new baby had arrived, making life harder than ever for the overworked man. He was stooped with age, yet the records at the welfare hall stated his age was only forty-two.

Jeanette had written her father about the Hokes and their great need. To her surprise and disappointment he disapproved of her calls and said in a letter, "Now Jeanette, don't be mixing with those dirty Niggers. Your grandfather was very angry when he read your letter. The Negro slums is no lace for a young girl. Here is a check. Give it to you teacher for the Hokes. You keep away from them!"

But she could not forget them and their needs. So occassionally she went with Elsie on her visits, and she continued to share her allowance money with them and help Miss Hamilton make over garments for the children.

At last vacation came. Sullenly Lucile told her sister good-bye and returned to Novinger, declaring she would win Ben away from her if she didn't watch out. But Jeanette had no fears of losing him, besides she knew Lucile wanted Howard Everet.

Elsie Hamilton and her daughter spent three months together in cabin in the deep forests of Canada. In reality, it was a summer in paradise for two love-starved women. Every minute was precious to them and they wasted no time in social pleasures with other people, but spent every moment absorbing each other's love.

CHAPTER XI

All too soon the Boston Girls' Seminary was again in full swing. It looked as if Lucile Barke was to continue to be a very popular girl, especially in the younger set. She was really more beautifully and expensively dressed than the previous year. 'Overdressed' was the verdict of the teachers and the better class of girls of the college.

Much to her chagrin, Miss Hamilton learned Lucile was to continue her music under her. She knew the girl had neither love nor talent for the subject. Only envy of her sister did she enroll in the department.

She not only was a poor student in music, but she was unkind and rude to Miss Hamilton, realizing that Jeanette was her favorite and close friend. Another reason for Lucile taking music was because she had heard that Howard Everett was a great patron of music.

One of her friends had said, "Howard Everett attends all of the very classical operas in the city and sometimes even comes to our musical recitals."

"Girls, do stop telling me about this prince of a man unless you intend to make it possible for me to meet him," Lucile cried excitedly.

"My dear child," said Margaret Sonne, "you are too young to attract that man. He has been abroad! He must be at last twenty-three years old, while you-"

"Won't I be eighteen in a short time. Margaret Sonne, you know that men like their women young. Now you and Jeanette-pooh! He wouldn't even see you, for you are too old, especially if I were present. Just wait and see."

Lucile had worked herself up to a frensy, and she said, "Oh girls, imagine what it will men to live on Fifth Avenue in a brown stone front.

I'll have diamonds and rubies and pearls, and millions of dollars, counting the millions Grandpa Barke gives me for a wedding present, of course."

"Now let's see, we will spend most of our time abroad. Winters in Naples, or is it Florence where the elite spend their winter months? We will own a gondola and a yacht, a plane, of course, and well everything that fashionable people have.

"Our children will have nurse-maids, governesses, and there will be a footman, a-a butler and I must study up on just what we will do."

One of the girls said, "The Everetts move in the most select circles."

"Reckon I better begin to practice to move so-so. Girls, meet the future Mrs. Howard Everett." She gave an extravagantly haughty bow to her admiring friends.

Finally Lucile and her set did meet Howard Everett, yet much to their indignation he didn't seem at all impress with the sparkling Lucile. Instead, it was the demure Jeanette who carried off the trophy.

But when the poor girl reached her room her sister couldn't say enough mean things to her. "Jeanette Barke," snapped Lucile in the presence of a group of her friends, "why did you hang onto Howard like a leach? Mother would have been so humiliated. Actually he appeared bored to death. I'm going to write mom about it."

Not long after this Howard was seen with Jeanette at the opera. She was so careful not to seem possessive that under the critical eye of her sister she became almost indifferent to the man. The less interest she evinced, the more attention he showered upon her.

Lovely flowers and huge boxes of candy found their way to her room. He became her escort wherever she went. In spite of her sister's cruel treatment, she began to regain her happy poise.

Jeanette said to her teacher, "Oh Miss Hamilton, I never dreamed life could be so sweet. "Don't you think Howard Everett is the most charming man you ever saw? And he is so fine and noble."

"Y-e-s, Mr. Everett is handsome and fine, I hear, but to my mind he is no finer or better looking than Ben Hooper. What about Ben?"

A cloud flitted across the girl's face for a moment, then cleared. "Ben understands. All my life he has been my friend and protector, yet he has always known that I loved him only as a brother. I confided in him right away about Howard, and he admitted he is a splendid young man."

Elsie was pleased for Jeanette's sake that a man of Howard's character had been attracted by her, yet she looked upon such a marriage with apprehension. She remembered that she too had laid here heart at the feet of the man she loved, only to have it trampled upon. "Will Howard some day discard my angel daughter? Cast her aside like a tattered garment?"

Then she thought of Ben Hooper. "Never would he desert her no matter what might happen. But was she correct in her judgment of the boy? How would she know, or Ben himself just how would he react should his wife bear him a mulatto child? Could he endure the test? No one can answer that question until faced with the issue.

The beautiful, but haughty Mrs. Everett was pleased with her son's choice. She said to him, "Howard, I had despaired of you ever selecting a girl suited to your worth and station in life. But Miss Barke fulfills my dreams beyond expectation, for she is not only beautiful, but cultured and delightfully gifted in music."

He stooped and kissed the cheek of his fastidious mother. "It is gratifying to hear you say this, mother, for Jeanette is an angel in goodness and sweetness. Surely two such creatures were never created."

"Son, think of your lovely, talented children with such a girl for your wife."

He blushed and laughed. "But, mother dear, we aren't married yet, In fact, Jeanette and I are not even engaged."

"Howard Everett, what do you mean by dilly-dallying? Suppose some other man discovers her? What about that wealthy, handsome Ben Hooper?"

"Don't worry. Ben is a real man and as rich as Croesus, but he hasn't a chance He is just a big brother. Jeanette told me so."

"Do not delay too long," she warned with a sigh. "For I consider her one girl in a thousand. But there is one thing I must speak to you about. I cannot tolerate that coarse, loud-mouthed sister of hers. How can such a creature be related to Jeanette? Why should our exclusive seminary admit a low-bred girl of her character?"

"Lucile is only a half-sister. And I feel toward her much as you do, for she does grate on my sensibilities. However, she is a very popular young lady."

"Money seems all that counts these days," said the woman indignantly.

Then the girls in the college saw the brilliant stone on Jeanette's finger, knowing she was to marry Howard Everett, although the engagement had not been announced.

The pals of Lucile gathered in her room to discuss the event. One of the girls said, "I hear that Mrs. Everett is delighted with her son's choice. Lucile, she was heard to say that your sister is the most perfect lady she ever met."

"Thanks, pal for the tip. What would that dame say if she knew the facts about my sister's background? Ah, well, I know how to be the sweet, affectionate little sister. Keep an eye on my technique from here on."

"Given up the chase, Lucile?"

"So long as there is life, there is hope. My dream of becoming Mrs. Howard Everett has not entirely faded, yet."

"Many a slip between the cup and the lip." quoted a dark-eyed girl comfortingly."

The social column carried an elaborate account of the engageent of Miss Jeanette Bark, the heiress, to Howard Everette. Elsie saved every picture and word from the newspaper about her daughter.

Harriet Kieth also saw the Boston paper and remarked, "Such a beautiful girl, but not one bit more attractive than her mother twenty years ago." But she wondered what would be the outcome of such a marriage. "Maybe she will find security and happiness by marrying into this old Boston family," she said to the spinster Miss Hardesty.

Miss Hardesty, snapped, "Yes, if her children don't show their Negro strain."

Miss Kieth felt alost resentul tht Jeanette should have so much and Jerry seemingly almost nothing. Wasn't the boy nearly an outcast in society? At least he must be forced to go about explaining or apologizing for his parentage. Always he was under suspicion. True, Jeanette had had her persecutions too, but for the past two years she had had her mother, and Harriet Kieth supposed the girl was very happy.

As the fiancee of Howard Everett, Jeanette's popularity quickly returned. Even Lucile and her youthful crowd would be stupid to snub the future Mrs. Howard Everett. Especially since his mother took great pride in introducing her to her most exclusive friends. For the time being Lucile seemed stunned since the tide had changed against her nefarious activities.

Howard's devotion, merry smile, and infectious laughter began to ring the roses back to Jeanettte's cheeks. She lived in a new world, a realm high above Lucile and her scornful smiles and malicious thrusts.

Miss Hamilton was delighted to see her daughter gay, buoyant, and vivacious again, almost forgetting that there could be anything but supreme bliss for her pretty little girl.

The wedding was to take place in June at the Barke mansion instead of at Jeanette's home. For at last John had had his eyes opened to the wicked behavior of his wife and her daughter. He was determined that his beautiful eldest child have a wedding day unclouded by sinister influences.

Mrs. Howard was to be present at her son's marriage. Even Elsie had consented to be a guest, too. She had taken to wearing dark, heavy shell-rimmed spectacles which made her feel very secure from being recognized as the former Lucy Barke.

Lang Smith had chided her, saying, "You look like an old maid school ma'am."

"My maiden aunt," whispered Lucile spitefully to her friends, yet loud enough for Jeanette to hear.

"Oh, Miss Hamilton, those glasses just spoil your beauty," protested Jeanette.

So with the various comments, the teacher considered herself in no danger, and with pleasurable anticipation looked forward to the trip to Novenger. It made her feel more secure to know that Lang Smith would be a guest too. And of course there would be other mutual friends like Ben Hooper and his parents. The boy seemed more like a brother to her daughter than ever.

Just as soon as Jeanette had had time to complete her shopping for the important event after commencement, Dr. Cunningham would fly to Boston for the two sisters to bring them home. Elsie planned to meet the doctor at that time, eager to test her guise, yet having no fear of recognition.

Commencement week arrived. Miss Hamilton was busier than ever, for she spent her leisure time for days helping Jeanette with her trousseau, and planning her new life. It gave her great pleasure to think that the young couple were to make their home in Boston after their honeymoon in Europe.

She was unusually rushed with school work, for there were more than the usual number of graduates from her department. Each of these girls required special supervision for their recitals. Besides, she was not sleeping well because of the overwork and extra responsibilities. Subconsciously, it was her own instead of Jeanette's wedding she was preparing for. John Barke's image filled her mind night and day.

Then one day Miss Babcock, the dean of women, burst into her studio without knocking and gasped, "Miss Hamilton, come! It's Jeanette Barke!"

CHAPTER XII

The blood drained from Elsie's face as she cried, "What? Tell me! Where is she?"

"She is in the dispensary. We couldn't find you! An hour ago she fainted in the cloak room, dropped to the floor like dead! She is still unconscious!"

The women ran as fast as they could. There on a small white cot in the dispensary lay Jeanette. The school doctor and nurse looked grave. Lucile stood by her sister's side, her face ghastly, her eyes terrified but with a strange gleam in them.

"How is she?" Panted Miss Hamilton.

The physician said, "We hope it is only a faint, yet it does not seem to be an ordinary swoon."

Elsie turned to Lucile and asked, "Was Jeanette ill when she left your room this morning? Do you know what caused her to faint?"

"No, Miss Hamilton. Yes, no, well-I don't know a thing about it!" The wise woman noted the shifty eyes and great agitation.

The girl in white uniform signaled for Miss Hamiton to follow her into the adjoining room. Then closing and locking the door she said, "I have told this to no one, but you should know, Miss Hamilton. Jeanette's former roommate told me, and she loves Miss Barke like a sister and has watched Lucile's treatment of her the past two years, and it is growing worse every day. Last year she started insinuations about her birth-"

"Her birth?" interrupted Elsie aghast. "W-what do you men?"

"About her mother. The story has been in circulation again this year, but was hushed up for a time after the announcement of Jeanette's engagement to Mr. Everett."

"W-what did Lucile say about her m-mother? Tell me," whispered Elsie.

"I can't its too horrible." The nurse stopped and wiped her eyes. "She-said-that her mother was part Negro. That Jeanette has a Negro twin brother. At first no one believed the story, but then some one saw her with you when you visited the colored family down in-"

Miss Hailton managed to get to the window and opened it for air, holding onto the ledge for support.

The nurse continued. "Lucile is madly in love with Howard Everett-all the girls know that. Now she has renewed her efforts to get him by broadcasting this story bout Jeanette, hoping it will reach the ears of Howard and his mother and prevent the approaching marriage.

"Knowing that her sister was in the cloak room Lucile and her crowd deliberately discussed the story in all its boldness in the hall, wanting her to hear what was being said about her."

"But when Jeanette dropped to the floor as if dead, the girls became alarmed and some one called the doctor. Margaret, Jeanette's former roommate, wondered if she should tell the doctor and I said you should know the story first and decide what to do."

All night long Elsie sat by the side of her child's bed, wishing she might die for her daughter. The school nurse flitted here and there administering remedies to the still unconscious girl. The physician had left orders to be called if there were any change in his patient.

Near the break of day, the sick girl opened her eyes and stared about vacantly. Quickly Elsie bent over her, but no sign of recognition came into the lovely eyes.

"Jeanette, dear," whispered the teacher softly, "don't you know me? I am Miss Hamilton."

"Who are you? I want my mother. Mother, my poor mother! Lucile, it is not true! I won't believe you! Don't you tell falsehoods about my dead mother. Howard, don't believe her." The tired eyes closed again.

Lucile Barke became more terror-stricken than ever as the hours dragged on and her sister had not regained consciousness. Early in the evening the doctor sent her from the room, for her presence made his patient worse, that he could easily see. When she was near, Jeanette tossed and turned and moaned.

What a relief it was to Elsie when she knew Dr. Cunningham had arrived. It had not seemed best for the college to send John Burke a telegram about his daughter, knowing that his physician would soon be coming in his own plane.

Miss Babcock explained briefly to the doctor that Miss Barke had suddenly taken ill the day before. Elsie started to flee in terror, then she remembered her disguise, and that it had been nearly twenty years since he had seen her.

The nurse in charge merely reported the present condition of her patient, handing him the chart which he carefully scrutinized.

"How strange," he said, a deep scowl between his shaggy eyebrows.

The nurse introduced Miss Hamilton. Did he give a perceptible start, or was the little teacher letting her imagination get the best of her?

"Ah, Miss Hamilton," and he took the teacher's shapely hand in a warm embrace. "The family has talked so much about you, I feel I know you."

Elsie breathed a sigh of relief. That was over. She was glad Dr. Cunningham could take charge of the case, feeling that if any physician could help Jeanette, it would be this man who had cared for the Barke family for almost a half a century.

As she looked at him she thought to herself, "Astonishing! He appears little older than when he left me and Jerry at that Lawton Hotel in Alabama almost twenty years ago."

Her thoughts were interrupted by Jeanette's shrill cry. "Lucile, tell me the truth. Don't say those wicked things about my dear mother. I won't believe she was a Negro. Howard, please tell your mother it is not the truth. Ben, make them stop talking. Miss Hamilton, you don't think my mother was a colored person, that I have a Negro twin brother!"

The doctor turned to Miss Bryan, the the school nurse, "How long has she kept this up?"

"Intermittently for hours."

Elsie signaled for the nurse to tell the doctor everything for the girl's life depended upon the circumstances, then she left the room.

Miss Bryan told him everything and he said, "Too bad. Too bad. Keep Lucile entirely away from this room. I am glad Miss Hamilton knows the truth of what has been said by Lucile. Perhaps we better not permit Mr. Everett to visit her, at least for the time being."

"Yes, doctor. Those were the orders to Dr. Smith, the school doctor, and we have been carrying them out, although her fiance is almost frantic. He has remained at the hospital since we transferred her."

"Miss Bryan, do all in your power to ease the mind of Miss Barke; assure her that everything is all right. When she asks questions about her mother, tell her the story she hear in the cloak room is false. Her life may be at stake."

Jeanette's fever rose to the danger point. She had been taken to the best hospital in the city, placing her in a private room with two nurses in charge. A consultation of physicians followed.

"Brain fever," announced the specialist. Dr. Cunningham and Elsie felt sure it had been brought on by Lucile's cruel persecution during the past two years. The cloak room episode was but the climax that caused the final break.

John Barke and Lulu Simpson soon arrived by plane. Elsie thought her knees would give way under her when he came to the hospital, and her heart pounded until she wondered if he could recognize her. Yet she made no attempt to escape.

When he was presented to her, he showed not the least sign of recognition. To be sure he was grief-stricken and could think of nothing except his sick daughter.

No one was admitted to the hospital but Miss Hamilton, John, and the numerous nurses and physicians. John Barke and Elsie watched over their child, bound by the subtle cord of parental love.

Howard Everett haunted the hospital. No one could persuade him to leave long enough to obtain sufficient food and sleep. A mutual respect and liking sprang up between the father and the young lover.

John thought to himself, "Here is a man who will love and cherish Jeanette no matter what may come. Howard has no yellow streak in him. He would scorn to be the weakling I have proven myself to be."

Ben Hooper practically lived at the hospital. He scarcely ate or slept while the girl he had loved all his life lay at the brink of the grave. Night and day he was at or near the hospital.

He sat on the old stone seat just outside the door. He said to himself, "Jeanette imagines it is Howard she loves, but how could I care so much she did not love me in return? She calls her feelings for me but a sisterly affection.

"Well, darling," he cast his eyes on the light in her room, "I'm here if and when you need me."

Howard did not resent Ben's devotion to the girl he expected to make his wife, if she lived. He admired and pitied a man who could love so unselfishly. Strange as it may seem, these two princely men were a comfort to each other in their deep anxiety.

Always Lucile lurked in the shadows, pale, sullen, terrified, for she wondered if she had killed her sister. "Not that I care, unless I am found out. Who can be trusted these days? Some of my own gang might turn yellow should she die."

"Of all people I know, I fear that Margaret Sonne most. She is sure that I am to blame for Jeanette's illness. I wonder if she has told daddy and Miss Hamilton what she knows? It frightens me the way Doc looks at me, but no one can prove anything on me," she said to herself defiantly."

"Why did she have to be my sister, anyway? I hate her. Always she has been the shadow between me and the light. With both papa and grandma it was ever the sweet, accomplished, angel sister."

"Then there is Ben Hooper. I could have loved him but no, he saw only her. Now the man of all men, Howard Everett, must choose her for his wife. Jeanette knew very well I had picked him out for my husband before I even saw him." Hot bitter tears stung her cheeks.

She stationed herself on a bench far out in front of the hospital, expecting to catch a glimpse of Howard as he visited, or hoped to visit, the girl he loved. She continued to cry saying, "Oh, Howard, why didn't you choose me? If Jeanette never wakens, you soon will forget. Men are like that. Then you shall marry me."

But she had a nature that rebelled against waiting; she couldn't wait to see if her sister lived. Besides, she had forgotten she had had the same chance as her sister with Howard, and he did not give her a second glance. So she continued to hang around the hospital, hoping to trap the man she wanted. Once to the disgust of his mother, he did drive her home.

"Son," said Mrs. Everett sternly, "promise me you will never be seen again in the company with that vulgar, wicked Lucile Barke. She is cheap, scheming, and low-bred. You could get in serious trouble with a girl of her character."

Howard promised, although again and again she tried to force herself on him as she had the night he had driven her home. Often she accosted him in the the hospital halls where escape was impossible. She took neither a slight or a snub.

After ten weary days and nights Jeanette's fever broke, and she opened her eyes with the light of understanding, but remembered nothing that had taken place. She asked weakly, "Where am I and why are you here, daddy? Why am I in the hospital? Such a bad dream as I did have. Miss Hamilton, you are here too." Then she closed her eyes in normal sleep.

With a sigh of satisfaction Dr. Cunningham said, "Jeanette will live. The crisis is past." But as her mind began to clear and her memory return, she wore a perplexed epression, which soon turned to a troubled look.

She sobbed into her pillow. "Now I remember. Why didn't I die?" Again her fever shot up.

John turned to the music teacher and said helplessly, "Miss Hamilton, can't you do something? She loves and trusts you. When no one else could do a thing with her, when she was at her worst, you could calm and quiet her. It is you who have brought her back from the jaws of death. You must save her now." He went out of the room, softly closing the door behind him, leaving Elsie and his daughter alone.

Miss Hamilton took the thin white hands in hers and said, "Jeanette, dear, you must believe me. The story you heard Lucile tell in the hall is a malicious lie." She felt justified in making this statement, hoping to save the girl's life.

Jeanette seemed to believe her, and again showed signs of improvement.

Before Howard was permitted to visit her, he filled her room with the loveliest flowers. Every day he sent her a letter, assuring her of his love. Mrs. Everett also sent her loving cards. The girl was blissfully happy.

The day finally came when Howard could visit her. "Oh my darling," he cried, "it seems like an eternity since I last saw you. If you never had awakened!"

She asked anxiously, "Howard, have you been ill?" And he did look as if he were convalescing from a long sickness.

When Ben Hooper visited her he shamefacedly hid his face in the bed-covers to keep her from seeing his tears of joy. He was unable to speak a word, while she said, "Oh Ben, I missed you so."

Lucile was still barred from seeing her. It was not that she cared to see her sister, she resented the insult, as she called it. Yet the doctor and her father knew Jeanette's recovery was too important to permit this hateful girl to be near her until she had completely gotten over her illness.

This attitude of her father, as well as her impatience caused her to decide the time had come for her to act-she dare not wait longer. She must have Howard!

CHAPTER XIII

Yes, Lucile Barke decided she could not wait longer. Until now, she had expected, hoped, her sister would not regain consciousness. With her rival out of the way, she felt confident that her charms could win Howard Everett. Now it seemed certain Jeanette would live.

Hoping to make herself irresistible, she dressed with the greatest of care. The evening was lovely, an ideal time for the conquest. As she strolled leisurely down the hospital walk, she knew exactly what her strategy would be. But a few minutes before she had seen the object of her dreams enter the building to visit her sister and knew that before too long he would be coming out again.

For over an hour she waited impatiently beside the path, then she heard his car approaching. He had eluded her too often, she was determined he should not this time, so she forced him to slow down to keep from running over her.

"Oh, Howard, it is you," she said in mock surprise, with a little-girl pathetic smile as she pretended to take a step. "I have sprained my ankle. O-o-h! How it hurts! Her face registered great distress as she hobbled along.

"You poor child! Get right in and I'll take you back to the hospital and find the doctor. Forgive me, I will get out and help you in the car." Although she evinced great agony, she refused to be taken to the doctor, she more important matters to attend to.

He did not remember his promise to his mother, probably would have disregarded it had he remembered. By nature he was a very gallant young man, and this was an emergency. Besides, the girl was only a kid and soon she would be his little sister.

He seemed to be seeing the girl for the first time, seeing how very beautiful her dusky-white skin looked against her scarlet dress. He hadn't remembered she had lovely curling eye-lashes, or that her neck was smooth, white and full, showing strikingly above her low-cut dress. One dark curl hung tantalizing just in front of a tiny pink ear.

Tonight, the man felt very generous toward the world. Wasn't his beloved Jeanette rapidly recovering? His darling whom he had feared never would awaken was soon to be his bride. Dr. Cunningham had assured him it would be only a matter of a few weeks until she would again be normal.

The birds twittered in the tree-tops in the balmy New England twilight, while the air was fragrant with the breath of the flowers. Howard Everett was so absorbed in romancing he completely forgot the girl beside him.

He wondered why he had been so lucky as to win a girl like Jeanette. "I have met the charming women of London and Naples, talked with the lovely belles of the South, and danced with the fascinating girls of California, but none of them compare with my Jeanette.

"Mother was a genius at judging character and it makes me smile to hear her laud her charms and accomplishments. If only I can be worthy of such a wife."

"Howard!" He gave a perceptible start and was rudely brought back to earth. "I-I-have something to tell you," and the siren dabbed her eyes with a filmy bit of lace.

Moved by her tears, no man can endure to see a woman cry, he asked, "What is it, little sister? Solicitously he bent toward her, his arm over the back of the car-seat.

"I-I don't like to tell you. It is something that is going to hurt you, for it is about-my-sister-" Here she choked out a sob, while Howard pulled his car off the pavement and stopped, his arm dropping to the shoulders of the weeping girl.

"My-my-sister-I just can't bear to hurt you. Once you know-you-never-never will look at her again and that will-will break sister's hear-"

"Stop!" Lucile Barke, don't say another word! The words came out like a pistol shot. "Don't you dare say another word about Jeanette. I know all you would say." He jerked his arm from her drooping shoulders as though he had received a blow. "You are but a serpent in the Garden of Eden, but you shall not wreck our happiness."

His foot slammed down on the starter and the car lunged forward onto the broad boulevard.

"But, Howard, how can you be so cruel to me? Can't you see I love you with all my heart? Can I help it if my sister's mother was part Nigger!"

"You lie! I have heard your miserable insinuations and falsehoods all this year and last year too. No one of any intelligence believes a single word you say. They know you are but jealous of your talented sister. They might believe you had tainted blood, but never Jeanette."

"Howard Everett!" screamed the girl, looking more like a small tigress than a refined young lady. "You shall pay for that remark. Yes, and you shall believe my story, too."

The following day Mrs. Everett's footman announced, "Madam, a Miss Lucile Barke is at the door."

"Lucile Barke? What does she want? Send her away. I will not see that ill-bred girl."

Soon the man returned. "Madame, the girl is most insolent, declaring she will 'camp' on the porch all day if need be."

"What can that hussy want? Show her in, if you must."

Dressed in flamboyant colors, as usual, and in a grand-eloquent manner, she sailed into the luxuriant reception room. Her eyes darted here and there, taking in every detail of the room and its furnishings. Mrs. Everett did not speak or offer her a seat, but stood haughtily waiting for her caller to begin.

With all of her boldness and arrogance, for once Lucile Barke was abashed. She wondered how she could say what she had come to tell this coldly proud woman. She cleared her voice noisily and twisted her handkerchief like an embarrassed little school-girl.

Mrs. Everett held a monocle to her eye and gave the girl a long scrutinizing stare, her nose elevated and asked, "Well?"

"I-I came, er-to, er, to say, that Jeanette's a Nigger! Her words came out in a tumbled, jumbled, almost incoherent roll.

The woman gave not the slightest sign she had heard, but continued to stare as if the girl before her were some new specie of humanity.

Lucile gritted her teeth, determined not to let the woman squelch her. "That most cultured, refined girl you think so much of and your fine son has promised to marry has a twin brother who is black. Their mother was part Nigger, that's why dad got rid of her and married my mother." She stopped for breath.

Mrs. Everett turned to her footman. Calmly she said, "James, kindly show this girl to the door."

With a very angry, red face Lucile started toward the door, then turned back and screamed, "I dare you to prove me a liar."

When the man returned the woman asked, "James did you hear what that hussy said to me?"

"Madame, it would have been impossible not to hear her brawling mouth."

"Call my attorney-have him come at once. He shall close that girl's mouth once and for all time. To think that she would dare malign her dear sister's name now that she has just been snatched from the jaws of death! Hand me my smelling salts-hurry!"

Alvin Maxwell, the attorney, was absorbed in a new case when James walked into his office and delivered his employer's message. But when the Everetts called him, no matter how busy he might be on another case, he answered their summons without delay.

He now hurried to see the woman. He looked anxiously at her and asked, "Mrs. Everett, what is the trouble? I never before remember seeing you so upset."

"Alvin, that vulgar, wicked half-sister of my son's fiancee has been here telling the most scandalous falsehoods about sweet little Jeanette. She should be in a psychopathic ward! Should be locked up, put behind bars."

"She declared that Jeanette's mother was a Negro, that her twin brother was actually black, when the girl doesn't even have a brother."

"That girl must surely be mad," he declared indignantly, for he had met Jeanette and admired her very much."

"Now, Alvin, go at once and get sworn affidavits from Dr. Cunningham and his nurse, Lulu Simpson who were present at the birth of Jeanette, that Lucile's statements are falsehoods. The doctor and his nurse are still in the city, so see them immediately."

Not once did either Howard or his mother doubt that Lucile Barke was telling anything but the rankest lies. He increased his devotions to Jeanette, to try to make up for what he knew she had to endure from her sister. As he looked at her fine, delicate features and her wealth of hair that was like spun gold spread over the white pillow, he marveled at Lucile's audacity.

"How can she be so stupid as to charge this lovely creature with tainted blood? My love must compensate for all of the insults piled on her by her jealous sister and step-mother. Once we are married, I shall take her so far away that she never will see or hear from them again."

CHAPTER XIV

Elsie Hamilton sat in a low rocker on the front porch of her own little cottage thinking of the past few hectic weeks. Her mind was too dazed to really think clearly, for she lost so many nights of sleep while remaining at the bedside of her ill daughter.

First, it had been the mad rush of the closing days of school at the seminary; musical recitals, helping the girls choose their graduation dresses, and shopping with Jeanette for her lovely wedding clothes.

Oh, those exciting days in the best stores-days she supposed never could be hers. Then the crash! Followed by long days and longer nights of vigil, side by side with John.

At first she thought she never could go through with it, John so near, John looking just the same, only more handsome with his graying temples and the sad, deep lines about his eyes and mouth.

Those lines told he had suffered for years, not just since his daughter became ill. Seeing those lines she did not feel quite so bitter toward him for discarding her, and marrying Rose Garner. Then as the weary days and nights dragged on she found only forgiveness and pity for the man who had so brutally deserted her in her hour of need, when she was so helpless.

During the crisis of their daughter, he had always looked to her for the final word. It was she who had quieted Jeanette in her wildest delirium, he standing helplessly by her side. Dr. Cunningham, too, had treated her just as though he knew she were the girl's mother.

More than once the doctor remarked to John Barke, "Strange the power Miss Hamilton wields over you daughter."

John would answer with a puzzled expression his troubled face, "Doc, I don't understand it."

Elsie knew something of what the two men were saying and thinking about her, yet at that time she had no fear of recognition. But now she remembered the day her child was pronounced out of danger. Their tense watch relaxed. For the first time John seemed to really see her, and she often found his eyes upon her. It embarrassed her, made her uneasy.

Once he had said, "Miss Hamilton, I still marvel at the skill you showed in handling Jeanette. I cannot thank you enough. It was always you, not I, she seemed to want. Doc gets the credit for saving her life, but both he and I know it was you who brought her back from the brink of the grave."

Elsie remembered how she had blushed at the well-earned praise, then a dart had shot through her heart. She wondered what John would say and do if he knew her identity. Supposing it had been Jerry who lay at the point of death? Would he do as much to save his mulatto son as for his fair-haired daughter? It made her feel bitter toward the man.

While she sat resting and thinking on her porch, the postman handed her a fat letter from Harriet Kieth. She had not had a word for weeks, but until today she had been too worried about Jeanette to think of anything else. Moving her chair to a better light she broke the seal and read the letter.

"Elsie, commencement has been a busy time. But listen to this! Two weeks ago as I sat at my desk at the college making out grades, a rap came at my door. Not lifting my eyes from my record book, I called, 'Come', then set down my figures and looked up."

"'Miss Kieth, I believe!' boomed a voice. Before me stood a stalwart young man with sparkling brown eyes, dusky skin, and in the full regalia of a cow boy. By his side proudly stood a chunky, freckled-face girl with carroty-hair. The couple seemed highly amused at my bewilderment."

"Springing from my chair I cried in amazement, 'Jerry Randall!'"

"Miss Kieth, meet Mrs. Jerry Randall. Marvel and I were married last Christmas. Sorry not to have told you before, but we wanted to surprise you and it was impossible to get away before."

"'Oh Jerry, you handsome big boy!' I cried. 'Marvel, I am delighted to know you,' and I gave them each a motherly kiss."

Elsie fanned herself furiously. She couldn't believe what she had just read, thinking she must be in a dream This was just too much, with everything else that had happened the last few weeks. She felt her mind must surely fail her with this shock added to the others.

But with trembling hands she picked up the letter again and began to read, Elsie, that boy does not look at all like a Negro. His swarthy skin is a bit like that of the Spaniard or an Italian, but mostly like a coat of cowboy tan. He is not as dark as some life-guards at the beach. And I simply love that little snub-nosed wife of his."

"They begged me to take a ride in their new Buick sedan, but because a faculty meeting was scheduled to come immediately, I only ran out to look at the beauty, then had to tell them good-by and hastened to the meeting."

"Elsie, they stayed at the swankiest hotel in town, and came only to visit me and to let Marvel see the orphanages where he had lived. They invited me to visit them at Sheep Run, Wyoming, fifty miles from a railroad. They asked me to tell you to write to them and for both of us to visit them."

"What will be the outcome of such a marriage, Elsie?" Harriet had asked. "He is supremely happy and she adores him. Westerners are very broad-minded, maybe their love will last."

Miss Hamilton sat lost in thought, worrying because her son had married. Yet she realized it would be no worse than Jeanette marrying, for they had the same blood in their veins. She felt sure that should Marvel have a child that showed its Negro strain that her people would be more sympathetic than a woman like Mrs. Everett.

"Yet, must such young people remain single all their lives?" She knew that there was no solution, that it was not a matter of superiority or inferiority of race, or dominance of one race over the other, it just didn't work. It could not bring happiness to intermarry."

She knew that both races must take the responsibility of keeping that race pure if happiness was to follow. Children curse their parents for their indiscretions, their lack of good sense, when they intermarry, Children must suffer so long as adults throw common sense to the winds.

CHAPTER XV

Mrs. Everett had asked Alvin Maxwell to prove Lucile Barke's statements false and he immediately went to work on the case. He called Dr. Cunningham and Miss Simpson and soon obtained the desired information, then returned to his office. He dropped heavily down into his swivel chair and sighed, while a frown drew his handsome face into an ugly scowl. "Now what am I going to do?" he asked himself.

Mrs. Everett impatiently awaited his coming. She wanted to get the matter settled and off her mind. Finally she could stand the delay long and said sharply, "James, telephone Alvin Maxwell. Tell him to come at once. I can't understand why it is taking him so long to achieve the small task I set before him."

For once the great attorney was reluctant to respond to the Everett's summons. Finally he climbed into his car and slowly drove to the great mansion. With lagging feet he walked up the steps to the door. The footman ushered him into the presence of Mrs. Everett. He spake and sat down, wondering what to say.

"Well?" asked the stately lady imperiously. "Why sit there like a statue?No doubt the good doctor and his faithful nurse laughed at you for your strange request. They must have been very surprised."

"On the contrary, Mrs. Everett, it was I who was surprised. What shall I-" This man of the world, used to meeting all sorts of situations, seemed unable to continue. "My dear woman, I do not-know what to say-"

"Alvin Maxwell, what in the world is the matter with you? Have you been drinking? I never knew you to become intoxicated, but do stop your stuttering and sputtering and come to the point. Didn't you call on the doctor and nurse? If so, give me those affidavits!"

"There are no affidavits, Mrs. Everett. That girl, er, did-not lie!" He buried his face in his hands.

"You are drunk, although I smell no liquor. Or are you ill? Straighten up and give your report. If you failed to get the signed the statements, go after them right now. I want to get this off my mind."

"I am trying to make you understand, that Lucile Barke told the truth about her sister. Jeanette's mother was part Negro, and her twin brother was a mulatto. It is thought that she committed suicide and took his life too when he was but an infant. Of course Jeanette does not know a thing about her mother, but it is the truth."

"The reason Jeanette fainted in the cloak-room was because Lucile wanted her to know this story and was telling the girls in the hall, just so she could hear it. That is what caused her illness. But to save her life Miss Hamilton made her believe her sister's story was only one of her falsehoods."

"You can't make me believe such a fantastic tale. That siren Lucile has bewitched you. Go after those statements right away, and don't come back until you have them."

The man arose and paced the floor. "I tell you, there will be none. The doctor will confirm my statements."

She called her footman. "James, send for Dr. Cunningham, and don't delay. Not that I believe one word Alvin is telling me, but I shall get to the bottom of this story. Send Howard in, for this is his problem."

"Yes, madame," and the footman bowed himself out of the room.

Howard rushed in. In astonishment he looked from one to the other. "Mother, what is it? Are you ill?"

"No, son, but if what Alvin tells me is true, it can be more serious than illness. That Lucile Barke is spreading the most scandalous tale about your dear little Jeanette."

"I know, Mother. She has been slandering her both this year and last year, too. She even came to me with her sordid story, but I shut her up fast enough."

"She came here to my house and told her story, and I sent Alvin to get sworn affidavits that the tale was false. Now he returns and informs me she told the truth. He infers that the doctor will substantiate her words, and James has gone to bring the physician."

"Let him come! All of the people in the world can not convince me that Jeanette Barke has tainted blood. It is only a frame-up."

Dr. Cunningham arrived and the four sat in conference for two hours.

Howard jumped from his chair and stalked up and down the room. "The story is unreasonable, fantastic!" he declared. "Yet if it were true, no power on earth can prevent me from marrying Jeanette."

"Don't try to be mellow dramatic, Howard. Of course no Everett is going to marry into a family with tainted blood."

The young man replied curtly. "Mother, I am of age and am perfectly capable of making my own decisions. I shall do as I think best."

"Howard Everett, you are acting and talking as an adolescent. YOU shall not marry a girl with Negro blood."

"Say and do what you will, but I shall marry Jeanette, regardless of what Dr. Cunningham or any other person may say about her birth." He spoke vehemently. He had never see his mother in such a rage before.

Her face was livid as she said, "Son, if you marry Jeanette Barke, I shall not only disown you, but shall broadcast her story. The tale coming from a school-girl like Lucile, bears little weight, but spoken from my lips will fill the ears of every home in the land. Neither you nor she would dare walk on the streets. While I love and pity the girl, I love my honor more."

"Howard," said the attorney with great concern, "you better heed your mother's words. She means everything she says. You would not want Jeanette's name to become a by-word on the streets."

"Howard, my boy," the doctor spoke sympathetically, "Lucile's story almost sent Jeanette to her grave. The certified announcement from your mother's lips would kill her outright."

A death-like silence pervaded the room. A silence no one felt like breaking. Only the loud ticking of the clock on the wall could be heard, besides Howard's labored breathing.

Finally he said, "I can't give her up! I can't!" He groaned aloud.

The doctor spoke softly, "If you love her, you must save her from the cruel gossips."

"For Jeanette's sake to save her from vile tongues, I promise," he whispered hoarsely. "Yet how can it be done without breaking her heart? Putting her to open shame for me deserting her, jilting her?"

His mother now spoke calmly. "The wedding day must be postponed indefinitely. That saves her self-respect. No one need know the reason for the delay. Howard, you shall go immediately to your Uncle Louis Everett in London, and we will give out that he is seriously ill. In the meantime, I shall do my best to squelch any rumors about either the wedding or the story of the girl's birth."

Howard said, "Dr. Cunningham, if I consent to give up Jeanette, it shall be your responsibility to see that Lucile is sent away, that her sister never need live under the same roof or in the same town or city with her again. Never again must they attend college together, and do your best to stop the mouth of both the girl and her wicked mother."

The doctor admitted this might not be easy to do but he promised to try, then he went to tell John Barke what had taken place. He wondered if Jeanette had been snatched from her grave only to face a sorrow and disgrace more bitter than death itself. He hoped the facts might be kept from her, yet he doubted it.

After telling John he said, "This may put the girl right back where she was. A relapse can be serious."

"The sins of the fathers shall be handed down to the children unto the third and fourth generations," John quoted with white lips. "Of course it was not Lucy, but some of her ancestors who sinned."

The doctor and her father tried to send Lucile home immediately, but she had a mind of her own, and refused to go until she was ready. When they attempted to impress on her shallow mind the enormity of her sin against her sister she flippantly said, "Howard Everett would find it out sooner or later. Better now than later as in the case of her mother.

"But it may put her in her grave," explained the doctor.

"It won't kill my dear little sister. She is getting used to being talked about."

But because she sill had hopes of winning Howard Everett she promised to do no more talking about Jeanette in Boston and Novinger.

To get her away permanently the doctor told her that if she would go home she and her mother might spend the summer in Long Beach, California. "Next winter you may have your choice of the University of California or going with your mother to Florida."

"Swell!" she said. "After seeing California, I'll decide what about next winter."

John begged her to accompany him home to Novinger, but she insisted on doing elaborate shopping in New York City for her trip West before going home. He feared to leave without her.

Jeanette had been improving rapidly up to this time, but when Howard failed to make his daily calls, she became uneasy. When two days passed she decided he must be sick and worried the more.

The third day a brief note arrived by mail and with trembling fingers she opened it. "Dear Jeanette, I am suddenly called to the bedside of my sick uncle in London, but I will see you before sailing. Be a good girl, obey you doctor and get well, Howard."

She felt cold fingers clutching her heart. A premonition of impending danger filled her soul. She could not explain the feeling, but she knew something was wrong.

Then Howard visited her. Dark shadows circled his eyes. His face was haggard and drawn. "Darling, you are sick," she said anxiously. "Why didn't they tell me?

"I am not ill, Jeanette. Only sad that we must part. Good-by, my darling!" Hot tears from his eyes fell as he quickly pressed his lips to hers and was gone.

John Barke and Elsie Hamilton waited in the reception room of the hospital to learn the outcome of Howard's farewell visit. "Miss Hamilton, you go to her," he begged brokenly. "A woman knows what to say."

As John watched Howard Everett pass dejectedly down the walk he remembered another day. "Lucy must have felt even worse than Jeanette now feels, for she was cast out alone with a mulatto infant in her arms. A child she must love, and yet be ashamed of. No wonder she ended it all. Jeanette cannot, will not, commit such an act."

Finally John persuaded Lucile to go home with him, insisting she could finish her shopping for clothes in Los Angeles. Elsie and the doctor were to remain with Jeanette. Miss Simpson had gone already to look after the doctor's office. Dr. Cunningham urged John to send his wife and daughter to California as soon as possible. Of course Ben remained in Boston to be near Jeanette.

Yes, he began to again dream of a time when he might win Jeanette, knowing that Howard Everett had past out of her life forever. But he was wise, he would give her time to find out the situation for herself. In the meantime he would be near to give her what comfort he could.

"I am not glad she has lost Howard. I never could be selfish enough to gloat over another's misfortune or ill-luck. But as always, it has been my belief that Jeanette and I are destined for each other. She will be happier with me than any one else because I know her peculiar hereditary situation. I love her no matter if she should have tainted blood."

But will Rose consent to go with her daughter to California? Because of her contrary nature, she might think that Jeanette was pushing her out of her home.

CHAPTER XVI

Rose Garner Barke was delighted with the prospect of her and her precious daughter spending the summer in California, and alone. "Your father is so old-fashioned, child. When he is with us he cramps our style."

"Don't I know it. All of the time he was in Boston, I felt uneasy. You know how he is about a little drinking and smoking, especially women. And he doesn't like night-clubs. I am young but once, I believe in having fun."

Rose was maliciously happy because her daughter had so completely wrecked Jeanette's future. She was gleefully pleased to hear her step-daughter had been crushed and heart-broken.

The day the second-Mrs. Barke and her fashionable daughter arrived in Long Beach, California, the doctor's plane landed in Novinger, bringing Ben and Jeanette.

John insisted on carrying his daughter into the house. "You beautiful child, how much better you look."

"You are spoiling me, father, for I can walk if you help, only a tiny bit. I'm really almost well."

Jeanette and John had begged Miss Hamilton to spend the summer in Novinger. "It isn't because you need to be my child's nurse any longer," he assured her. Neither need you fear the Iowa heat, for dad's house is air-conditioned and grand-mother Barke would be delighted to show her gratitude for saving her favorite grand-daughter.

Elsie smiled ruefully at the irony at the situation. "Wouldn't it be a joke to be an honored guest in the very house where I was so shamefully pushed out twenty years ago?" she said to herself.

She declined the invitation, giving as her excuse that she was to spend her vacation with an old friend in Florida. John had seemed disappointed, saying he wished to do something to show his appreciation for her kindness.

Miss Hamilton packed her grips and boarded a boat for Palm Beach. "So much more fun to go by boat," she had said. "I love the ocean, and surely need something to lift my spirits, and put a bit of color in my cheeks." She smiled wryly at her reflection in the mirror.

Harriet met her at the dock in her tan roadster and said, "Elsie, you are prettier than ever. No wonder Lang Smith hangs on, you are lovely enough to wait for. Truly you have kept your school girl complexion and youthful figure."

"After all I have gone through with I can take a little of your flattery, even if I do know I don't deserve it." Then she related the story of Jeanette's broken engagement to Howard Everett and the part Lucile had played.

"How will it end? He can never return and marry her for fear of what his mother will do. Too bad she didn't marry Ben Hooper. He never would discard her even if she did bear him a mulatto child."

"How can you say that, Elsie? Ben would not know what he might do until he faced the issue. No one can be sure until he is put to the test.

"Here is the ocean! I'm glad your cabin is right on the beach, so we can go to sleep with the roar of the waves in our ears. And can't we roll out of bed and into our bathing suits and take a dip in the ocean before breakfast?"

When Harriet showed her the snapshots of Jerry and his wife she said, "He doesn't look at all like a mulatto. He is a Barke. He is the very image of J. B. Bark himself." Miss Kieth let her keep the pictures, also the ones taken since infancy, no need for secrecy any longer. If she chooses she might acknowledge him as her son. His future seemed assured, at least there was nothing she could do about it now.

Back in Novinger Jeanette decided she must be in Paradise with only her father and the housekeeper in the home. No scolding, scheming stepmother nor selfish sister to darken the skies. Grandmother Barke ran in whenever she felt like doing so.

In spite of the longing for Howard her health improved rapidly. Novinger seemed to know nothing of the marriage that was to have taken place. With Rose and Lucile gone, the townspeople show their real liking for Lucy's daughter, and this helped her face life.

The town had never accepted the second-Mrs. Barke. They did not like her personally, neither had they forgiven her for grabbing John so soon after Lucy's death or disappearance, they hadn't decided which.

The piano was a great joy to Jeanette, and there was Ben who ran in almost every evening and sometimes oftener. Maybe he came to talk to her father, but usually he sought her company without apology. Now that they were on their home bases, he felt more secure.

Life was so satisfying to the girl's weary body and soul that Boston, Lucile, Rose, Howard, and London seemed confused dreams. When her fiance's letter did not arrive, that seemed unreal also.

Yes, life to Jeanette was very sweet and comforting after two years of nerve-wracking days with Lucile in the seminary. For the first time in her life, she knew the meaning of home. Until this summer, home meant only abuse, nagging, deception, insinuations, taunts, and shame on the part of her step-mother.

Just one need seemed unsatisfied, that was the longing for Elsie Hamilton. Her letters came regularly and were a great comfort, but Jeanette wondered why she never mentioned Howard or her approaching marriage. Then she remembered neither Ben, her father, nor grandmother spoke about the wedding either. It seemed almost as if she had only dreamed of the whole affair.

Then she thought of Howard and his mother. It brought up memories of her heartaches, for always her love for the handsome man was shadowed by Lucile and her cruel insinuations. There was ever the fear that she would poison his mind against her as she had her most intimate friends.

Then too, memories of Howard brought up the horrors of her recent illness with its suffering and hateful dreams of her mother. So since coming home she had formed the habit of living in the present, trying to shut out the past with its hideous memories and and the future with its uncertainties. Gradually the man she had been engaged to marry faded into oblivion.

Yet subconsciously, she was still trying to solve the mystery of her birth. One day she announced, "Ben, I a going to ask father about mother. Those dreams I had while ill haunt me, then Lucile was was always taunting me about my birth. Every person has a right to know something about his background, who his parents are, I don't even have a photograph or snapshot to show I ever had a mother."

Quickly the young man said, "Please, Jeanette don't rake up the dead ashes of your father's past! You can't realize what he has suffered, for he loved your mother dearly; my parents know. Do not open his wounds."

But she did not give up. When she accompanied her grandmother to the cemetery to decorate the graves she carefully scrutinized the slab where her mother had supposedly been buried. "Lucy Barke, wife of John Barke, with the dates." That was all the information the inscription gave.

Jeanette seated herself beside the older woman and said, "Grandma, tell me about my mother. I know so little of her, and no one has ever told me about her. What was she like?"

"My child, you are her very image," she said, wiping a tear from her eyes with a small handkerchief edged with fine tatting. She never could speak of John's first wife without shedding tears.

"She was twenty when she came into the family, but she looked much younger. She was not only beautiful, but she was an angel and your father worshiped her. That is why he never talks about her; he has never stopped grieving for her. Of course you know she died at your birth."

"Sh! Don't ever tell this, but he never loved your step-mother. Everybody in town knows she tricked him into marrying her. Most men seem to be innocent and unsuspecting where designing women are concerned."

"Because your father loved you so much she pretended to be very fond of you, just to blind his eyes. So she trapped him into a lifetime job of caring for you, throwing herself into the bargain. Only she deceived us all, for I used to believe her profuse show of affection was sincere. But at last both John and I discovered what fools we had been."

Jeanette didn't think it would help matters to tell her little grandmother just how hateful and cruel Rose had been to her, for it would only grieve her. So she asked the question she wanted so much to know. "Did you ever see mother's parents, her folks?" She was remembering the story Lucile had told in the cloakroom.

"No-, I never saw them but your father and Doc have been in their home. They said that were nice refined folks, only rather poor. They live some place in Alabama. Your Grandmother Travis died not long after your mother did-"

"Travis? Was that mother's name before she married father? Were they dark skinned folks?"

"What a strange question, child! No, they did not look different from other people. How did you get such an idea? Your mother was a perfect a blonde as you, but her parents had dark brown eyes and black hair much like the Barkes."

"Did mother and father have other children besides me?"

"No dear. Your mother died right after your birth, and you were her first child. Too bad we don't have any pictures of your mother and grandparents. There used to be a number of photographs of them, besides the wedding pictures of your parents. In fact they became misplaced soon after your mother died."

"Do you suppose my step-mother destroyed them? Maybe because she was so jealous of mother, she made way with them."

"I would not put it past her, but I don't know."

As it happened Rose was not guilty of this crime, but, reader, I am sure you can guess. Ask J. B. Barke what he did with all of Lucy Travis' pictures. To be sure he will not satisfy your curiosity.

CHAPTER XVII

Lucile Barke and her mother, both extravagantly dressed, registered at one of the most expensive hotels in Long Beach, California. The woman had wanted to impress the public that they were the millionaire-Barques of Novinger, Iowa. They carried themselves with great haughtiness.

"Mom, isn't this the swankiest hotel you ever laid eyes on? Yesterday, I was palling around with a gal on the pike and she wanted to know how we could afford such a place. I made her understand just who we were. The way her eyes bugged out when I told her what we pay for rooms and meals she must not have much dough."

Soon it was noised abroad that an heiress from the Midwest was spending her vacation at the beach accompanied by her beautiful mother.

This was in the days when millionaires were not to be seen just any day. The women enjoyed being the object of many a stare from the public.

Now Count Von Lanier was searching anxiously for an heiress. In fact he was desperately in need of just such a one with her millions. He had come to the beach for this express purpose. And when he had heard the rumor that this particular heiress was accompanied only by her mama, the count was delighted, for he didn't care for papas, in fact he avoided them when possible.

"Ah, yes, this is the very lady for me!" and his watery, pale-blue eyes held a new light. He waxed his black mustache more carefully and brushed his last year's suit diligently, then polished his monocle and his gold-headed cane and set forth en conquest and to conquer.

"This should not be difficult," he laughed and gleefully, twirling his cane artistically. 'Midwesterners?' I hear they are very friendly and very approachable-gullible might be the word, so I hear."

The lady in question sat with her mother under a beach umbrella, clad in a scarlet, briefest-of-brief, bathing suit." Her web was spun, in her lair she awaited her victim.

The count was not an imposing or romantic appearing man, being short of stature and broad of girth. His scanty hair was of the hue of mouse's fuzz, his age something beyond thirty. But he had let it be known he was of the nobility.

"I must work fast. Heiresses are not crowing the beach in these days of depression." He realized he he was not the only fortune-hunter roaming the pike. "My creditors are becoming exceedingly embarrassing," he admitted to himself.

There was a flutter of excitement under the beach umbrella. "Oh Mama, look quick! There he comes. I know it is the Count. All counts carry a monocle and a gold-headed cane. Shall I fall into the ocean so he can rescue me?"

"Sh! He is sauntering down this way, but looking in the opposite direction. He doesn't see us. Quick, do something!"

Like a flash of lightening, Lucile sent her umbrella tumbling briskly in the direction of the little man. Dexterously she started in pursuit of the fore-runner of romance. It sped directly across the path of the Count. Being a bit near-sighted he did not at once understand the situation.

Lucile's form would have made an excellent bathing-beauty advertisement, while her raven curls fell in profusion over perfect cold-white shoulders. A pace in front of the man, she stopped, blushed a rosy-red, gave a fleeting glance with her sparking black eyes, then dropped her curling eyelashes, stammering an apology.

A weaker man than the Count might have dropped dead on the spot, or at least have been sure his heart was jumping out of his vest. But this man possessed a heart that was made of uncommon substance.

He lifted his natty straw hat with his right hand, tucked his god-headed cane under the other arm, placed his left hand over that heart, and bowed low.

Long before this, the Count had determined to marry an heiress, even if she was cross-eyed, fat, and spoke with a nasal twang. "But to see this stunning young beauty running directly into my arms! Ah! I cannot believe my eyes, for of course she is the heiress from the Midwest."

"Really, that child is literally throwing herself at my head. This luscious plum is mine for the plucking. Ah! And quick work it shall be." His small eyes became points of steel, and his smile was not good to see.

A few days after this novel beach episode, Lucile arrived at her hotel room in the wee hours of the morning. "Mama," she gurgled, "the Count is the funniest lover I ever had. He kisses my hands instead of my lips."

Rose replied, "My dear, he even kisses my hands!" Rose found that she was not too old to blush at the satisfaction this had given her. "You know, Lucile, counts are very proper in their manners. That's why I adore them."

"And remember this, when he proposes to you, he is almost sure to kneel before you and kiss you hand. Be sure not to show your ignorance by acting surprised, just pretend you are accustomed to being courted by the nobility."

Lucile adored colorful and scanty bathing suits and had purchased several of the most stunning ones to be found in the city of New York. She had planned on just living in them. A different suit for each day, perhaps.

Then what was her great disappointment to learn the Count refused to put on a bathing suit even once. She wondered why, but knew that if she was to bask in his presence it was worth any sacrifice she might have to make to get him.

Count Von Lanier was no fool, knowing his good points and his weak ones as well. Once he had seen himself in a bathing suit in a full-length mirror, never again did he suffer himself to try one on. He knew he looked exactly like a Brownie or a Kewpie.

Yes, the Count did work fast and nothing could please Lucile and her mother better. Many curious, envious eyes, followed them as they promenaded the pike or sauntered down the streets of Los Angeles.

Lucile lost no time in writing the exciting news to college friends and the home town. She was especially eager for them to realize what a fast worker she had been to capture a count in such a short time.

At the seminary it set the girls in a dither. "To think of her really landing a genuine live count," said Mayme Collier, one of her Boston friends. "But she is a beauty, and no doubt she let it be known she had money. Some girls have everything."

To Lucile the peculiarities of the Count were highly amusing. One night after a stroll along the beach in the moonlight she confided to her mother, "He pays me the most unusual compliments, calling me 'His little flower,' and 'His dream girl.' He insists he never loved a girl before. Mama, wouldn't Novinger think him loco?"

"Darling, the man is so very romantic, he surely is a prince and no make-believe. How lucky you have been." Rose complacently viewed herself in the mirror beside her bed. She was remembering her youth with its poverty and filth. "Now my daughter is to be a countess," she thought to herself.

Lucile broke in on her philosophizing. "I adore Hans. Don't you like that name. His full name is such a tongue twister; Count Hans Von Lanier. He told me tonight he had lived most of his life in Europe, and could have married more than one princess! When do you suppose he will propose?"

"Well, my precious child, he has practically asked me for you already. He told me all about his castle overlooking-I forgot what."

"Oh mom, why didn't you tell me before? Won't Jeanette be jealous? Think how envious the girls at the seminary will be. We better start making out the guest list today. Or should we go shopping for my trousseau tomorrow?"

Whom shall we invite? I would like for all of my class from the seminary to be presented. Some of them couldn't afford the trip, but we could send them tickets. Oh, I am so excited, I want to begin work on the list right now."

One month after meeting Lucile Barke, the Count formally asked Rose for her daughter's heart and hand in marriage.

The following day John Barke received a telegram from Rose saying, "Lucile is to marry Count Hans Von Lanier in two weeks. Give you consent or I shall sign the papers for you. Wire five-thousand dollars at once. Letter follows."

In the letter she explained that the Count needed money to put his castle in order for Lucile to live in. She was careful to say that when his mother had died she left all her money and jewels to her daughter, but she left the castle to Hans, which required some repairs. His mother had passed away but the year before, so had not had time to fix it up.

"John, dear, you must take into consideration that a girl can't catch a count with a beautiful old castle on the Rhine every day. You know counts are never known to have much money. Our precious daughter is not marrying for money, but for love and for the honor of becoming a countess.

"Darling," continued the letter, "do not fail us, but send the money at once. Of course I wouldn't expect you to leave your business to come to the wedding. I shall try to manage without you."

Rose received the consent to Lucile's marriage, also the coveted check. John was too pressed with business to leave the bank on such short notice. Although he did not like the sound of this hasty marriage to an unknown man, count or no count, he didn't know what to do about it.

With a gloomy frown on his face he said to Jeanette, "Even if I went to California, Rose would have her own way no matter what I said or did. When a woman has held the reins for almost twenty years, there is no use in attempting to loosen them from her hands now."

Much to Lucile's disappointment and her mother's indignation, the Count insisted on a small, quiet wedding. He knew that magnificent ceremonies with hundreds of guests cost a fortune, and that he could not afford such an affair.

"Every penny of that check for the castle must go at once to my creditors," he said to himself grimly. "Even that is not nearly sufficient, but maybe it will stand off the ones who are pushing me hardest until the next check can be filched from the banker."

Lucile had fully expected to sail for Europe immediately after the wedding, but her husband explained that it took a long time to put the castle in a suitable condition to receive his charming little bride.

The girl tried to cover her disappointment by boasting that she was now a countess. "Mama, I hope we meet Howard Everett just as soon as we arrive in London. Won't he be surprised when he learns I am Countess Von Lanier? Who are the Everetts compared to the Count? Howard will be sorry he spurned my love. Won't it be exciting to be present to kings and dukes and duchesses?"

Against the protests of both the Countess and the irate mother, a moderately priced small apartment was taken. "My sweet," purred the man, "we Europeans believe in simplicity. Too much elegance is not good taste, my child. And your charming mother must live with us, for we could not be happy without her."

But this was not at all in accordance with the women's ideas of living the life of wealth and splendor of the nobility. They had visions of luxuriant mansions with gorgeous furnishings and hosts of servants, a footman, a butler and all such things as story-books describe, and Mrs. Everett actually possessed.

However, from the first hour of marriage, and in fact before, Hans had ruled Lucile. Strange as it may seem, she liked it and made no protest. It has been said that each woman has her master, and when she finds him, she willingly submits her will to his, no matter if he be wise or a fool.

So now in every case, the head-strong, imperious Lucile defends her husband. "Mom," she said, "I've heard that European men are very different from American husbands, that always, they are the head of the house. Those women seem to like it. Soon, I shall be a European wife, so I just as well accept the custom of the country."

But there were some actions of her husband that worried her; his business seemed so very secretive and mysterious, taking him from home much of the time both night and day. In Boston she had had the protection of the college walls, and Jeanette. To tell the truth she was a bit afraid of her suave husband.

Rose marveled at the amount of money her son-in-law used to keep up living expenses. "But I don't know one thing about business," she acknowledged complacently to Lucile. "Your father attended to all such things."

"But, mama, Hans may be sending more money to Europe than he is telling us about. Perhaps he wants to surprise me with numerous fancy things in the house. I can hardly wait to see that old castle. I begged for pictures, but he insisted he wanted it to be a compete surprise to me. The Count is so thoughtful of me."

"Child, I hope you are right, but it seems to me all I do is send telegrams to John for money. If your dad won't become suspicious and make us a visit, or worse still, stop the flow of money to California!"

But two women sought solace in broadcasting the good fortune of the girl's marriage to a nobleman. Lucile sent her friends in Boston not only the announcement of her wedding, but each of them a copy of the Los Angeles newspaper account in the society column.

Likewise, Rose sent announcements and papers to her family in Ohio as well as to friends in Novinger. Since marrying John Barke, the woman had kept the uncouth, ill-bred relatives in the distance. Yet she could not pass this opportunity of gloating to them.

When Miss Babcock saw the announcement of the wedding she said, "I am surprised to think that coarse girl married a count."

Miss Clark, the English instructor replied, "But my dear, we haven't seen the count. The girl does have looks and money. Noblemen seem to have an affinity for American dollars."

"When I hear Lucile's name all I can think of is the way she treated her sister," said Miss Babcock. "Poor Jeanette's life is wrecked. Howard Everett has not returned from Europe, and it seems to be a well-known fact that he jilted her because of the tale her sister told about her birth. It is said she even went to Howard's mother and personally told her.

The English teacher heaved a sigh. "There seems to be no justice in this world. Lucile who is everything that is hateful and coarse is not a happy, distinguished countess, while her lovely, talented, angel sister is a broken-hearted outcast."

CHAPTER XVIII

Again Miss Hamilton, Jeanette, and Ben Hooper were back in school in Boston. Jeanette seemed to have recovered from her illness, and she returned to her classes looking attractive and almost happy.

Although not one word had reached her from Howard Everett, fiance, since he left for London, she had partly recovered from the disappointment before leaving Novinger. But her old school environment brought up a flood of memories, opening the healing wounds.

So before she had been at the seminary a week she began grieving for Howard, and thinking of the happiness her sister must be having as the wife of a nobleman. She often cried in her pillow at night. She wondered why fate had dealt her such a cruel blow. "Oh Lucile, you have love, protection, and everything. What have I done to deserve such a life?"

Ben never flagged in his devotion, continuing his role as a big brother. Both he and Miss Hamilton knew that the Boston Girls' seminary was rocked to its very foundations by her dramatic life story. How did the public learn her story, they wondered. Lucile had given her word not to talk, and Mrs. Everett would not.

Yet everybody knew that Howard had jilted Jeanette because she had Negro blood, and they had the full story. For they discussed freely the fact that her mother had carried colored blood and her twin brother was black, although both the mother and brother were said to be dead.

They also knew that John Barke had discarded his wife and sent her and his black son away, afterwards marrying the nurse, Lucile's mother who cared for Jeanette when she was an infant.

Can this story be based on facts?" asked Miss Babcock. "And how did it come to the ears of the public?"

Mrs. Clark said, "Rest assured Lucile had something to do with it. I doubt if there is any way to stem the tide of gossip. It must run its course, like any plague, but eventually it will burn itself out."

"I heard on good authority," said the dean of women, "that her father and the doctor bribed her to keep her mouth closed."

To be sure Lucile was the instigator of the story, and it was she who cunningly caused it to be broadcast, for this was what she wanted. With a few well-chosen hints from her alert brain, gossips were able to piece the story together.

On that last day in Boston, Lucile had gathered a large group of pals to her room, knowing this would be her last chance. "Girls," she had said, brushing an imaginary tear from her beautiful dark eyes, "you have cruelly condemned me for saying my sister is part Nigger, but I do feel very, very sorry for her. She can't help what her ancestors were. Some of you may think I made up this story-" she stopped and looked like a lovely martyr.

"Please, tell us the truth before you go. We won't tell a soul," begged all the girls in one breath.

"I'll not say another word, but time will tell. Keep an eye on Howard Everette."

"Do Howard and his mother know?" questioned the girls eagerly.

"Darlings," continued the vixen, trying to look melancholy, but her luminous eyes danced maliciously, "I am getting a swell trip to California pronto for keeping my ruby lips sealed."

As she was bidding her friends good-by she gave them a parting shot. "Girls, I failed to say that when you hear of Howard marrying Jeanette, don't fail to drop me a line." The gleam in the girl's eyes spoke volumes.

One of the girls sent for a subscription to the Novinger Times. And not long after this the Boston Daily stated that Howard Everett had gone to London to the bedside of his uncle. By September no account of Jeanette's wedding had been reported in the Novinger Times. Howard Everett had returned the United States.

Although Lucile's crowd had been struck with awe when the announcement came of her marriage to a nobleman. When Jeanette returned to the seminary people forgot her Lucille and centered their interests on Jeanette and her exciting history.

This became the subject of common gossip. Wherever she went she was conscious of staring eyes. Often she caught them whispering behind her back. Again her life seemed almost unbearable.

But like Miss Hamilton years before, she vowed to helping the unfortunate. Service for humanity would be her goal also. And she would not sit and wait for them to find her, but she would seek them out.

On Thanksgiving Day, she and Elsie made up an especially attractive and appetizing basket of food for the Hokes, the colored family down in the slums of Boston. It was no small task to fill a basket with sufficient food to satisfy thirteen hungry mouths.

Jeanette had looked forward to this day, here would be a few hours where she could be away from the gaping crowd about the seminary. Here she would be free from suspicion. But to her surprise and chagrin, both Mr. and Mrs. Hoke behaving strangely. Again and again, she caught them staring at her as if seeing her for the first time.

On their way home she said, "Miss Hamilton, is there no place on earth where folks will not stare at me? How can those people away down in the slums know that Howard jilted me?"

How had the Hokes learned Jeanette's story in full? Lucile had deliberately visited them and told everything, for nothing was too low or vile for her to stoop to do.

"Supposin' she does have colored blood?" snapped Mayme Hoke. "Colored folks is just as good as white folks!"

"But, my dear," said her husband, "the world doesn't see it that way. Besides even the better class of Negro disapproves of marriages between the whites and the colored races. The offspring of such marriages seem to be especially cursed for neither the white man nor the Negro want to claim them."

"Howard Everett would 'uv done powerful well to get that girl, black or white," was Mrs. Hokes verdict.

Christmas came. Jeanette despaired of ever seeing or hearing from Howard again. It was rumored that he had returned to the United States months earlier. No one said where he was, and he had not been seen in Boston, neither had they seen his mother.

John Barke visited Jeanette at the holidays. Although Elsie tried to avoid him, it was impossible to prevent seeing him since his daughter so much of her time with her in the studio or in her home.

Since Rose was still in California with Lucile and the Count, John had no reason for hurrying home. One evening he insisted that Elsie accompany them to the opera, along with Ben Hooper. Afterwards, he invited them out for refreshments.

She had feared to accept the invitation, but didn't know how to get out of it. While sitting in the eating place he leaned across the table and said, "Miss Hamilton, I just can't get away from the idea that I have known you years ago."

Elsie felt her cheeks go hot and cold. She stopped eating and clinched her hands under the cover of the table to hide their trembling.

"That reminds me of a story," she said, trying to regain her poise. "A man once remarked to a farmer, "seems like I have seen you some place before.' The old farmer squinted up one eye and replied, 'Spect you have, I's often there.'" She realized this was a poor stab at a joke, but anything to divert the man's attention from her.

But John Barke would not be thrown off the subject. "Do you know that you look enough like Jeanette to be her big sister. No wonder she is attracted to you."

Elsie knew the man was approaching too dangerously near the truth. It alarmed her. Supposing he did discover her identity? What would she do? Her daughter's story was serious enough as it was. Should the public learn she found her long-lost mother in the person of the woman who headed the music department of the college, it would be worse than ever. She could not let that happen.

"Ben," she said abruptly, almost rudely, pushing back her chair from the table, "my head is killing me. I am sorry to trouble you, but could you drive me home? Mr. Barke, I trust you and Jeanette will forgive me."

The girl was much concerned and insisted on accompanying her, but Elsie would not hear of this. John was sympathetic but showed keen disappointment.

Safe at home she thought to herself, "How foolish to take such a chance. John's mind is groping for an explanation for his hunch that he has known me before. Sooner or later, he will discover the truth. It must not be!" Hope was relieved when a few days later he left for Novinger, Iowa.

CHAPTER XIX

The word came to the Barkes from California that Lucile expected a child in early summer. It had been a great disappointment to her that Hans did not take her to their castle in Europe, for she was eager to show the Count to the Everetts, besides, she wanted the child to be born in a castle in royal fashion.

"Honey, you shall go to the swellest maternity hospital in Los Angeles," consoled her mother. She wrote this to her husband in Iowa. "Hans insists his child must be born right here in our home, but for once, since her marriage to that foreigner, I am running the show and shall take her to a hospital."

John answered and said, "Rose, you know father has always lived up to the tradition in his family that the children must be born under the paternal roof. Now that he is getting old, please do not worry him, but send Lucile home where Dr. Cunningham can see that everything goes off properly. Maybe he does have a complex being exchanged and lost at maternity hospitals, but you know he has a bunch of newspaper clippings to substantiate his feeling."

Rose lost no time in penning an answer, "John Barke, do you think the child of a countess is going to be born in a hick town of the Middle-West? What would the great social world to which we rightfully belong think of us? Just give old J. B. an aspirin to quiet his nerves. He isn't dictating to us on this affair."

Maybe the banker was growing older, but his fighting spirit had not lessened in the least. "I have always ruled my house and plan to continue to do so. No whipper-snapper grand-daughter and her mother can break Our great family tradition."

Immediately he wrote Hans Von Lanier a very forceful letter, offering him a fat check to bring Lucile home for the birth of their child. By now the Czar felt he understood the Count, that he was quite well acquainted with him.

Immediately came the telegram, We accept with pleasure your kind offer and my wife shall come to your home for the birth of our expected child." The message was sent 'collect.'

But Rose had lost none of her fighting spirit either. The very next day John received another telegram for him to pay for, "Send Hans the check if you wish, but Lucile's child shall be born in the St. Luke's Maternity Hospital."

To her daughter she said, "Darling, if you child cannot be born in Europe in a castle, at least it must be born in a great metropolis. As the Countess Von Lanier the Los Angeles press should give you and the child great publicity and honor."

"Oh mama, I do want Boston folks and Jeanette to read the account right from the newspapers. Think how envious Jeanette will be, gloated Lucile.

Hoping the Count might be able to influence his, J. B. Barke sent the promised check. Hans lost no time in getting to the bank to cash the magnificent check, knowing his wife and her mother were at that very moment making preparations for departing for the hospital. But the man couldn't be worried about such trivial matters as honor and keeping his word.

However, the old banker was taking no chances. So on the day that Lucile registered in at the hospital, Dr. Cunningham's plane purred to a landing in Los Angeles and he and the two Barke men taxied to that same hospital. Accidentally they ran into Rose in the hall.

"John Bark!" screamed the woman. "What are you doing here?"

"Don't you suppose we want to see Lucile and her husband as well as our new heir?"

The girl in stripes ushered the three men, accompanied by Rose into Lucile's spacious room. "Dad, you are not going to take me back to Novinger.

Mama, call the supervisor, quick! Where is the doctor?"

"Don't become excited, my child. We did not come to bring you home, but to visit you and see the new grandchild." John smiled ruefully at the grim faces of his two companions, hoping there would be no unpleasant scenes. But he realized that his father and wife were unpredictable.

While the family awaited the important event, John bought his daughter flowers and a large box of bon-bons.

"Mr. Barke," Count Von Lanier spoke in his smoothest tones, "you must not pamper my charming little wife. I am a count, not a rich American and do not wish to spoil the child."

John smiled tolerantly, but positively disliked this oily-tongued foreigner with his dialect. He reminded him of a snake slithering through the grass.

"Who is this fellow?" he wondered. And at once he asked Dr. Cunningham to have him investigated, knowing it should have been done before his daughter had married him.

The child was expected to arrive in a few hours. Rose had engaged the best-known obstetrician in the city, but he did not object to Dr. Cunningham assisting on the case.

"I can afford to be generous," said Dr. Sinseburough, the physician in charge of the case, thinking of the enormous fee he was receiving. It won't hurt me to cater to these small-town Mid-Westerners whose women-folk are so eager to make a splurge."

Since Rose was a trained nurse, she was grudgingly permitted to don a white uniform and take her place near the doctors and other nurses. Not to be left out in the cold, the Count stood in an ante-room where he could see all that went on.

While John and his father waited in the hall both were thinking of another scene twenty odd years before as John relived those hours and days of anxiety and horrors, he thought of his wife Lucy.

He wondered what had actually become of her and his infant son, censoring himself for his heartlessness in discarding her without a forgiving word for her deception. Yet he had the feeling she had not known she carried Negro blood.

Rose too remembered that scene and the birth of the twins, thinking gloatingly of her triumph and revenge on the girl-child. To her nothing was quite so sweet as revenge. Pride, jealousy, and revenge were the controlling emotions of her life.

She chuckled to herself with the malicious thought that Jeanette never would marry Howard Everett, for she had seen him but the week before at the theater in Los Angeles. He had been escorting one of the city's most exclusive socialites, who was both charming and beautiful. But the woman had been happy to notice that only sadness was to be seen in his face.

She had heard that Mrs. Everett was engineering the match, and it was only a matter of time until the engagement would be announced by the press. "I suppose that is why she is in the city," Rose had told Lucile. "Perhaps she is afraid her son will not keep his promise, but will try to take back Jeanette unless she marries him off."

Rose then sighed with the satisfaction as she thought to herself, "I doubt if the silly, sentimental Howard ever loves any one but Jeanette. He is exactly like John Barke. John never pulled the wool over my eyes, for I have known all along he loved Lucy with her Nigger blood instead of me-that is why I hate him."

Still waiting for Lucile's baby to come Rose let her thoughts travel in what she considered happy channels. "I'm glad to see Howard sad and heart-broken, just good enough for spurning my child's love.

"Wait until he reads about her child. Count Von Lanier's baby. He will be sorry and very jealous to think what he missed. I can hardly wait for him to get the news. Yes, and Lucile must send him an announcement. And won't the seminary folks in Boston be surprised to hear of the baby! Money talks, even to the press.

"Jeanette will be cut to the heart, for she always loved babies, and she never will dare have one for fear it might be a Nigger. And another thing, as soon as Lucile is able to get out she plans to have Howard meet the Count." The woman was lost in blissful reverie.

Her thoughts were here interrupted by Lucile's mumbling to herself under the influence of the anesthesia. Her words were incoherent. "I-hope-it-is-a girl. I-I'll call her Abigail. Born-to-Countess-Lucile-Von-Lanier. Wish Jeanette-could be here-won't she be jealous. Reckon she-is-weeping— good enough-"

The nurses almost forgot their ethics, having to avert their faces to keep from showing their cynical smiles. The patient and her mother were too vain and conceited to receive the respect of the institution. More than one patient has made a fool of herself, reveling her innermost thoughts and desires, while under the anesthetic.

The Count decided to give Lucile a lecture when she came home, while Doc wanted to shake her, and even Rose wished she would stop talking.

The Czar waited impatiently out in the hall, sometimes stalking about indignantly. John tried to curb his impatience and show more self-control. Both men thought how much better it would have been had Lucile come home for the event.

Nurses often turned to stare at the older man with his beastly brows and queer behavior. But they looked at John Barke too, for while he was not a young man, he was a most striking, and handsome man with his iron-gray hair and the bearing of a soldier.

The nurses whispered among themselves in the blanket-room. "Isn't this the strangest case you ever have witnessed?" asked one girl in stripes to another.

"I never saw an old man come to see his grandchild born," giggled another nurse. "But that old banker is as rich as Midas himself, I hear."

"Well, maybe we don't know too much about countesses and millionaires having babies. I reckon they can do as they please, for the hospitals charge them ever so much more than other folks," said a third girl.

CHAPTER XX

In a tumbled-down shack of the Boston slum area, where black-faced children swarmed like flies, a heated discussion was in progress.

"Charley, what is you goin' to do about it" Charley Hoke isn't your name a tall. Mayme stood with her hands on her broad hips, emphasizing her words by many nods of her graying head.

"Wife, I can't decide what to do," said the man patiently. "I don't have the heart to make that poor girl more trouble. She has had too much all ready."

"That money rightfully belongs to us," she answered emphatically. "Ain't you been shamefully cheated out of parents, money, and a name? Why? Pride and vanity."

Then the black-faced woman shook her fat sides with laughter. "Won't I make a splurge when I gets my hands on that money? I can jest see myself struttin' down the street and everybody staring at me in a new yaller silk dress and elegant Frenchy heels."

"Mayme, dear, we must first think of our children. Food, clothing, and medical care for our little ones must be had before we buy any finery for ourselves.

"Mister Charley Hoke, you hain't bought me a new dress for nigh unto twenty years. Charity clothes is all I has. I'm tired of them. A fine provider you is."

"I'm sorry, dear. Haven't I tried? Haven't I worked from four o'clock in the morning until five at night?" asked the man meekly.

"Sich pore management. When we gets our money. I'm gonna manage it. For once in my life, I'm gonna enjoy myself.

He wondered how long a few thousand dollars would last his wife. If his Uncle Ted were correct there might be that much coming to him, but he had said it would mean a lawsuit.

The letter from his Uncle Ted telling about the money that had come a month before. He had not mention it to his wife, wanting to try to decide what to do about it. Now Mayme had found the letter's hiding place.

"So you has secrets from your lawfully wedded wife?" she had said, and the irate woman had shaken the offending letter under her husband's nose. "You think you is somebody, don't you? But we hain't what we seems. I hain't Mrs. Charley Hoke no more, I's gwine to be a fine lady."

"Honey, we are used to doing without money. Can't we just go on as we are?" pleaded the man.

"Man a-live, is you crazy? Why I has most of that money spent already. Just since findin' the letter this mornin' behind the pitcher on the wall."

"But do you want a law-suit? We must hire an attorney, have a lot of publicity, then run the chance of getting nothing but a disagreeable name for ourselves and for our children. Law-suits are expensive and uncertain."

After Charley had gone to work the next morning, Mayme reread the letter. How she did want that money! There were so many pretty dresses, hats, shoes, and other things for herself she longed for. Of course she knew nothing of law-suits, but she felt she nothing to lose and a chance of getting what looked to her like a heap of money.

She collared the postman and asked him numerous questions. "Hey, mister, who is the biggest lawyer-man in this town of Boston?" He looked surprise, even if he were accustomed to the woman's strange questions.

"Alvin Maxwell is considered the most competent attorney in the city, I understand, although I have not had any dealings with him. Are you in need of legal advice, Mrs. Hoke?" he asked jokingly.

"We sure is. My husband is about to get a fortune and we needs a lawyer-man who can talk big and won't take no sass. My ole man is bein' cheated out of this money by a rich old guy that's as mean as dirt. So we gots to get a lawyer who knows his business."

"Good luck to you." The postman was unimpressed.

"Huh, he don't think I knows what ise talking about. He can jist wait and see."

All day she thought and thought about that letter. But that night neither she or Charley mentioned the letter, Uncle Ted, or money. After going to bed she thought some more, in fact she hardly slept for trying to figure out what to do to get the money. Of one thing she was convinced, her husband never would lift a finger to get it.

The next morning after Charley had left for work and while the children were sleeping, she slipped the letter from its hiding place behind the picture on the wall and read it again. She nodded her head, put it back behind the picture saying, "I'll do it."

Hurriedly she pulled her many children from their beds, gave them a meager breakfast, hurried the older ones off to school, then admonishing the others to behave themselves while she was gone, ran over to the near-by grocery store. She managed to wangle the merchant into making an appointment with the attorney the postman had mentioned to her.

She raced back home, highly elated to think she was on the road to riches. Donning her best charity dress and hat she started for the bus, on her way to her first interview with an attorney.

As would be expected, Mayme Hoke had difficulty in getting by the office girl. But because she insisted she had an appointment with Alvin Maxwell by telephone, the girl reluctantly admitted her.

She laid the matter before his judicial eye, gave him the letter in proof of her statements and said, "Now Mister," she tossed her head importantly and smiled, "I'll pay you well for getting' me this money."

The man read the letter in amazement, then reread it, a deep scowl between his eyes. "How strange! Imagine that!" He gave the woman a long, scrutinizing stare, shaking his head.

"Don't you believe what Uncle Ted writes, Mister?" she asked curtly.

"It was not that, madam, But, Ms. Hoke, I regret to say, it is impossible for me to handle your case." He arose as a signal for her to leave.

But she held her ground and asked, "Why, Mister? Its a swell case and you can make a pile of money for yourself. If you gets us five-thousand dollars, you gets fifty dollars. Ain't that fair?"

He tried not to smile at her statement of generosity, but he had difficultly getting rid of her. After she was gone, he was lost in thought. "What a story for the press, if only I dare give it out. To think of a man of such rich heritage being tied to a woman of her type. I wouldn't dare handle that case," he said to himself.

Mayme Hoke was disappointed but she was not beaten yet. The following day she put one her charity dress again and went in search of another attorney. But her manners and appearances were against her, besides, she was a Negro. Then, too, her story sounded like a fairy story or a tale from the Arabian Nights.

She went to office after office, but all to no avail. However, she was enjoying the experiences more and more. It was a relief to get away from the responsibility of the home. Then too, she was acquiring a feeling of importance.

As she stood scanning the directory at the foot of the elevator of a large office building one day she said, "The kids can just look after themselves. I'm not goin' back without findin' a lawyer-man. Reckon this name might be all right. I'll give him a try."

The oftener Mayme told her story the more convinced she became that Charley Hoke's Uncle Ted's letter had stated facts. She determined to let nothing dampen her spirits, for she had started something and she would finish it. Surely some man would take the case.

By much questioning of various business people she gained fair rating of attorneys. Finally she decided Warren Hanford was the man for her to see, and she called at his office.

He sat in his private office tilted back in his big swivel chair, wondering how to find business during the worst days of the depression. Then Caroline, his faithful office girl, announced Mrs. Charley Hoke.

"Show her in," he snapped curtly, disgusted that he was forced to give such a person a hearing.

After a few minutes he dismissed the woman, then said, "Caroline, you know I can't afford to accept Negro clients. If I start it, there will be no end. Anyway who wants such trash as that woman?"

"But, Mr. Hanford," insisted Caroline Miller, "supposing all attorneys took that attitude? Besides, the woman declared her husband is a white Negro. The letter verified the fact that he is half-white."

"That story had no foundation. The woman has been attending too many cheap movies." So he dismissed her and her letter from his mind and went on worrying about the lack of business and the depression.

But Caroline could not forget the woman and her strange story. While she was young and attractive, she carried a wise little head on her shoulders. More than one of the attorney's cases had its turning point because of her keen brain.

Unknown to her husband, Maybe continued her search for a lawyer. Just to keep up her courage in the matter, she spent some time window-shopping, occasionally she entered some of the most expensive dress shops. "I just want to see what swell folks wear," she apologized to herself.

Her slum neighbors became intensely interested in her story and adventures with the legal world. Because the women all believed her tale, she found herself much courted, for it is human nature to bow to wealth and royalty. To these simple folk five-thousand dollars looked like a gold mine and and its possessors millionaires.

Mrs. Alexander, her next door neighbor, was one of her admirers in this great enterprise and one day she said, "Mis Hoke, won't you come with me to the show this evenin? My Gold can look after your kids."

"Thanks, but I hain't got the money. Honest, I spent my last penny on trolley fare trying' to see a lawyer-man. Yesterday, I had to borrow money of the milk man to get down town. Yes, sir, that's the truth."

"Come on, Mis Hoke, I have enough for both of us." So the good neighbors vied with each other to serve the future-rich folk.

Strange as it may seem, Charley was still blissfully ignorant of his wife's maneuvering in the legal world. Each night she carefully placed the letter behind the picture on the wall. Often the man would take the letter from its hiding place after super and reread it, shaking his head solemnly, replace it, then roll into bed.

Mayme watched him in disgust. "If he had half the brains I got, he would find a lawyer-man. Then he would not have to get out of bed at three or four in the mornin' to go on his garbage wagon." Then eyeing him cautiously she said to herself, "Ole man, you is waitin' for a surprise. It won't be loo long either. You will see."

CHAPTER XXI

A breathless silence pervaded the delivery room of the St. Luke's Maternity Hospital in Los Angeles, broken only by Countess Lucile's almost incoherent babbling. She was mumbling, "My sweet-baby-Abigail-born-C-"

Then the child arrived. At the sight of the infant Rose gave a wild scream and dropped to the floor. Dr. Cunningham recognized her cry and ran to her and dexterously picked her up and carried her to a private room and laid her on the bed.

He turned to the nurse in charge and said, "As soon as she comes to, give her a sedative to keep her quiet."

Rose struggled to a sitting position and screamed, "Oh, no, Doc you don't give me your dope to keep my mouth shut!" She tried to get out of bed, but the nurse forced her back on the pillow. "You and your Barke tribe won't make way with me and poor little Lucile as you did with Lucy and her brat."

"Mrs. Barke," said the nurse in a business-like tone taking the woman by the arm to administer the hypodermic, "Lie down. Soon you will feel better. Take this shot like a good girl."

She jerked away, "Let me out of here. Where is John? Let me find that low-bred husband of mine. He shall pay for this disgrace-" and with that she was out of bed and on her feet, having prevented the girl in uniform from giving her the sedative.

Hans Von Lanier had taken but a second glance at his daughter to make sure his eyes had not deceived him. Then while Dr. Cunningham was carrying Rose from the room, like a bolt of lightening he shot from the room and out of the hospital.

The old doctor from the Middle-West left the hysterical woman with the nurse and went in search of John Barke. He quickly told his father about the new-born infant.

"Doc," said the younger man hoarsely, "it is the Barkes who carry the tainted blood, not the Travises. Why did you deceive me?"

"Y-you-have guessed right," said the physician sadly, "B-but-"

"Why did you and dad commit the dastardly crime of branding Lucy and wrecking the innocent girl's life? I not she, am the guilty one." He stared indignantly at both men. J. B. Barke immediately left the room without a word.

"Your father is a proud man, John. He had hoped you might never marry, if you did, we planned to make way with any colored child that might arrive before either you or its mother saw it. That is why we have insisted all births should be born in the Barke home, but Rose double-crossed us both times."

"What are you going to do about Lucile's mulatto child?" asked John.

"Your father has gone to make terms with the physician and the hospital authorities-we must work fast. Try to pacify Rose, somehow, while I find Hans."

"Say, where is the Count? He was right here a minute ago, now he has disappeared."

"He is not a count and never was, but a noted gambler from Boston. All he is after is money. Detectives are on his trail. But I must go look for him and find out what he is up to."

"Doc, I am glad you have unearthed this much about him, for we should have investigated him before the marriage. Yet after letting Rose hold the ropes for twenty years, it is discouraging to attempt to lift my voice against anything she wants. I better go to her before she does something rash."

As he entered the room where Rose was she shrieked, "John, you miserable, low-lived Nigger! Why didn't we know it was you and the Barke tribe who carried the tainted blood? Such a stupid fool as I have been. You with your limpid black eyes, wavy dark hair! Any one with the brains of a child would have known old J. B. Barke is a Nigger with his buck-head and course lips and thick neck."

"Don't you dare 'Rose, dear' me. Nurse, telephone the best attorney in the city for me and send him to my room here. This miserable scoundrel and his precious father shall pay for this disgrace, and so shall Doc. The world shall know the truth about Lucy and her kid."

In vain the nurse and John reasoned with the infuriated woman. "I'm going to Lucile," she declared, but was unable to walk. "She must not know the truth, not yet anyway. And where is that count?"

Lucile was slowly coming out from under the anesthetic and was mumbling, "Won't folks be envious of me and baby Abigail? Born to a countess-" then she was awake.

"Where are mama and the Count? Has the baby come? A girl? O, I's so glad it is a girl. Little Abigail! Bring her to me, I must see the little darling. I want mama!" she demanded imperiously.

"Your mother will be here soon," explained the nurse. "Your daughter, er, must not leave the nursery-yet."

"Why? I want to see her. "Isn't she all right?" Every mother is haunted by the fear her child may be born blind, crippled, or with some other abnormal condition.

"Yes, no. The doctor will be in soon and you may talk to him." The girl in uniform was glad to escape without shouldering the responsibilities of explaining so precarious a problem to this high-spirited young mother.

J. B. Barke and Dr. Cunningham hurried to the office of Julius Longstreet, the private detective they had engaged soon after arriving in the city to keep track of the Count.

"What are we going to do now? Asked the doctor. "Rose will stop at nothing. We may just as well prepare for the noose."

"Doc, you talk like a fool! We are not licked yet. Think of the narrow escapes have had over the past half-century. The disgrace is horrible, but it could have been avoided had Rose cooperated. But money still talks, especially in these depression days."

"With the hospital crew knowing the truth, what can we do? Lucille's child looks more like a Negro than did Lucy's boy."

"Can't the hospital let a nurse take the rap" suggested the Czar with his accustomed assurance. "Can't the authorities of the institution give out that a little young student nurse mixed babies? I had a few words with the physician and and the superintendent of nurses and they seem to be willing to listen to reason, and accept the enormous check.

"But there are no colored mothers in that maternity hospital, surely-"

"Couldn't one be imported? This is the least of my worry that is their problem. Doc, money will do anything these days. Well, anything but give Rose brains and a spirit of cooperation. Yet, in order to cover her daughter's disgrace, she should be induced to listen to reason."

The the attorney arrived and put an end to the conversation between the men. He said, taking a packet of papers from his case, "Mr. Barke, your man is an interesting character. As I said before, he is no count, and Hans Lichtinberger, alias Count Von Lanier, is wanted in several localities in the country. The New York police want him for forgery." He handed them a photograph sent by the detective from that city.

"That's the man all right," Dr. Cunningham said. "But how could he grow that luxuriant mustache so quickly?"

"It is no doubt removable. Where where is the man? He has given us the slip. And the Los Angeles police find they want him for boot-legging. Last but not least, his wife in Chicago is eager to locate her lawfully-wedded husband."

So the man is a bigamist!" snorted the old banker. "Now Lucile has neither a husband nor a father for her child."

The doctor mumbled under his breath, "Surely Rose and her spiteful daughter are being paid in their own coin."

Someone handed the detective the latest edition of the newspaper and he carelessly glanced at the headlines.

NEGRO CHILD BORN TO COUNTESS VON ANIER HEIRESS OF THE BARKE MILLIONS. COUNT SUES FOR FIFTY THOUSAND DOLLARS DAMAGE.

Rose and her daughter had coveted publicity and notoriety. Boston would get the news, straight from the press.

The detective, Julius Longstreet, placed the incriminating packed of letter and pictures in his case and literally rolled up his sleeves for the fight before him. "Mr. Bark, this is the work of no other than the clever Hans Lichtinberger. We must locate the scoundrel immediately."

In one of the most luxuriant homes in the residential section of the city of Lost Angeles Howard Everett and his mother sat eating breakfast. As their trim maid set down the hot toast she handed the man the morning paper.

He carelessly glanced at the headlines, a piece of buttered toast half-way to his mouth. He drew in his breath sharply and dropped the toast, passing the newspaper to his mother, watching her intently.

She too saw the headlines, but turned to her son and said placidly, "Lucile's crime against her sister is avenged."

"But, mother, that doesn't bring Jeanette any nearer happiness nor lesson her disgrace," said the man sadly.

The news of the birth of Lucile's child reached the Boston's Girls Seminary by way of the press just as Rose and her daughter had hoped it would. "Good enough for Lucile! Declared Miss Babcock. "Too bad it still involves Jeanette."

Miss Clark said, "To think that John Barke, that handsome, cultured man, has tainted blood. Oh, the suffering caused by intermarrying of the the two races. Both races are to blame, but it is the succeeding generations that pay the penalty."

Virginia Norris, the librarian, asked "Miss Babcock, do you think it is a sin for a white person to marry a Negro?"

"That's not for me to say, Virginia. What I do say, is that it is not expedient, for it brings anguish and humiliation to both races. It is not good sense. A seventy-year-old woman might marry a thirty-year-old man and it could not be called a crime or a sin, but everybody would say she was using poor judgment, for it would bring only unhappiness to the contracting parties."

"However, in the case of racial intermarriage, it may not be the couple marrying who suffer the most, but their innocent, helpless offspring. They are the victims of their parents' stupid and silly behavior," said Miss Babcock. "Mind you, I am not condemning the Negro more than the white man."

Strange as it may seem, Jeanette did not read of the birth of her sister's child. Like some busy college students who carry heavy work, she seldom looked at a newspaper. No one wanted to tell her, feeling she had trouble enough.

But Elsie Hamilton did read that account with gladness in her heart. "I'm not a Negro after all! My blood is not tainted! The curse is lifted from me. But my poor Jeanette is no better off than before. If only she won't read about it.

"How cruel I am, but I can't find it in my heart to feel sorry for Lucile. Neither do I pity the old Czar. But John is not only disgraced, but he will suffer remorse for his cruelty in discarding me."

"Now I am free to marry Lang. I have often wondered why I could not say yes to his many proposals. He is so good and noble. He has waited long enough, he shall wait no longer."

CHAPTER XXII

In Boston Warren Hanford sat in his law office with his feet on his desk, his hands locked behind he head, a heavy scowl on his handsome face. "Will this depression never end?" he groaned.

Caroline Miller handed him the morning paper. "Here's the Boston Times." She had said nothing but the paper was opened conspicuously to the account of the birth of the child of Countess Von Lanier, mentioning the fact that the mother had been a student at the Boston Girls' Seminary.

"Caroline, wait!" boomed his voice as soon as he had read the headlines, scrambling to get his feet off the desk. "You brainy kid! As usual you are right. Wish I had taken that old fat woman's address, just my luck, for by now she is sure to have a lawyer."

"Mr. Hoke is a city garbage man. Shall I call the city hall?"

"By all means. What would I do without you? Here's my chance to make a haul. I'll take the case only on commission, and shall take plenty too. That old gal doesn't know the first thing about business."

The home address of Charley Hoke was obtained, a letter written, and a messenger boy given the missive.

The attorney said, "Now, kid, give this letter to no one but Mrs. Hoke, the fat colored woman of the house. Should her old man be there stick around until you can slip her the letter. Understand?"

Turning to his secretary he said, "My hunch is that Charley may not be too strongly in favor of this suit."

"My guess is, that he knows nothing about it, or that his wife is scouring the city trying to scare up an attorney. You may be safe, for she won't get one easy, too many are as unwise as you."

A few hours later Mayme was at the office, beaming her toothless smile. "You sent for me, mister? You wished to see me?"

"Be seated, my good woman. Some time ago you were here I believe, about some legal business for your husband, if I remember correctly." How he did hope she had not found another attorney. This case would be a snap. He held his breath for an answer.

"Yes, sirree. I was here about Charley's Uncle Ted. It is a mighty easy case. Its one you can easy win if you had experience in that line at all-"

"Well," he said, interrupting the flow of words, "I might consider taking the case-"

"Yes, sir, let me tell you. Uncle Ted is a brother of J. B. Barke, the millionaire-maybe you have heard about him. Their father was white and their mother was a colored lady. Uncle Ted is black like his ma-"

"As I started to say, madam, I might find time to take your case on a fifty-fifty basis. I am very, very rushed with business, but would try to look after you suit. On a fifty-fifty basis, Mrs. Hoke, that means-"

"Is you askin me to give you twenty-five hundred dollars if we gits five-thousand dollars? Give you all that for you jest knowin' how to use some big words and do some loud talkin'? Nothin doin'. Another lawyer-man will take it for a third, but the grocery man said he is cheatin.' A feller-"

"But you see-"

"A feller in the post office says he lows ten percent is enough for such a easy case. That's five-hundred dollars. Uncle Ted is brainy like his brother that owns the bank and all that money and he says-"

"Madam, my time is very limited, but just to help you," he stopped, assumed a judicious air, cleared his throat and continued, "I handle only big, important cases. Your case will require expense and perhaps a great deal of traveling and hard work. But as I said, I wish to help you, so I might consider taking it, for, say thirty percent, but not any less-"

"Remember then, you gets only thirty percent, not a penny more. Here's Uncle Ted's letter, but you dassant lose it. Do you have a safe place to keep t? Charley, that's my husband, don't know I has it. It tell just how to go about getting' the money. Youse knows the J. B. Barke, the rich old guy? His granddaughter has been to our house lots of times-"

"Sign here-"

"You hain't getting me to sign nothin'. The mailman tole me to sign nothin'. Thems his very words to me. Say, mister how soon will I get my five-thousand dollars? My clothes already bein' held for me. That's my new hat, you see."

"Madam, it may be months, even a year before you receive a penny."

"Hurry, won't you? Take good care of the letter-"

Warren Maxwell smiled blandly, suavely he almost closed the door in the woman's face as she tried to back her way out of the office, talking glibly all the time.

"Caroline, to think that Charley Hoke is the long-buried Jerry Barke, son of old J. B. Barke. Pretty slick! Cheated his own son out of his name and inheritance. Suppose he would have done the same to John had he showed his Negro blood."

"So the father of Ted and J. B. married a pretty Negro girl while he was a fur-trader in Africa. Later he returned to Canada where he died, leaving his wife and two small boys. So when the white boy grew up he came to the United States and passed himself off as a white man, while his brother stayed to care for his mother. But why has Ted waited all these years to tell his story?"

"He had promised his mother to make no trouble so long as she lived. She died a few months ago and now he is trying to right the wrong to Charley Hoke."

"But I don't get it. Why was Jerry supposed to be buried?" asked Caroline.

"I forgot to say, that because J. B. never told his wife he carried colored blood, he and the old doctor had it made up between them that should a mulatto child be born, Dr. Cunningham was to take it to his grandmother and Uncle Ted in Canada, reporting it had died in infancy."

Then the office girl read the letter for herself. "So the boy was told he was the adopted child of Ted Barke. Well, the poor Charley Hoke can surely use some money to bring up that house full of children. But won't the fur fly when you get your hands on the old banker!"

"Caroline, I remember reading about the disappearance of Lucy and her child, but never dreamed I would have a part in unraveling the mystery.

I wonder if she did commit suicide and kill her child?"

It did not take much time or work to verify the records and get a report on the two empty graves in Jamestown, Iowa. Since all of the statements in the letter had been proven true so far, Hanford took a plane to Nova Scotia to visit Uncle Ted Barke himself.

He found the man living in a two-room shack of unhewed logs. "I'm glad you came, Mr. Hanford," said Ted Barke, a little old man with woolly white hair, a bent figure, and a face as black as tar. "I have been guilty of a great wrong against Jerry but for her mother's sake I kept quiet. While J. B. lived in luxury ad elegance, his son existed in dire poverty."

The attorney sat gingerly on an old cane-bottom chair, wondering if he dare take a full breath lest the chair give way under him.

Ted was saying, "Until my health failed, I sent small checks to Jerry each month. It is not fair, my brother has always been a good manager and seemed to coin money. But he grabbed all of father's wealth, while I was left to care for mother.

"When Lucy and her other twin were discarded I wanted to expose my brother then, but mother begged me to spare him. She seemed to realize she had been as much to blame as my father for their ill-advised marriage. I've kept close tab on J. B. through all the years and know about his many crimes and meanness."

As Hanford nosed his plane toward Boston he thought of the sorrow such marriages brought into the world. "Without doubt the story is true. Poor Ted, he has never married because of his parents indiscretions. The man is intelligent, fine and noble in spite of his black skin, but life has cheated him. He has missed happiness because of his parent's mistakes. He would not want to marry a Negro woman lest he have a white child and embarrass her, and he dare not marry a white one, even if he could."

Arriving at his office he remarked to the girl, "Caroline, everything is moving fast. The case becomes more exciting every day. Now to get the district attorney to prove the Barkes and Dr. Cunningham, their henchmen, murdered Lucy and her child. Say, nobody needs to prove they committed murder. Those men must show us they did not kill the woman and her infant. The burden of proof is on them, not us. In plain words, they must find her and her son."

"How about Charley Hoke's case? She asked.

"That is too easy to waste even a second thought upon. It is self-evident J. B. tried to defraud Ted of his share of the estate. When J. B.'s wife had her mulatto son, Jerry, he was taken to Ted to raise. J. B.'s wife was too ill to know. He was pronounced dead. As the nephew of Ted, he was raised by Ted; he was named Charley Hoke and when he grew up he moved to Boston and raised his family, as a poor garbage hauler. So Charley as well as Ted should have had a share of the estate left by J. B.'s father."

"Take a look at this," Caroline said as she handed the attorney the latest issue of the Los Angeles Daily, for she was keeping tab on the news of that city. The headlines fairly slapped him in the face.

ST. LUKES HOSPITAL DENIES COUNTESS VON LANIER GVE BIRTH TO MULATTO CHILD. REWARD FOR INDENTIFICATION OF PERSON WHO MADE STATEMENT TO PRESS.

"Huh," said the man, "that must have cost the Barkes a heap of money. They are making a fight to squelch the scandal. But it is going to cost them more money than they can find to stop the broadcast I am unearthing."

Not long after this the same newspaper stated that the millonaire, J. B. Barke and son, John, accompanied by Dr. Cunningham, their physician, had returned to their home in Iowa.

Soon Warren Hanford was walking into the doctor's office in Jamestown, plying him with poignant questions. The aging physician had lost his fighting spirit. He was old and broken. His soul was weary from the Barke trouble in California. Hanford's task was easy.

To the queries the doctor replied without protest. "Yes, I was the attending physician at the birth of Jerry Barke, son of J. B. Barke. I did sign a death certificate knowing him to be alive and with his grandmother in Nova Scotia."

"Did you sign a death certificate for Lucy Travis Barke, wife of John Barke, knowing her to be alive?" Asked the attorney.

"Yes," groaned the snowy-haired man.

"And Lucy's infant son?"

"His birth was never recorded, for only the two nurses, his parents, grandfather and I knew of his birth. Hence no death certificate was needed. The grandmother has known nothing of our work. Since she does not know her husband is half-Negro, his one fear in life is that she may discover his secret."

"Dr. Cunningham, do you know the penalty for signing a death warrant for a person you know to be living?"

"Yes, Mr. Hanford," whispered the man, his lips livid.

"Now for Lucy and her child and their disappearance," asked the lawyer, taking notes as he he went along. "You acknowledge taking them secretly in your plane at dead of night to Alabama?"

"Yes, but I swear I did not harm a hair of their heads. What became of them is a mystery I can not fathom."

"My good man, you and the Barkes will fathom that mystery or go to the electric chair!" cried the questioner hotly.

J. B. Barke sat in his luxuriant office at the Citizens' Bank of Novinger, Iowa, feeling especially elated. He chuckled complacently to himself, "That St. Luke's Hospital case was a close shave. But my old head got the best of them. Even Doc lost heart and left me to figure it out, but wisdom and shrewdness along with a bit of cash is all one needs in life to be a success."

"Now there is my brother Ted, always worked like a slave. But he's a miserable near-pauper. No brains, no wisdom, and soft. Forever taking care of someone. My policy is, take care of J. B. and let the other fellow look after himself. Brains, and I have them." He leaned back in his big chair and gazed across the town-even most of its inhabitants belonged to him.

"Since Hans Lichtinberger, the so-called-Count, is safely behind bars we have nothing to fear from him. The hospital did a magnificant job of covering up our disgrace. Cost a fortune, but it was worth it." The bank president chuckled some more. "My brain and wisdom handled it. Bah! No need of poverty and misfortune."

"If that silly Rose keeps her mouth closed, Lucile need not know she gave birth to a mulatto." Her woolly-headed girl had been exchanged for a white infant at the city foundling-home. Rose had gladly consented to the deception to save the disgrace, but she still swore vengeance against the Barkes. Had the Czar known what she had in her mind, he would not have smiled quite so complacently.

But the man was blissfully unconscious of the impending danger that hung above him like a deadly dagger that swung by a single thread. All of his life he had stood with his heel on the other fellow's neck, he imagined danger could not trap him, his brains were too sharp to permit him to fall.

At this psychological moment the fatal messenger of tragedy stalked into the Novinger bank and served papers on the two Barke men.

"But you can't do this to us!' blustered the grizzled old man, jumping angrily from his chair, "You can't bring murder charges against us for the death of Lucy and her kid. Just name the amount. This can be settled right now."

"Oh, no, my good fellow. At last justice is catching up with you. Put away your check book, for the time being at least. Later it may come in handy, but no bribing me. We have the goods on you, at least it looks that way to me."

"You can't prove a thing. You are bluffing and you know it," snorted the old man, dropping into his chair, livid with rage and fear. Like all bullies, at heart he was a coward.

When he saw that the man before him meant business and seemingly had his evidence, the Czar, not looking at all like one, turned white and tears streamed from his eyes, eyes-that had never shed a tear, even in the death of a relative. "Please, have mercy. Think of my age and gray hairs-spare me this disgrace. My beloved wife is not well, for she is afflicted with heart-disease. She must not know!"

"Father, we can put up bond, we do not have to go to prison, Besides, we can clear ourselves." But he did not feel so brave as he sounded, yet he could not endure to see his father in such distress.

"Your son is right, for bail can be arranged for yourselves and Dr. Cunningham. As for pity, Mr. Barke, when did you ever show mercy to anyone? Haven't the widows and orphans always been your victims" Now you blubber like a child when forced to face the results of your pride and greed."

J. B. Barke put up bail for himself, son, and the doctor, then set his head to clear themselves. The bail had been made exceptionally large because the feeling was strong against the men. They were considered criminals, in fact murderers. Warren Hanford was doing his job well.

CHAPTER XXIII

Out in California, Lucile took great pride in her child. "Now, Abigail Von Lanier," she said, for she loved to talk to the infant, "you must remember that you papa belongs to the nobility. Your mama is the Countess Lucile. Darling, any one can tell by your looks you are of noble birth-that you are a genuine blue-blood.

Knowing the background of little Abigail as she did, Rose felt she must scream if Lucile did not stop her silly jabbering. "How soon dare I tell hear the truth about Hans? Would it be safe to let her know the baby is only a founding and not her own? Yet any minute she could find out the truth. What a blessing she never reads the papers."

"Mama," asked the fond mother, "did you ever notice how much like the Count she looks? Same eyes, same mouth, same nose."

"Yes, yes, child!" Rose answered impatiently.

"How soon do you think I can make an ocean voyage? Hans insists it may be quite a long time. "I'm dying to see our lovely old castle. It must be magnificent by now, we have put so much money in it."

"And do you ever see Howard Everett? Just as soon as I am able to appear in public, I want to show him Abigail and the count. He spurned my love, now it will be fun to show him how much better I did than to marry him."

Rose feared to attempt to answer any of the questions lest she get into deep water and unable to get out.

"And, mother what is the matter with the mail? Why doesn't a letter come from Hans? He should get most of his sister's estate since she was unmarried. It is almost a month since you told me he left for Europe." The Barkes had told her Hans had been suddenly called to Germany by the sudden death of his sister the very day of the birth of Abigail.

"Mom, do you suppose he could have been in a shipwreck? If he is all right why didn't he cable the day he arrived?"

"Don't worry, dear. You are likely to hear from him most any time now." And Rose was afraid of just that and wondered how she could prevent it.

Lucile continued. "The Count has always been very dilatory in writing ever since we were married. Before that, he wrote me every day."

Rose decided to engage an attorney and begin divorce proceedings against her husband at once. The suspense was driving her mad. She made an appointment with Curtis LaGrange, one of the noted divorce lawyers of the city of Los Angeles.

She called on him and laid her case before him. He was intrigued for although he didn't mention it to her, he had read all about the Count and the Negro child in the news. And like all attorneys he had the facts about Hans Lichtinberger. Rose gave him another link in the chain of the mystery story.

He agreed to take her case on a commission basis, provided she advance him a sizable amount in the beginning.

"You see, madam," he explained in his smoothest tones, "there will be a great deal of work and expense attached to your case, more than the usual ones. I will require funds to begin work. When your decree is granted and you get your alimony from your husband, the amount you advanced in the beginning will be cheerfully refunded and deducted from my total fee."

Rose didn't like the idea and told him so. "It will take almost my last dollar to write you so large a check."

"Then, my dear lady, be wise and write your husband for a large check before we file divorce papers against him. That way you will be far ahead. Or maybe you prefer to wait to start proceedings."

"Oh, no, I do not want to delay one day. Begin at once and I will write tonight for more money." Then she wrote the attorney the size of check he had demanded, admitting to herself she despised him.

"Why don't you wire for money, madam?"

"I prefer to write." She couldn't tell the lawyer she was ashamed to send another telegram to Novinger for money, for she had set too many already for her son-in-law, that 'miserable Hans' she now called him. Like all small towns the villagers discussed in full anything that was of public interest, and Rose knew it. Besides, it could make her husband tighten his purse-strings.

Mr. LaGrange lost no time in cashing the check Rose had given him, but he made no haste to begin work on the woman's case. Maybe this was one of the man's weakness or perhaps it is a trait of all attorneys.

That very day Rose wrote a letter to John asking him to send a large check by return mail. "Dear Hubby," she began, for she knew how to get what she wanted, "we are almost down to our last dollar. You can't realize much it costs to live in a large city, especially with a child. Please, John, hurry. With love Your little Wifie."

She was glad the attorney had thought of her writing to John for money, for whatever she got would be just that much more. He had promised to make him pay for the divorce too. She hoped he would get a large alimony, supposing he would make a greater effort since he had taken the case on a percentage basis.

"Once I get the divorce and the money we are ready to get the rest of the Barke wealth. How? Blackmail, Mr. LaGrange laughingly calls it. But the Barkes are giving me all I demand or I send Doc, John, and the old man to the electric chair or the gallows, whichever they prefer for the murder of Lucy and her brat.

"This is going to be fun!" and for the time being, Rose forgot the predicament of her daughter and the baby. The second-Mrs. Barke had a nature that thrived on revenge and crushing those she didn't like.

She hoped to do as successful a job on the rest of the Barkes as Lucile had in crushing Jeanette. She felt if she could accomplish this, her happiness would be complete. "Even if my poor little girl is saddled with that brat and no husband, we'll go to Palm Beach or maybe England or France and live like the real blue bloods."

She knew that with the millions she hoped and expected to get out of the Barkes they would be accepted most any place in the world, for the great depression still stalked the land. And seemingly the one thing that all people desired most was money.

Rose was building high castles in the air, unmindful of the rumbling tornado that swirled toward her and Lucile, threatening to draw them into its great devouring mouth.

While she was gloating over her anticipated good fortune she thought of Jeanette and wondered how she was facing the the scandal that would be confronting her. She knew that even the Everetts dared not return to Boston because of the things people were saying about Howard jilting Jeanette because she carried Negro blood. It gave Rose real satisfaction to think of her step-daughter's humiliation.

Jeanette did face great humiliation in her social life at the seminary, but even gossips tire of the same subject and finally turn to fresher scandals. She became almost content again, for she was with Miss Hamilton much of her leisure time, and then there was Ben Hooper.

However, the tall handsome man from Novinger was becoming weary of his role as big brother, and was pressing his suit for the heart of the girl he had loved and courted all his life.

"Jeanette, you know Howard Everett's engagement to that Los Angeles belle has already been announced. Do you still hope?"

"No, Ben, I gave up Howard long ago, but it does not seem fair to give only what is left of my heart. You deserve something better."

"Dearest, one tenth of your heart is worth more to me than all the hearts in the world."

"Wait, Ben just a little longer. Besides if I have colored blood as Lucile said in the cloakroom, you do not want me."

"Jeanette, never say that again to me. You know that Lucile tells falsehoods. Yet should she be right, I love you just the same and want to make you my wife, for I love you better than my own life."

He did not tell her what he had read in the newspaper about Lucile giving birth to a mulatto child. Although he had seen the denial also, in his own mind he was convinced the first notice was true and that J. B. Barke and the doctor had squelched it. For a long time he had thought the Barkes, not the Travises, carried the Negro blood. But he wanted Jeanette just the same.

Lang Smith, too, was growing impatient of the long delay, for he felt sure Elsie Hamilton loved him and of late he had been more encouraged than ever. So he renewed his suit with greater ardor. But all of a sudden and without apparent reason, the woman became more distant than ever. He couldn't figure it out.

Elsie had been so relieved and delighted to think she had no tainted blood when she saw the notice in the Los Angeles paper telling of Lucile's mulatto child. But the second notice left her sick.

Which notice was correct? She wondered and worried. How could she be sure if it were she or the Barkes who carried the Negro blood? All she could do was to wait for further developments. She must not encourage Lang Smith, of that she felt sure.

Down in the slum area of Boston, Mayme too was growing tired of waiting. Almost every day she put on her one charity dress and hat and waddled to the attorney's office. "I wanter see the lawyer-man," she would demand of the office girl. Mayme called her 'that man's watch dog.'

"Madam," Caroline would answer impatiently, "Mr. Hanford is working hard on your case. It takes time. Please, Mrs. Hoke, be reasonable and do not come again until he sends for you. When you are needed I will notify you."

"Now, Mis, he has had the case long enough to have my five-thousand dollars. Any man with brains could have had it before this. How does I know he hain't run away with it?"

"Mrs. Hoke, you know has not collected one penny of your money yet. Good-by!"

"But the store wants to know when I can get my yaller dress they is keepin'"

Charley was still in ignorance of his wife's legal maneuverings. For she had demanded the lawyer give her back the letter to hide behind the picture on the wall. He sometimes reread it but came to no decision of what to do about it.

CHAPTER XXIV

Lucile sat in her Los Angeles apartment gloating over her good fortunes.

She never tired of boasting to her child. "Now, Abigail, you must understand right now that you are a lady. Born a lady, and you must never associate with common, trashy, children. Children of nobility are too good to associate with ordinary kids. Yes, you are a true blue-blood."

Rose had gone to call on her attorney. She was frantic. John had failed to send her a check, had not so much as answered her letter. That was not at all like him. The suspense was more than her impatient nature could endure. She considered sending a telegram, thinking maybe her tricky lawyer had sent the divorce papers to be served on him.

Curtis LaGrange did not offer her a chair but smoothly said, "Mrs. Barke, it takes time. No, your husband has not been notified of the impending suit. Your letter may have miscarried-you better send him a telegram at once."

Following his advice Rose hastened to the Western Union office. "John dear I'm desperate stop No money for the next meal stop Please wire money at once lovingly Rose stop.

To the girl at the desk she said, "just send 'collect'."

She felt relieved and instilled with new courage. On the way to the apartment she stopped and purchased herself a lovely evening gown and cloak to match. Haughtily she said, "Charge to the account of Mrs. John Barke." Then she tripped out of the store, smiling complacently. She told herself she needed something to lift her moral.

After spending two hours at the beauty salon and charging it to her spouse, she explained to her conscience, "I must not let myself get run down at the heel, for I really am a young woman and still have a future, once I get money. Soon Lucile must go to get herself some new clothes, then we can go into society."

She gave an unusually big order at the open market and grocery combined. "Just charge to John Barke." When the clerk hesitated she gave him a cold stare and asked, "You don't know the millionaire-Barkes of Novinger, Iowa?" Her scorn made the man burn with shame for his ignorance and not inducing her to make it a bigger order.

While her mother was away, Lucile continued to play with her child. The morning paper lay unopened on the library table. Although Rose knew her daughter was not in the habit of reading the news she usually took no chances but kept the papers out of sight. But in her haste to leave this particular morning, she had forgotten it.

As Lucile reached for another chocolate from the box on the table, the newspaper fell to the floor and sprawled at her feet. As she carelessly picked it up the headlines caught her eyes.

HANS LIGHTINBERGER ALIAS COUNT VON LANIER TAKES OATH FROM PRISON CELL IN LOST ANGELS JAIL THAT NEGRO CHILD WAS BORN TO HIS WIFE LUCILE. CLAIMS REWARD FROM HOSPITAL. LICHTINBERGER BEING HELD FOR BOOTLEGGING.

Lucile read breathlessly on. "A wife in Chicago....for forgery in New York City." She felt her throat would choke her. Running to the crib she gave the infant a scrutinizing stare and spitefully kicked the bed with her toe. The startled child shrieked its protest. But she ignored its cries and carefully reread the account in the paper, huddled in her chair.

She pieced events together; the disappearance of Hans, the strange behavior of the nurses and the hospital attendants, and the fight between her mother and the Barkes. "Why had I been such a stupid fool? Of course it is the Barkes who carry Nigger blood, not Jeanette's mother!"

She walked over to the crib. "Where did this kid come from? What did thy do with my Nigger brat?"

She sat down in the chair, trying to figure it out. She wondered where her mother could be, and opened the door to look down the street. Deciding it might pay to read the newspaper she scanned the pages from cover to cover, finally her eye caught the divorce notices.

"So! Mom is suing dad for a divorce and that is why she is away so much of the time. I don't blame her. Who wants to live with a Nigger?" Then she stopped aghast. "I'm a Nigger, too! Oh! I can't stand it!:

She walked the floor, crying and wringing her hands, watching anxiously for her mother. When finally she did see her coming she threw open the door, screaming, "Mom, why didn't you tell me? You let me make a feel of myself over this brat. Where did it come from? Where is my Niger kid?"

"Lucile, darling, don't blame me. I wanted to protect you." She tried to put her arms around her infuriated daughter.

"Don't you touch me nor don't you darling me. And get this youngun out of my sight before I bounce it into the street. I hate you and Hans and the kid and dad and grandpa and everybody. I'll kill myself too like Jeanette's mother!" She threw herself on the couch and kicked and screamed like a ten-year-old.

Rose tried to console her by telling her everything. "Darling, I'll get my attorney to dispose of the brat right away. Cheer up, sweetheart, for it will not be long until we have millions of dollars to spend as we want to. I haven't told you, but I am going to get a divorce form your dad-"

"I saw it in today's paper. I don't blame you one bit-"

"You saw it in today's paper? Then Curtis LaGrange lied to me. He told me this morning he had not yet file the papers. Maybe my wire will get to Novinger before the notice reaches John. I hope so, for we must have money or we will starve."

"Dad never did fail us. You say you did shopping? You surely have a lovely hair-do. I must get one as soon as I get this kid out of my sight."

"Lucile, as soon as I get my divorce and the Barke money we will go so far no one will ever hear of the past and know you carry tainted blood. If necessary we can assume another name. Think of it, baby, with no jobs or money for anybody, you and I will roll in the old man's millions."

But money did not come in response to her telegram and already the business firms had seen the divorce notice and were shutting down on her credit. The lawyer dilly-dallied about disposing of the child, Abigail, and the money had been spent.

For some time Rose was unable to get an appointment with her attorney, but he kept putting her off. Finally he did admit her to his office.

"Mr LaGrange," she smiled guilessly, "I've decided to withdraw my suit. If you will be so kind as to give me back my money-" She was desperate, and if she could get that money, it would tide her through until she could get money, then she would file again for the divorce.

"My dear woman, it is too late now to stop divorce proceedings. And of course I can not refund your money. My fee is the same whether you accept your decree or not. You see I have already done all of the buildup on your case. From here on there is little work." The man was very affable but exceedingly firm.

"Then you won't refund my money?"

"No, Mrs. Barke. I am sorry," was the suave reply.

"When can I have my divorce?"

"I do not know until I look at the court calendar. I shall notify you, madam, just as soon as it is discerned when you case is coming up for hearing." Curtis Lagrange stood smiling graciously for the woman to depart.

At the door Rose turned and asked, "When are you coming to get the child we are keeping?"

"I shall have my secretary notify you just when to expect me. Right now I am very, very busy."

Rose hurried home, indignantly denouncing her attorney and all lawyers in general. She must have money. Even though she had already dismissed the nurse-maid and all other domestic help earlier, she still could not make it.

The minute she opened the door to the apartment she announced, "Lucile, we are not waiting longer for that smooth-tongued attorney. Abigail is leaving at once. "I'll not feed her another day."

"What are you going to do with the kid?"

"Never you mind," and the woman went about her duties with her lips set in a firm line, a strange gleam in her deep-set eyes. That night the child was fed and put to bed as usual and the girl decided her mother had only been bluffing.

At three o'clock the next morning she quietly arose, dressed, and fed the baby. The she wrapped it in a heavy blanket and stealthily slipped from the house. She climbed into a waiting cab and gave a number.

"Shall I wait for you?" asked the driver when he let her out.

"No, thank you, sir." She walked two more blocks and stealthily stepped on the front porch of one of the most magnificent homes in the city. Carefully she deposited her small bundle containing the sleeping child close to the door, then crept down the steps and disappeared, chuckling maliciously to herself.

"The kid can't suffer," she mumbled to herself as she boarded the trolley for home. "It is sure to be found before feeding time, and it is warmly wrapped, besides the weather is mild."

Lucile was waiting at the door. "Mom, why didn't you tell me you were going? I awoke when you closed the outside door. What did you do with her? Throw her in the ocean?"

"Of course not, silly. She is in safe hands," She laughed with glee, refusing to divulge the secret.

The newspaper next day carried an interesting notice.

INFANT FOUND ON DOORSTEP OF MRS. G. A. EVERETT. CHILD TAKEN TO POLICE QUARTERS AWAITING IDENTIFICATIN.

By now Lucile had found it wise to read the news. When she saw that notice she said, "Oh, mom, you are too cute for anything. Can you imagine Howard picking up that kid?"

The comfortable apartment was given up, rather, the landlady ordered them out because they were behind on the rent and she had to evict them to get them out. They were compelled to take one room on third-floor in the poorer section of the city.

"Mom," whined Lucile, "this onion smell is horrible."

"I don't mind the onions so much as the garlic odor."

"It is so hot and stuffy. Why must we live here?"

"You might try finding something better with what we have to pay in rent, for had I not visited the pawn shop we couldn't even have this place. Tomorrow I'm taking a position. I am certainly happy to be a graduate nurse and command seven dollars a day."

"Oh, do you have a position, mom?"

"Not yet, but it's be easy to locate one. Aren't nurses always in demand?"

The next day Rose tramped the streets from early morning to late in the evening. At each place she was told she must be a registered as a nurse in California.

Night after night the proud woman wearily climbed the rickety three flights of stairs with only failure and dejection written on her face.

"The rent is due tomorrow," cried Rose.

"Let the old woman wait. Who cares whether she gets rent for this dark, dirty hole or not?"

"She can turn us into the street!" snapped the tired woman.

"Then why don't you get a job?" retorted the girl impudently. "Bet I could get a job."

"Try it, my charming daughter."

The next day, dressed in her gaudiest finery Lucile, the proud, sallied forth to try her fortune. But like her mother, night after night she returned weary and beaten. Yet, the depression was no worse in Los Angeles than elsewhere. In fact its inhabitants boasted it was less severe than elsewhere.

"Mom," said the girl one day, "think of it, I was offered a job in the Dime Store. But no pay for a month until I learned to sell needles and pins. The employment office told me they would get me a job but the fee must be paid in advance.

Rose had sent repeated telegrams to John, but neither check nor a reply came. Although she continually tried to see her attorney, her efforts were vain. When she reached him by telephone, he simply put her off with promises, never keeping any of them. Rose was now a regular patron of the pawn shop. By nature she was extravagant, and long before this her credit had run out. The two proud women were having some experiences they did not appreciate. However, they tried to keep up their spirits by looking forward to the millions they would get from the Barkes when her suit was actually settled. She felt sure it would not be long.

CHAPTER XXV

As soon as Warren Hanford, the attorney for Mayme Hoke, had left the office of J. B. Barke, the old man had called in his son and had him telephone for Dr. Cunningham to come to him at once.

He said to his son, "John, your mother must not know. Go immediately to her and tell her our aunt Minnie is ill and wants her to come at once. Doc will take her to the farm and it is so far out in the sticks she will never her the scandal until it has all blown over."

Minnie Hanson was no relative, only another tool of the old banker, not that she wished to be, but because he held the mortgage on her farm and she had choice but to do his bidding. That day before the sun sank in the west Mother Barke was settled in her new living quarters, there to stay until and if the trouble was settled.

With Mrs. Barke disposed of, the three went into conference behind barred doors in the Czars private office to his own home. The banker was roaring angrily, "Doc, what has got into you? You act like a whipped dog. Get busy and find Lucy and her brat. Dead or alive, find them immediately. Do you understand?"

Dr. Cunningham stared with glazed eyes, for he had scarcely slept since the visit of the attorney to his office. His broad shoulders sagged.

"Say something! Yelled the grizzled old banker, "John Lieullen Barke, if you had any backbone, you would tear up the earth to find Lucy and her black son."

"Father, since Lucile had her mulatto child and I found out that I have Negro blood I care little what happens to me. Since I have contaminated blood, I'd rather be dead than alive. But for the sake of mother and Jeanette I will go with Doc on this wild goose chase. Yet after twenty years what can we do?"

The banker had engaged the best legal aid he could obtain in Chicago, promising him any amount of money to clear them. But Thomas Stoneberg showed little fighting spirit, thought the old man.

"Mr. Barke, he said, your case looks dark. Your only hope is to find the missing woman and her son. I shall do my best to get you a light sentence."

John and Doc flew to Lawton, Alabama for evidence in the case of the missing Anna Travis and her son.

After the two men left, J. B. sat in his office in a daze. He said to himself that surely this couldn't be happening to him, thinking it must be only a hideous dream and soon he would awaken to find it only a fantasy of the mind. "I've outsmarted the world too long to be trapped by my black brother and a fat old Nigger wench, and she is my daughter-in-law, too.

Ah, yes, Mr. Barke, Ted Barke has brains too, even if his face is black. Mayme Hoke has plenty of brains also, even if she doesn't look it. You are just as much of a Negro as is Ted upon whom you look down upon.

When Rose's letter arrived John had already left to look for Lucy. His father broke the seal of the letter from Rose and read, saying, "I am glad he is not here, for he is so soft he no doubt would send her another check. We had left her enough money to last for months. For a year all she has done is wire for money for her and the Count. Old gal, you shall be disappointed this time." He tore the letter to shreds.

Then her telegrams came, begging for money. He was more indignant than ever. What have they done with that money? Let them starve! I am surely glad John is not here.

When the divorce notice came for John the old man said, "Huh, so that is her game. No wonder this miserable woman wants money. A nice time for her to be bringing a suit, but we might as well have all our troubles at once. Guess John won't shed any tears because of losing her. Money is all she wants If we can't find Lucy and her boy she may not get much."

John Barke and Dr. Cunningham went direct to the little hotel in Lawton where Lucy had been left with her child. But even the stupid hotel proprietor had left for parts unknown.

When they looked up the detective who had been on the case twenty years before he smiled at their belated investigations. However, they did not satisfy his mind as to why they were trying to rake up new evidence. As yet the press had not been given the story.

They called on Mr. Travis and told him they had been mistaken about his daughter Lucy having tainted blood, saying they were very sorry.

The frail old man was furious and said, "After twenty years you acknowledge your lies. Get out of here before I turn a mob loose on you."

In a kindly tone John said, "We are leaving at once, but first tell us if you have ever heard from Lucy or son."

"Of course not. Get out of here!"

J. B. Barke made a flying visit to see his wife at Minnie Hanson's. He felt quite sure he could trust the woman but he was taking no chances. She met him at the car and said, "Your wife is getting along fine, do not worry about her."

"Now, Minnie, inform the neighbors the doctor has given strict orders that she must have absolute quiet and not one caller, understand?" (Some old woman could tell her the whole story.) "Minnie she sees no one but you."

"Mother Barke was much concerned about her husband's health and said, "Father are you sick? You have looked peak-ed ever since you returned from California, now you appear positively sick. Take me home with you. Let me doctor you. Minnie is not very sick, she can get some one to look after her."

"Ma stop your stewing, for I'm all right. Should I get sick Doc can fix me up quick enough. You must stay here and get Minnie well. She is alone and too far from a doctor to be alone." He gave the door a healthy bang and started for the car.

The hard-headed old banker was worrying more than he would admit even to himself. He knew he looked sick and did not like to be told so. He realized that to be charged with Negro blood was one thing but to be arrested for murder was a far more serious situation.

Dr. Cunningham and John returned from their southern trip, failure written all over their faces. The old man shot them one look then stormed, "You sissies! Tomorrow, Doc, you and I are flying south. "I'll show you what I can do."

"Your attorney can do far more than two old men," complained the doctor. "Twenty years ago the best detectives in the land were on the case while the trail was still warm. Did they find Lucy and the boy I'll tell you J. B., we have reached the end of the road!" His words fell on deaf ears.

Then the divorce papers were served on John Barke. He said, "Let her do her worst. She can't hurt me now. I never did love her, now I have lost what little respect I might have had. But she won't get the millions she expects, although I shall not protest her case or appear against her."

It was with a feeling of relief that John came to the realization that no matter what else might happen to him, he was at last free from Rose and her tyranny. For almost twenty years she had hung like a millstone around his neck, not only crushing out his life but that of his daughter Jeanette.

The following day his father and the doctor left for the South. But it did not prove any more profitable than did the former trip.

Then the press blazened the headlines that J. B. Barke, the millionaire banker of Novinger, Iowa, and his son, John and Dr. Cunningham, their long-time physician, were charged with the murder of Lucy Barke and her son. Lulu Simpson and Rose Garner Barke, wife of John Barke, were named as conspirators.

But down in Boston's colored town, one family was blissfully ignorant of what newspapers were saying. Wooly-headed children fill the small house to the bursting point. A ragged, bent, old man sat dejectedly on a bench in the crowded, cluttered kitchen.

"Mayme, why isn't supper on the table?" he asked impatiently. "It is now nearly seven o'clock and no signs of a bite to eat. When a man leaves for work at four o'clock in the morning he must get to bed early. Take off that dress and those ridiculous high-heel shoes and give us something to eat. The Children are hungry too."

"Don't you jest love this dress? The old supper can wait." She strutted gingerly before the cracked mirror in her pinchy shoes and new silk dress.

"Stop making a fool of yourself! How did you get money for that stuff anyway? Or did someone give them to you?"

"You would like to know? The big departmental stores sez my credit as good as J. B. Morgan's whoever he might be. See that finery on the bed?" She giggled girlishly.

"Look, dad," called one of the girls. On that dirty unmade bed lay gay colored dresses, a gaudy hat, fancy shoes and an evening gown. All for the slatternly Mrs. Hoke.

"Mayme," groaned the man, "are you crazy?"

"How do you like this pink formal? Taffeta and Lace with only straps or shoulder and no back!" She tossed her grizzled head coquettishly and smiled her broad smile, showing her missing teeth. "Ole man, I am getttin' jest a few necessary garments to wear, for soon we is sure to be rich."

"A fool and his money are soon parted," quoted Charley. "Only the fool doesn't have his money yet, and maybe never will have it." The Boston garbage man was still in the dark. For he ate, slept, worked, then started all over again, and he knew little else. His horizon was not too high.

But just then a neighbor dropped a bomb in the shape of a newspaper on the doorstep of the Hoke home.

"Pop, look, a paper," said Johnny, the ten-year-old son.

Were supper ready, Charley probably never would have opened the paper. He might not have read it even then, had not the strange head-lines caught his eyes. The world had read the story, in parts the day before.

So now as the man saw those glaring words he turned to his wife and demanded, "Mayme Hoke, what have you done?" He jumped from his bench and confronted her with, "Read this!"

In tall headlines was the man's story. The reporter had made a feature story of Charley Hoke, Boston garbage man. Jerry Barke, known as Charley Hoke as heir to millions while his eleven children were sick for want of food and proper clothing.

With a smirk she red the headlines, then said, "Now, Mister Jerry Barke, hain't you glad your wife took this here business into her capable hands? We is millionaires. Heaps more than a measly five thousand dollars. That hain't nothin'. See why the departmental stores want our business?"

"But look what you have done to Jeanette Barke. She has given us food, clothing and money. The newspaper states her father and grandfather are to be tried for murdering Lucy and her son. Think what you have brought on the girl, for her father may go to the electric chair and you are to blame.

"You mean your scheming old father and your brother are charged with murder-"

But he grabbed his hat and ran for the door before his wife could finish her words, the newspaper held tightly under his arm.

"Whar you going' Charley Hoke? She demanded, but he neither stopped now answered.

Soon he stood at the doorway of the seminary. With his battered hat held awkwardly in his hand, he said, "Miss Jeanette Barke, please." He forgot his ragged overalls in his anxiety for the girl.

When she came into the room and saw him she asked, "What is it, Mr. Hoke? Is little Marian sick?"

"M-miss Jeanette, where can we talk in private? It is very important." She led the way in silence to a small sitting room and closed the door.

The man sat a fully minute, nervously fingering his tattered hat. Then he cleared his throat and asked, "Have you read the papers lately" Have you seen tonight's paper?" She shook her head, looking more puzzled than ever.

"Please, Miss Jeanette, before you read this paper, believe me when I tell you I had nothing to do with it. Until I read this newspaper tonight I never dreamed my wife had consulted an attorney and given him Uncle Ted's letter, authorizing him to take legal action."

She stared at him in wonder, trying to understand what he was driving at. But when he handed her the paper, her eyes widened with amazement that turned to horror as she red on. "Then I'm a Negro as Lucile said. Daddy is a Negro instead of mother. You are father's brother who was supposed to have died in infancy and have a tombstone beside mother's."

The man sat in paralysed fear, wondering what she would do.

"Look! Father and grandpa are charged with murdering my mother and brother. I did have a brother, a mulatto brother! Oh, poor daddy. Can't somebody do something to save father?"

"Jeanette, just one thing can save them; that is to find your mother and brother! Whatever money may be coming to me from this suit, is at your disposal to help free your father."

"I must find Ben. He will know what to do. Please find Ben Hooper over at the university. Send him to me as quickly as you can. I am now going to find Miss Hamilton and send Ben to her home."

"And, Jeanette, you don't blame me?"

"No, no. I don't blame anybody. Hurry and send for Ben and help me find a way to save father."

CHAPTER XXVI

Elsie had just finished reading the evening paper and her heart ached for he daughter, knowing that she would not only feel disgraced but would grieve for her father. Then she wondered if John had known all the time it was he and not she that carried tinted blood. But she decided only his father was capable of such vileness.

From what she read in the paper she knew Lucile must have had a mulatto child just s the first notice had stated. "And good enough for her. Now I am free, free! Free to marry Lang at last.

She went out on the porch to tie up some wisteria vines, happily humming a tune under her breath. Lang Smith was to take dinner with her and life seemed very sweet to her at that moment.

But she stopped singing, chiding herself for experiencing happiness when her daughter lived under such a tragedy. "Does she know?" she wondered. But remember she never reads the newspapers.

Just then she saw Jeanette flying down the street toward her, her face telling its own story. The woman tried to think of some comforting words to give her.

"Have you read the paper?" panted the girl.

"Yes, Jeanette. Come in, dear." She took the girl's hands in hers and kissed her smooth cheek.

Jeanette threw herself on the couch and sobbed. Lucile was right all the time, for I am a Negro and do have a mulatto brother. Was that why Howard jilted me, Miss Hamilton?"

"You see Lucile went direct to his mother and told the story. Although the woman liked you and felt sorry for you, she declared her son could not marry a girl who carried tainted blood, demanding he give you up. When he persistently refused, she told him she would broadcast your story. To save your name he gave you up, but Lucile broadcast your story, in spite of her promise to your father not to."

"I am glad to know, and of curse he could not marry a Negro, neither do I really blame his mother. In my heart I always knew Howard was good and noble. But here I am thinking of myself instead of trying to prevent daddy from going to the electric chair." Again she burst into tears.

"Miss Hamilton, what can I do to save father? I have sent for Ben; he may think of something to do. Did any family ever have such heart-breaking troubles as ours?" She walked the floor, wringing her hands. Elsie watched in great distress.

Finally she could stand it no longer and suddenly came to a decision.

"Jeanette, do not cry, for your father shall be saved."

"What do you mean?" she asked, her eyes wide. "Do you know what became of my mother and brother? Are they still alive? Where are they?"

"Wait, dear. I hear some one at the door. Lang is coming for dinner."

Elsie went to the door. "Ben," she whispered, "I am glad it is you, for I must talk to you alone. If you have read the evening paper, you know why Jeanette sent for you. Come back at ten this evening. Tell no one. Lang is coming for dinner but I shall send him home early and she must be in the dormitory by ten."

When Jeanette saw Ben she went into his outstretched arms. "Oh, Ben! You know all about father and grandpa. What shall I do? I can't bear it. I have tainted blood, so does daddy. Charley Hoke is my uncle, all of his black-faced children are my cousins. My own brother is a mulatto." Quickly she pulled away from his arms. "Ben, how can you come near me?"

"Jeanette, for a long time I have been sure there was mixed blood in the Barke family some place. But, dear, I love you just the same." He pulled her back in his arms.

She tried to smile through her tears. "Ben, what would I do without you? But I must think of daddy. How can we save him? He did not kill mother, I know he could not for he wouldn't hurt anybody. If anybody killed her, it would be, maybe-grand-"

"Don't worry, for we will find a way to save them," assured the man, although he had no idea just how.

Promptly at ten o'clock Ben Hooper returned to Miss Hamilton's small house. She sat on her cool front porch waiting for him.

"Miss Hamilton, Jeanette intimated you might have a solution for her problem. As you know, unless Lucy Barke and her son be found or accounted for, her father and grandfather are sure to receive a strong sentence."

"Yes, Ben, that is why I asked you to come this evening." She hesitated, she knew what it would mean to reveal her identity now. He noted her pallor and her agitated manner.

"Ben are those men worth saving?" she asked barely above a whisper.

"Old man Barke deserves punishment, but maybe not the electric chair. He has not only sinned against Jerry, Lucy and her child, but he has caused John to turn against his wife and child. Doc is putty in his hands."

"Besides, think of the sorrow he has brought to Novinger folks by his greed, scheming, and dishonest dealings. Some people would rejoice at his execution. But John is a prince of a man inspite of the fact he didn't show much strength of character when he was induced to discard Lucy. Yet he has repented, for he has suffered much through the years."

"From what I hear, he had a small Hades on earth with the second Mrs. Barke."

"You are right there."

"But, Ben, can we save John and Doc without rescuing the old man from the electric chair? He deserves punishment, but all the men are involved in the murder charge." She walked back and forth across the porch, her hands clinched and her face drawn and white. He watched her curiously, marveling that she was suffering such anguish for her student.

Ben finally said, "We can not save the other men without saving the old man. But, Miss Hamilton, what is the use of talking? None of the men can be freed unless we find Lucy and her son."

"Ben, I am Lucy Barke."

"You? You Lucy Barke? John Barkes wife?" His eyes widened in amazement and he took a step toward her. "Of course! Why did we never guess it before? Why hasn't Jeanette realized the reason for her being drawn to you? She is her image!"

She sank down in a rocker. "But, Ben, the sacrifice is too great."

"You would not be doing it to save John Barke, but for your daughter's sake," he said softly.

"Yes, yes! Let me think. Go now, but come in the morning. Let me sleep over it. I shall know in the morning."

"Just one thing first, the son?" he asked anxiously. So much he wanted to know, yet dared not ask her now.

Jerry is alive and living in Wyoming. I named him for his Uncle Jerry whom I supposed lay in the Jamestown cemetery. Later I will tell you all about it, but not now.

"Can you go after Jeanette and bring her here for the night? She had to attend a committee meeting at ten o'clock, but it should be over by now. She must not be left in the dormitory to face the barrage of curious or gloating eyes," she said to Ben.

That night as Jeanette lay sleeping on her mother's arm, Elsie lay staring into the darkness. So much involved if she revealed her identity. Jerry with his tainted blood and striking features must be acknowledged as her son.

Charley Hoke, a fine intelligent man, yet black, would be her brother-in-law a fact all the world would know, and Maybe her sister-in-law oh, no!

The college must know she had married a part Negro. As Miss Hamilton she was respected and loved, been looked up to by both students and faculty. It would not only bring her into open shame, but call up all of the old sorrow and heart-ache.

"I can not do it! I have suffered for twenty years, enough for a lifetime, suffering that almost sent me to the bottom of the river to my grave. Then there is Lang. What would he think? No, no, I cannot sacrifice myself to save John Barke and his criminal old father."

The light of morning dawned, showing her Jeanette's white, tear-stained face beside her. "Darling, I want to save you, oh, I do! What shall I do?" She stared at her daughter, struggling with herself. Tears streamed from her eyes.

Then she remembered that long ago at that bridge when she was about to take her own life she had pledged to live for others, to dedicate her life to serve humanity. "Daughter, I will not fail you. This shall be my supreme sacrifice. I am free! I can face the world with a clear eye, for my blood is pure. Because I have suffered, I shall know how to shield my daughter.

"Jeanette shall live in her rightful home. No longer will I shun my responsibilities as a mother to my son. Dear Lang, you shall wait no longer.

Father shall spend his declining years with me. Just let the press blazen the news. Let the seminary talk. I shall be happy having my daughter with me and nothing else matters."

Her secret of the past twenty years had been as a great canker gnawing at her soul; this she now realized. Now she could be her real self-no more acting, no further subterfuge.

She was too overjoyed to lie in bed longer. Slipping quietly from her daughter's side, she took an invigorating shower and dressed with care. Jeanette must not be ashamed of her mother.

Too excited to wait for the maid, she set about to prepare a delicious breakfast, using her choicest linens, china, and silver. This was an occasion to celebrate. Yes, she must have flowers from her own lovely garden to bedeck the table. She laid three places, feeling sure that Ben would show up in time to eat.

And in Miss Hamilton's rose-tinted bed-room, Jeanette was opening her eyes to a cold, cruel world. But she buried her face in the folds of the pillow and sobbed passionately. "How can I go back to school and face everybody? And father must be saved."

"Darling," whispered Miss Hamilton softly, "dry your pretty eyes, jump into the shower, take the dress you like best from my closet and hurry into breakfast. A surprise awaits you."

For the past year Jeanette had been in the habit of wearing any dress that struck her fancy from the teacher's wardrobe. Miss Hamilton still had the figure of a school-girl and her dresses exactly fit the girl.

In a short time the young guest entered the dining room, wearing Elsie's prettiest pink morning frock, her golden hair in soft curls on her neck. Her face had lost some of it's haggardness.

When the door-bell rang shrilly Elsie said, "Please go to the door, dear," feeling sure it was Ben.

As the young man walked into the room, he quickly scanned Miss Hamilton's face. Yes, she had decided; he could tell by the happy expression she wore. How he did admire her, realizing something of the sacrifice this must mean to her, a sacrifice to save the man who had so cruelly discarded her.

"Just in time for breakfast, Ben," said Elsie, feeling very gay and light-heated. "Don't tell me you have already eaten, for your eyes give you away."

"Jeanette tells me you have a surprise for us," he said. Miss Hamilton blushed and dimpled like a girl awaiting her first lover as they looked expectantly at her."

They had just seated themselves around the delightfully tempting breakfast table when the telephone gave an insistent peal. Ben hastened to take the call. "For you, Miss Hamilton. A Harriet Kieth of Pankhurst College, Alabama calling."

The color drained from the woman's cheeks. She was thinking of her father and wondering what had happened to him, for he as getting old and never had been too strong. With trembling hands she took the receiver.

"Yes, Harriet. We read it last night. I was planning to tell them. Oh? I-I-I-promise. What Jerry? When did it happen? I'll catch the first plane-"

Elsie's lovely breakfast went begging. She snatched only a few bites, while Ben and Jeanette ate in troubled silence. Else told them a dear friend had been seriously injured and might be dying, that she must catch a plane in an hour to Wyoming.

Neither Ben nor Jeanette had the heart to mention the surprise that she had promised them.

Ben drove her to the airport, Jeanette went to school. They rode in silence, finally broken by Elsie. "Ben, keep my secret until my return, for it is Jerry who is injured. I can think of nothing else now." She bade him good-by at the airport and boarded the plane.

CHAPTER XXVII

Rose Barke had to accept a night job of cleaning floors at the county hospital. Anything to tide them over until the divorce was granted and she received the large alimony she expected, besides the millions of hush-money not to tell about the Barkes making way with Lucy and her son.

The deputy sheriff stopped in front of the tumbled-down building, looked at the number and scratched his head. Surely this can't be the residence of the woman wanted. This couldn't be the living quarters of the millionaire-John Barke's wife. I saw by the paper she is suing for a divorce, but even at that she would not live in such a place." He climbed the rickety stairs and raped on the door.

Rose lay on an old cot in her third-floor room, trying to sleep. At the sound at her door, disheveled and with great circles around her eyes, her skin sallow and dirty looking, she looked out.

Drawing her soiled robe close she snapped, "We don't want to buy anything!" and started to slam the door in his face.

He was too quick for her, and put his foot inside the unlocked screen. "Are you Mrs. John Barke?" He asked, still in wonderment.

"Yes, What do you want with me?"

When he served the papers on her, explaining what they meant she was furious. "And you are the deputy sheriff? There must be some mistake. Why are you serving papers on me for the murder of Lucy Barke and her kid? I never did a thing to her." Her anger was turning to fear, and she was half-crying.

"You must tell that to the prosecuting attorney, madam. We must strt for Boston immediately by plane."

"I-I-I-don't want to go. I haven't done anything."

"I will wait outside while you get dressed and your things ready to go," he told her curtly.

"Mom, I am going too," said Lucile tryig to mend another run in her best rayon hose.

"You can't. I haven't a cent for carfare."

"I'm going to that trial if I have to hitch-hike." And hitch-hike she did. Yes, the lovely heiress to the Barke millions set out on foot for Boston. The The haughty Countess Lucile Von Lanier donned her only fancy pair of slacks and put out her dainty thumb.

And strange as it may sound, just five days after Mrs. Rose Garner Barke and the deputy sheriff landed by plane in the city of Boston, a dirty, bedraggled girl in a pair of once-rose-colored slacks climbed the steps to the Boston Girl's seminary and swaggered inside.

"Miss Babcock, may I go to Jeanette's room?" asked the vagabond when confronted by the dean of women. At first the woman was going to call the police to report an intruder, finally she recognized her, the girl who had prided herself on being the most expensively dress girl at the seminary.

"Lucile Barke!" exclaimed Miss Babcock in consternation. "I didn't recognize you. What kind of a prank is this?"

The girl tried to throw it off as a huge joke, but she didn't succeed in deceiving the woman. For she had a worn and hungry look on her pinched face.

As she went up the stairs Miss Babcock thought how the girl had scorned her sister, heaping humiliation on her. . . "Now, my dear girl, you are proven to be part Negro and you did have a mulatto child, besides, you never had a real husband. That man you lived with and by whom you bore a child is now behind bars. Still you hold up your head and are unashamed.

"Now you come sniveling to Jeanette for sympathy and money. Yes, and the silly girl is sure to take you in and give you whatever you ask for. I'd like to give you a piece of my mind," said Miss Babcock indignantly to herself.

When Jeanette saw her sister standing in her door, smiling and smirking, she feared she was going to drop to the floor. "Lucille, why did you come here looking like a tramp? You have done me harm enough, now you want to disgrace me farther.

"Jeanette, how can you talk to your sister like that? The only sister you have. I thought you would be glad to see me. Now all you do is to scold me," and she began to bawl. "Don't you know I have no clothes? That daddy won't send mother a penny?"

"How did you get here?"

"Hitch-hiked! I was mighty lucky too! Two swell guys brought me most of the way in their fine new cars." At the memory of those drivers Lucile forgot to shed any more tears, and smiled in her old boastful way.

Jeanette said, "You ought to be ashamed of yourself! Have you lost all of your self-respect? Do take a shower, for even your hair is filthy as well as your face. Why did you come back here, anyway?"

"I came back for daddy's trial, of course. When does it begin?"

"Wednesday morning. Here is your mother's dress. She had the audacity to send for me, and of course I went. You may wear this dress of mine. Since you are much slimmer it should fit you. When you are ready, I will take you out to eat."

Jeanette clothed and fed her sister and gave her money to reach her mother. "Why, oh, why didn't she stay on the west coast?" she cried to herself bitterly.

As Elsie Hamilton winged her way to Wyoming, her mind was in a state of turmoil. Events were transpiring entirely too rapidly for her peace of mind.

John and his father and the doctor being tried for murder, Ben knowing her secret, and now Jerry at the point of death.

She tried to figure out how it would end, remembering that in five more minutes, had Harriet Kieth not telephoned, she would have made her identity known to Jeanette and saved John's neck. Harriet had read the account of the case in the news and when she phoned Elsie she tried to extract a promise from Elsie to let the secret go with her to her grave.

Miss Kieth had said, "Let those scheming men go to the gallows, for they deserve it, let them take their medicine."

Elsie pushed the problem from her, thinking she would decide later, for she kept wondering if she would find her son alive.

As the plane landed she had found no answer to her questions. She climbed out of the plane and into the mail truck that was to carry her fifty-miles to the small town of Sheep Run. After her speed in he skies and with fear clutching her heart the vehicle moved so slowly she wanted to scream. Even the fresh tang of sage brush that filled the land filled her with disgust.

"Ya say you're stopping at the Sterling Ranch, Miss? Mighty fine folks.

Too bad about that handsome son-in-law getting' half-killed. Ain't supposed to live, I hear. You some kin to the folks?" Queried the loquacious mail carrier.

"I'm a close friend of the young man's family," she answered evasively.

"Ya say you live in Boston? Cum quite a ways just to see a friend, ain't ya? Reckon you might like for me to drop ya right at the ranch door."

In the midst of miles and miles of barren hills covered only by dull-looking sage brush sat the house. It was a great rambling white house surrounded by beautiful evergreen trees. Back of the house sprawled the barn, surrounded by the corral.

A short, chunky girl with flying red curls ran out to get the mail and greet the newcomer alighting from the truck.

"Howdy, Marvel. How's Jerry? Any change" asked the old truck driver sympathetically.

"He is just the same. He has never rallied since he was thrown ten days ago," she said, wiping her eyes with the corner of her blue apron.

"Miss Kieth telephoned me yesterday; I hope something can be done for him-"

"Oh, Miss Hamilton, I am so glad you are here. Just the fact that you are here will help him recover sooner.

Marvel led the way into a large living room, modernly furnished. While removing her wraps Elsie said, "Tell me abut the accident."

"Jerry was attempting to ride papa's outlaw-stallion. Jerry is so daring and brave. He wanted to be the first to ride him, but he was thrown, and on to his head. It may cost him his life."

Elsie's heart ached for her handsome son who lay so still and lifeless. She would never have guessed he carried a trace of Negro blood, and he was the image of his grandfather Barke, yet he reminded her of John at the time of their marriage.

"He has lain like this ever since he was hurt," said Mrs. Sterling, a tall, dark kindly faced woman. "X-rays show us nothing. We have had the best specialists from Denver. They give us little hope, and if he does live, they tell us his mind may not be right. The two nurses are from Denver, also. And Marvel is expecting almost anytime."

Miss Hamilton was glad she had was here. She liked Mr. Sterling as she did his wife. He was a giant of two-hundred pounds with red hair just like his daughter. Elsie Hamilton could see that Jerry was getting the best of care and that no expense was being spared for his welfare.

Two days after Elsie's arrival Jerry opened his eyes and asked, "What am I doing in bed?" He attempted to raise himself from the bed and succeeded only in almost tumbling out on his head.

The nurse hurried to her patient and ordered, "Mr. Randal, you must be quiet. It is very dangerous for you to attempt to try to get out of bed, for you were thrown from you horse."

"I was! That's funny I don't remember a thing about it. Where's Marvel?"

The nurse went to the kitchen and whispered, "Mrs. Randall, go to him, his is calling for you. But be very careful what you say to him so as not to excite him, for he is not out of danger yet."

Instantly she was by his side. "Jerry, dear," she said softly, "kneeling by his side of the bed and gently taking his hand in hers.

When Elsie saw that look of love and devotion in their eyes, a sacred fire, she prayed that her son's life might be spared. His poor starved heart had found its home.

It was surprising how rapidly he gained and his mind was perfectly clear, only what had happened to him was a black-out. The physician soon pronounced him beyond danger and one of the nurses was discharged.

Finally Elsie was presented to him. At first, Jerry was distant and fomal in his manner, for he was debating in his mind why she had never made herself known to him years before when he needed her so much.

But he managed to say, "Miss Hamilton, it was swell of you to come." He tried to hide his real feelings. "I want to thank you for looking after such a miserable little scamp all those years. As soon as possible I shall begin to pay you back the money you put out for my keep."

"You do not owe me a penny, Jerry. Forgive me for not visiting you before."

"Sure! But when I was a kid at those old orphanages, I used to cry myself to sleep because you didn't come to see me."

"Oh, Jerry, you don't know how sorry I am." Tears rained from her eyes as she kissed his broad forehead.

She hastily went to her room. Jerry turned to his wife and said, "Marvel, isn't she swell? I just love her."

"I'm jealous. She is too young and attractive to be kissing my husband." She laughed mischievously.

"Say, honey as soon as Doc and the nurse give me permission, I want to talk to her about father and mother."

"Yes, dear. But not yet,"

Then the baby arrived, a cute little roly-poly girl. She was a veritable Marvel with her round face and silky red curls.

Elsie said to herself with a wry smile. "Now I am a grandmother, but why should I mind? Surely I am old enough, but it gives me a strange sensation-I've posed being young so long."

Jerry said to his wife, "Dearie, don't you think the baby's name should be Elsie!"

"No sirree, Jerry Randall!" She retorted. "Long ago we agree that it should be Harriet. Who was it that visited you and loved you all the years everybody else was cuffing you about? It was your dear Harriet Kieth."

"Well, you have the right to say," he said resignedly. "After all, it is your baby."

"Silly, it is your baby too."

"But dads don't count much." Then he sat straight up in bed. "Marvel, I've got it, Let's name her "Harriet Elsie'."

"A bright idea. Harriet Elsie Randall sounds like a story-book name."

When Miss Hamilton was told the baby's name she said, "Oh, you darlings, and she hastily wiped her eyes. "Forgive me for being an old goose."

Soon the young man was able to sit up in an easy chair and read for a short time, and the new baby and her mother were in perfect condition.

Elsie asked herself why she stayed on, knowing she was not needed and her daughter did want her desperately. But she reasoned that her Jeanette did have her father and Ben. Finally she acknowledged to herself that it was heaven to be on this peaceful ranch, and that she loved her son and wanted to know him better. "I know how grandmothers feel, for I adore that baby."

Always she was confronted with her problem. Should she keep her secret as Harriet advised or should she divulge it? Subconsciously it was in her mind both day and night, even dreaming of telling her children. Maybe this was the reason she did not return to Boston, knowing Ben would put pressure on her to tell. If she were going to make her identity known to Jeanette and Ben then she must do so to Jerry while on her visit. Around and around went her thoughts, until she felt almost dizzy.

CHAPTER XXVIII

"Say, folks," said Jerry Randall one day as he was sitting in his chair reading the evening paper, "are you following the Barke murder trial? While I was down and out I missed some of it." Elsie gave a start but made no reply.

"Strangest case I every herd abut. I've followed it ever since that mulatto kid was born to the Countess girl in California. Say, Marvel, would it hurt if I talk to Miss Hamilton about my folks?"

The girl puckered her brow. "We must ask dad and mother first. They know what the doctor told them. You know, Jerry, you get so wrought up when you talk about that subject and we must play safe."

"Somehow," continued the young an, "this Barke case makes me think of my own. Tainted blood can give a guy plenty of uneasiness."

Elsie held her breath in amazement. Why was he saying such things befoe his wife?

He went on to say, "This Barke case is sure to go on for months. I wish I could hear it."

"Honey, maybe Miss Hamilton would like to look at the paper." Both women could see he was becoming too excited for his good.

As Elsie read the account of the case she commented to herself, "Lucile will try to disgrace Jeanette, for the paper sites she is attending the trial and that Rose divorced John. Poor man, he must be paying dearly for his ill-treatment of me. Yet he must be relieved to be free from that woman."

She sat lost in thought, then her heart turned right over. "John is free! Free to marry again. Oh, no, I never could marry him again. Once I laid my heart at his feet and trampled on it, and he let them spit on me. Never can he mean anything to me."

"Miss Hamilton," said Marvel a few evenings later, "daddy says it is all right for Jerry to ask you abut his parents."

In alarm she wondered what she could say, but finally decided to wait and let him do the talking.

"Miss Hamilton," began the boy anxiously when she went with his wife into see him, "Marvel and I want you to tell us everything you know abut father and mother. Who am I, anyway?"

She felt her face go hot and cold. She dare not tell this young man just recovering from a serious head injury the truth. It could cost him his life.

Noting that the woman hesitated, Marvel said, "You need not fear to tell us everything. Before Jerry asked me to marry him, said he might have Negro blood, so we are prepared for the worst. We prefer cold facts to suspense and mystery."

Elsie sat in amazement. Her son had done a noble, honorable thing, and Marvel was standing by. Yes, she must try to tell them the truth.

"Jerry, you and Marvel are grand, and I believe you are able to hear the truth. You have followed the Barke case-"

He interrupted her, demanding, "Tell me, quick! Am I involved in that case?"

As she looked at his flushed face and sparkling eyes she wondered if she dare. His hands were shaking, and should he have a relapse, she would be responsible. She must talk to Mr. Sterling first.

"Jerry, excuse me a moment, my throat is dry. I must have a drink before I begin my story."

She gave Marvel a warning, then went in search of the man. His wife told her he had gone to the corral and started to the door to call him. She said, "Don't bother him, I will talk with you, Mrs. Sterling. It is about Jerry.

Jerry wants me to tell him about his people, but already before I start he has gone into a frenzy. His hands are shaking and his cheeks flushed-"

"I think I better call my husband." When he came in they discussed it in full, wondering what was best to do.

Marvel burst into the room. "I know you are questioning the advisability of telling Jerry the facts about his life. Don't you think it will worry him more not to satisfy his mind?"

Finally it was decided Miss Hamilton should tell him the story of his parents, and she planned to be very brief. As she reentered his room he said, "I'll try to hold on to myself. Please go on. You were telling me I was involved in the Barke case, maybe you didn't actually say it in words, but I know it is true. Am I the missing boy-"

"Y-y-e-s."

"Then I am John Barke's son, I am the lost baby, the kid that was lost with his mother in Lawton, Alabama?"

"Then his name is really Jerry Bark?" Marvel wanted to know.

"Yes, you were named for your uncle Jerry K. Barke, known as Charley Hoke."

"So, I am a Negro after all!" He bowed his head in his hands, sobs shook his frame. A long painful silence followed, Marvel wiped her eyes, her hands trembling.

Finally Marvel went to her husband and bent over him, planting a kiss on his cheek. "Jerry, I still love you. Didn't I promise to love you even if you found you had mixed blood? It is only the baby I am thinking. Oh, Miss Hamilton, do you think she might have a mulatto child?

"Dear your physician is the one to answer that question." Yet in her heart she knew the girl's fears were well-grounded. For it is a well-known fact that the Negro is the dominate race, and its strain might show up for many generations.

At that the girl cried harder than ever. "I wish we had never had a child, I can't bear to think of her suffering. But Jerry, you are not to blame, for you cannot help what your ancestors did."

The boy gained self-control first and leaned back in his chair, still pale and tired appearing asked, "What became of my mother? The inference is she committed suicide. Did she?"

At last she was face to face with the question. What should she say? How would he react? What would he think of her? "Your mother did not commit suicide-"

"Is she alive? Do you know where she is now living?"

"Y-e-s, Jerry."

"Then you know my mother? Where does she live? Miss Hamilton, you-you-" Forgetting that he was convalescing, that he had been on the brink of the grave such a short time before, he jumped from his chair and and stood towering over her. He peered down into her colorless face.

Half-fainting, he staggered back to his chair. "No, no" you couldn't have deserted me. You couldn't have been so cruel. I needed you so!"

Elsie ran for a glass of water, holding it to his lips, fanning him vigorously with the other hand. Rudely he pushed the glass from him and averted his face.

"Don't come near me," he cried brokenly. "I can't bear it. I've longed for you and prayed for my mother all these years. And to think you were making money, wearing pretty clothes, surrounded by friends and having a jolly time. It is harder to have my own mother desert me than to know I have colored blood."

Miss Hamilton hurried to her room and threw herself across the bed. Dry sobs shook her as she upbraided herself for her seeming-selfishness. She knew that she had welcomed Jeanette and taken her gladly to her heart because she was white, but let Harriet persuade her to desert Jerry because he looked like a mulatto.

"Jerry is right, and he never will forgive me, and I love him so," she said to herself. All night she cried and tried to decide what t do. Early the next morning she packed her grips, read to start to Boston. "Jeanette needs me, Jerry does not, neither does he want me. He will be happier without me."

She ate a few mouthfuls of breakfast, then announced her intentions of leaving at once, providing the mail carrier were able to accommodate her.

"Miss Hamilton," said Mrs. Sterling in her motherly way, "the children have told me about last night. Forgive the lad, he is not himself at this time. They are eager to talk with you, and as soon as they have finished their breakfasts, go to them."

After the girl had removed the trays from the sick room, Elsie went in and Jerry said, "Mother, I am sorry and ashamed for my rude behavior last night. Please forgive me. You were given no chance to explain your side of the question."

"My son, Miss Kieth advised me and I know she believed she was doing the right thing and so did I at the time, that you would be happier to never know you had white parents. Now I know we made a mistake. Besides, for safety reasons, we thought the Barkes would be less likely to follow us if you were in a colored institution. At that time we feared old J. B. Barker might do us bodily harm."

After she had related to them the facts of the past twenty years, and of her meeting with Jeanette and her tragic experiences, the boy had only sympathy for her. He said, "Mother, you and sister have had even harder lives than I." He looked fondly at his wife and said, "I know I am happier now than either of you can ever be."

"Please, do not think of leaving us, mother," said Marvel warmly.

Jerry said, "Of course you are not going, now just as I have found you. And remember, I shall keep you for a while too. But the biggest question before us is what are we going to do with the Barkes? Shall we save John Barke's proud neck, or shall we let him take what is coming to him?"

"There is but one side to that question," snapped the fiery, red-headed wife. "I think that he and all of his conspirators should be given the full benefit of the law."

"But, Marvel, look at it from Jeanette's viewpoint," reasoned Elsie. "All her life she has known little but persecution, and she idolizes her father. He is very dear to her. Unless we save him, then it is a severe sentence, maybe execution."

"What had you decided before coming here, mother?" asked Jerry.

"When Miss Kieth telephoned me of your accident, we were sitting at the table, Jeanette, Ben, and I. I had revealed the secret to Ben the night before and in five more minutes she would have known also. But Harriet had read the press account of the Barke case, and she begged me to let my secret go to the grave with me, insisting the criminals deserved punishment-"

"She is a wise woman," put in Marvel.

"Now I don't know whether to follow her advice and keep out of the fray and let the law take its course or to do what I can to save them from execution."

"Wife, we could use some of that Barke money," said Jerry. "It is ours for showing up, that is all we need to do. I'll bet that old cowardly banker would be willing to fork over every cent he possesses to save his hide."

"Dad can give us all we need!" snapped the girl.

"But, honey, he has done too much for us already. I would like to be on my own, I have been dependent on others all my life."

Elsie knew Jerry had had too much excitement for one day and said, "We don't have to decide right now."

Week glided into week at the Sterling Ranch, a haven of rest for the tired little music teacher. It seemed another world after the bustle of life in a city, especially with all the trouble she had experienced for others. Here she had few problems. There she had been attempting to smooth out the tangled webs for Jeanette, Ben, Lang, the Hokes, and many others.

CHAPTER XXIX

While Elsie Hamilton was living a quiet, tranquil, life on the Wyoming ranch, the weary weeks of the trial dragged on for the Barkes. All the newspapers were filled with comments on the case, but always much the same.

It had taken but short time to substantiate the claims of Charley Hoke, now known by his own name of Jerry K. Barke. Old J. B. Barke had no defense. The paper stated that the family were preparing to leave Boston's tumbled-down area for a location more suited to their new status of living.

The murder case hung fire for more evidence that Lucy Barke and her son had been murdered. The defense attorney had begged for an extension of time in which to locate the missing pair.

Fabulous awards were offered through the press for information about them. Amusing incidents were reported of persons purporting to know of their whereabouts in order to claim the reward amounted to a small fortune.

Harriet Kieth wrote frequent letters to Miss Hamilton, urging her to remain on the ranch and not divulge her secret to the accused men. In one letter she said, "Sit tight Elsie, and don't become sentimental. Stay where you are, for if you return and attend the hearings your soft heart never could endure to see John Barke suffer."

And Elsie did pity John from the bottom of her heart, knowing it had been more the fault of her father than his, but she worried more about Jeanette than anything else. Yet, she felt it would be embarrassing to attend the trial since her husband had a divorce from Rose.

Ben wrote her begging her to come to the rescue, "Jeanette's heart is breaking. Now that Jerry is well on the way to recovery, why do you not come to the aid of the daughter that you profess to love?"

After reading that letter she turned to Jerry and said, "Son, I must take the next plane home. I can't endure the suspense another day."

"Now mother, be sensible. If you return, Ben and Jeanette are sure to persuade you to give in to them. We have suffered too much to let Doc and the Barkes go unpunished."

So she listened to her son and remained on at the ranch. She hoped for her own sake as well as for Jeanette the trial would be settled before school opened in September. She was sure she did not want to see too much of John Barke.

Early in August the press heralded the glad news that the missing pair had been found. Large photographs of them were shown along with glaring headlines.

AT LAST! LONG LOST WOMAN AND SON FOUND ALIVE!

A feature story followed. The woman had been found twenty years before wandering in the mountains near Lawton, Alabama. She was carrying a Negro infant in her arms. She did not know who she was or where she came from or where she was going, for she was a victim of amnesia.

The main witness, Louis Kreuer, had found her and had given her a cabin to live in on his tobacco plantation. Here she had lived ever since. For want of a better name, he had called her Lora Smith, and her son Jack.

"When the Barke case came out in the newspaper," testified the man, "Mrs. Smith sat day after day pouring over the story. I marveled at this because I had never before seen her read anything."

"About a week ago, I found her sitting in her yard with the paper in her hands, laughing and crying hysterically. Then she told me she was Lucy Barke, the lost woman, and Jack the missing boy. She declared that just as soon as she read the story, it all came back to her as clear as day."

"Mrs. Smith, I mean Lucy Barke, told me how she had started walking with her baby into the mountains twenty years ago right after the doctor's plane left town. Then all at once her mind went blank, and she could remember nothing, or who she was."

In spite of their indignation at the impostors, Elsie and her son laughed until they cried at the two ludicrous pictures in the papers. The purported Lucy Barke was a large, square-built woman with grizzled hair, fashioned in a bun on top of her head, several front teeth were missing, and she had weak, squinting eyes.

Jack was an ugly buck, black, and too old to fit the case. His head was large and covered with the kinkiest of black wool. Both he and his mother were dressed as genuine hill-billies.

"Dad, do you reckon, it would hurt me to drive my Buick to Boston" My fingers itch to get hold of that old impostor Jack," declared Jerry hotly.

"Son," said Max Sterling kindly but firmly, "don't think of such a thing. You are not yet entirely out of danger. The court can handle those impostors.

Surely the Barkes are too smart to use such evidence. Stay at home and watch the fun."

Soon the court did dispose of the woman and her son. The newspaper stated they only were after the award, but were not wise enough to deceive the law.

The Jerry K. Barke family were awarded a large sum of money and all of the Barke property in Novinger, Iowa. According to the paper, they were preparing to move into the old banker's mansion, while Jerry generously provided for his Uncle Ted by giving him the bungalow formerly owned by John Barke.

"Mrs. Mayme Barke," said the press, "is rejoicing in the fact that she can at last have room enough for her large family of thirteen. The J. B. Barke house boasts of having twenty-seven rooms, all air-conditioned."

Reluctantly Elsie finally left the ranch at Sheep Run, Wyoming, for home. But when Jerry said good-bye Jerry had said she would see him driving up in front of her door in the Buick before snow flew, "And remember, mother, don't let them wheedle you into disclosing your identity. Make those men take their medicine."

Seemingly the Barke murder case was drawing to a culmination. Dr. Cunningham had been given life imprisonment for the murder of Lucy and her son. J. B. Barke and John as instigators of the crimes had received heavy fines, court costs, and ten years imprisonment at hard labor.

For being cognizant of the crime, Lulu Simpson had been given a light fine, while Rose Garner Barke did not get off so easy. Because she soon married Lucy Barker's husband was evidence in the eyes of the law that she had a motive for her silence in the case, and was sentenced to one year in the women's reformatory.

The defense appealed the case, and were promised another hearing late in September. The attorney for the defense increased his efforts to find the missing woman and her son.

Jeanette and Ben Hooper met Elsie at the air-port in his car. Tears rolled down the woman's face when she saw Jeanette's haggard face, for she was but a shadow of her former self. "Oh, Miss Hamilton, if only I could go to prison for father." Miss Hamilton felt Ben's reproachful eyes on her face.

Then it was time for the seminary to open again, and Jeanette was to have been a senor in the school of music. But she refused to register, saying she had no money for school and if there was any money it should go to help free her father.

However, Jeanette did enroll later for part time school work, for Miss Hamilton secured a place for her as assistant piano instructor. For some time Elsie had needed another helper and Jeanette Barke was her most talented student.

Much to her chagrin, Rose and Lucile persisted in calling on Jeanette at the dormitory. Not only had those women done everything in their power to wreck her life, but now their cheap, gaudy attire and low coarse behavior were very humiliating to the refined girl.

One day before a group of girls Lucile said, "Jeanette, it is oodles of fun to work at the Dime Store. I see many of my old pals but most of them pretend they do not see me, but I just yell, 'Hi there!' and they have to return the greeting." She laughed loudly at her own stupid wit.

"And you should see her boy friends," added Rose proudly. "A new one every night. They simply keep us in candy and gum. Not one of them know who Lucile is or was married or had a baby. Of course they never heard of the Barke murder case."

Some folks always seem to find something to gloat about no matter what circumstances they find themselves in.

Occasionally Else saw Doc and the two Barke men. Their changed appearances shocked her, for the old banker looked ten years older, and the doctor seemed even more decrepit, for he was feeble and broken in spirit. She wanted to cry when she saw John's pathetic face. Surely the men were paying heavily for their folly, and they would pay more.

CHAPTER XXX

When the Jerry K. Barkes left their tumbled-down shack in the slums of Boston, Maybe was confident she would be supremely happy in her new home. She had large plans and smart ideas for her future living.

She said to her friends and neighbors, "Folks we is going' to live in a mansion, the finest house in town. We is goin' to have servants too, white servants. Guess they call them hired girls in Iowa.

"Good-by, good-by, all of you. Don't fail to visit us just as soon as we get settled. Before too long I'm goin' to have a party for all of you Boston folks. It will be a swell affair too. I'll let you know in plenty of time to git here."

The small Iowa town was dumfounded when the new owners of the Barke house arrived. The village folks had never seen quite so many people in one automobile. The new red sedan was full to overflowing.

"Thirteen persons in that one car." said the butcher's wife. "There comes that truck with four coons in it, making seventeen Niggers in our town!"

"See!" cried a grocer man's wife. "A little white girl-I heard there were ten black children and one white child. The little old man with white hair and black face must be old J. B. Barke's brother. The tall man with the yellow skin and thick lips is Jerry K., the banker's son and John's own brother."

"Yeah, and the one who has been buried in the Jamestown cemetery beside Lucy for forty years," giggled Mary George, another neighbor.

The depot agent's wife asked, "How do you folks know who is who among our new neighbors?"

"Didn't you red the Eastern newspapers during the trial? I saved every picture."

Finally the colored folk were settled in their new homes and three of the men drove away in the truck. During the time of unpacking and getting settled the children were exploring not only their own premesis, but the entire town. They had never set foot before out of the city of Boston, having lived mostly in their own slum area. Besides the older boys had worked.

Three days after landing in the town of Novinger, Mayme announced, "I must find a housekeeper for Uncle Ted." She dressed in her gayest new frock, placed he favorite hat at a rakish angle, and waddled down the street to see and to be seen.

"She is coming to my door!" and Edith Larkin quickly turned the key in the lock.

Mayme pounded with her big fist, making the door rattle as if a tornado had hit it. Receiving no response she tried the knob as was the custom in the slum community. And as in her own neighborhood, she walked around to back door.

Here she knocked even louder but with the same results. When she tried the knob it opened and she walked into the cozy kitchen were Edith and her neighbor, Blanche Hays, huddled behind the table.

"Hi, folks!" announced Mayme, grinning her toothless smile. "Didn't want you to feel we is stuck up because we has more money than the rest of you and lives in the finest house in town."

Only stony stares and compressed lips met her warm greetings.

Mayme was unembarrassed as she rattled on, "Uncle Ted needs one of them housekeepers, and I could use some white servants. Top pay, plenty of good grub, and a room all by themselves, or if lonesome with one of the kids. They don't kick too much." She had not been offered a chair, but had plopped down in one. Still no response from the two women.

"Neat little kitchen, but awful small. You know how spacious my kitchen is, about five times the size." She arose, craning her neck to see into the rest of the house. "Don't you have a parlor? How you ever have a party?"

While he women were trying to think of some way to get rid of the intruder, Myme said apologetically, "I'm sorry I can't stay longer." Receiving no response, she walked around to the back door.

The minute the door closed behind the woman Mrs. Larkin said, "What shall we do? It is worse than I anticipated."

Blanche Hays said, her black eyes snapping, "It looks as if our peaceful town is completely ruined. If we must sit with barred doors night an day, we are selling out. But with colored folks here, who would buy? And at what price?"

"Bill Smith told us last night the kids are everywhere, even playing ball in his backyard. Maybe in Boston where they lived, children played wherever they liked."

Then there was another rap at the door. "I'm afraid to go to the door," she whispered, tiptoeing to turn the lock. Stealthily she peeped behind the shade. "Oh, Mrs. Grinell, it is you," and she opened the door to let her in, explaining why the door was locked.

Mrs. Grinell, the grade-school principal, sighed heavily as she said, "You are not the only one who has trouble. We are having plenty of strife and warfare at school. Fights all the time. But the white children started it by called the new children 'Coons'. Like their grandfather, old J. B. Barke the colored Bark boys fight to kill."

"John Wallace says the men come in for groceries and he thinks they are fine fellows. Of course Ted and Jerry are only part Negro. He is nice to them, for he says they buy about as much as half the town put together. The store that caters to them will get a big business, for that woman has come into our midst declaring she will take no sass from pore white trash."

"I heard that they bought fifty dollars worth of canned goods yesterday," laughed Blanch.

Sunday morning Mayme was up bright and early, rousing everybody out of bed. "Out of there Jerry. You and the kids ain't sleepin' this mornin'. We are all going to church. Jim, you hurry and dress and run over and see if Uncle Ted is up. Tell him to come here for breakfast. We got to make a good impression on this town, besides, we want to see the preacher."

As fourteen scrubbed and combed persons in their new togs with squeaking shoes filed into the small church, Reverend Thomas caught his breath in wonder. "Brother Larkin, please get some one to help you bring chairs from the hall." Then he shook hands with Mr. and Mrs. Barke and uncle Ted.

"Welcome to our church. Mr. Barke, there are a few seats over there." he said, giving Uncle Ted a seat in front. You girls may sit here. Boys, more chairs are on the way."

School began to move more smoothly, rather the tough black Barke boys had fought their way into recognition, if not into the hearts of the village boys. Every normal boy takes off his hat to any other chap who is a more efficient scraper than he. The new boys were champions in their field.

Before Mayme had lived in her new home a month she began planning a party. Not finding any white servants or hired girls in the town she had sent to Des Moines for colored people to help, so now she felt she was ready to launch out in her social venture and prove to the town she was not stuck up or felt herself above them.

She christened it her 'Reschepshun' for the Novinger folks. "They seem kind of timid round us. I am goin' to welcome them to my mansion and prove rich folks can be sociable."

As another piece of social strategy she loaded her offspring with candy, popcorn, gum, and peanuts to give out at school. "These are for your friends. Don't you give a thing to the kids that tease you and call you names."

Finding that the scheme worked admirably she added apples, bananas, oranges, and licorice which seemed to be the favorite treats with the younger members of the crew. The colored children were learning the power of money.

However, Mayme centered her efforts on plans for her reception. "Let's see," she said, chewing the end of the pencil while the baby tried to climb into her lap, "this is to be a swell affair. It's to 'stablish our society statis. What's the name of them fancy foods?"

She sat lost in thought. "I remember Welch rabbit, avy coddy salad, angel cake, and I'm going to decorate it with red hots. Strawberries from Floridy, and some real food too-hot biskets and corn beef and cabbage.

I'll get the cater-man from Chicago. It don't sound big enough to get one from Des Moines. He'll know how to make them buffy suppers, how to put on the dog that will 'stablish us as rishtocrats and bein' real blue-bloods like old J. B. boasts of."

When Jerry K. realized what his wife was up to, he rubbed his eyes in amazement. "Mayme, what do you think you are doing? Colored do not settle down in white communities and try to make a splurge. How many have you invited to the party?"

"Everybody in town."

"Woman are you crazy? There must be over six-hundred people in this burg. We can't afford to feed such a mob. Besides, don't you see these people don't want to associate with us-they are prejudiced against colored folks."

"Jerry, you talk just like a man. The folks are afraid of us because we is rich. "I'm going to show them how common we is."

Like many another husband Jerry K. had learned it was a waste of words to argue with his wife. So he picked up his hat, and started for the door with but a parting warning, "Don't be extravagant, dear. Our bills are mounting sky-high."

"Pore old man, he is so used to skimpin' he forgets we is rollin' in dough. Didn't I tell him away back in Boston I expected to enjoy myself when we got the money?"

It was not only the cost of the food, but the caterer from Chicago insisted he must have trained assistants and would bring them along with him. To entertain six-hundred guests meant work.

Then there were the decorations-elaborate decorations. The flowers alone cost more than Charley Hoke had been in the habit of receiving for a full-month's work.

The night of the party arrived. The children were more excited than Mayme. For days and weeks they had talked of nothing at school but what ma was going to feed the white folks at the reception.

The children had been scoured and scrubbed until their faces shone, hair slicked down as well as could be expected, and dressed in their best wearing apparel. Each child had been instructed carefully as to where he or she should stand or sit, what to say, and how to act.

Maybe had lined them all up and said, "Now, kids remember not to disgrace your daddy's fair name. Show this town you is a real Barke blue blood and has got manners."

Eight o'clock came. Eight-thirty. "The folks is tryin' to be fashionable late," Mayme explained. "I tole them specifically the time was eight."

At nine o'clock the children were crying for food. Jerry's feet were killing him for his wife had insisted he wear his pinchy shoes.

Mayme's new pink formal with no back and straps for shoulders, was wet and soiled. The cold sweat of apprehension stood out in drops over her tired face and fat body.

"All the folks couldn't have forgot, because I had it in the newspaper twice. Wish I had sent cards like I wanted to but the ole man wouldn't hear it.

Said it cost too much."

At ten o'clock the children were fed and put to bed. "Those pore white trash can't snub me!" she screamed with righteous indignation. Turning to the caterer she said, "I'm going to give a party for colored folks in Des Moines."

The invitation was given out that the Barkes were prepared to entertain five-hundred guests, mentioning the food to be furnished. A great cry of rejoicing went up at the other end of the telephone.

At sunrise the next morning, Novinger, Iowa, witnessed the greatest spectacle any self-respecting village ever laid eyes upon. Colored folks came for tens and twenties, some arriving in good cars, others in jalopies, many in trucks, others hitch-hiked, showing up later in the day. One old couple came driving a bony gray mule.

"Yes, one-hundred strong came to Mayme's house-warming party. And such rejoicing as went on. Had the town people been wise they would have attended the reception themselves, for this taste of gay life inspired the woman to give repeat performances which the villagers strenuously objected to and was the undoing of Jerry K. Barke.

Mayme declared she had not been so happy since she left her tumbled down shack in the slums of Boston, and that she was very, very glad the white trash had snubbed her.

The house, the basement, the barn, the garage, Ted's house and garage, every nook and corner were filled to overflowing with happy, noisy colored guests eating to their fill.

"Jerry K.," called Maybe, "hurry to the store for more corn beef and cabbage. Buy all they got. Welch rabbit and avy cody may suit white folks, but it's fried chick, and biscuits and corn beef and cabbage for refined colored folks."

"Good-bye, good-bye! Yelled Mayme to her departing guests at four o'clock the next morning. "Come back again!" The town rang with their happy voices. The hostess was weary enough to drop, but supremely happy, realizing that when she wanted a good time she would seek her own kind, her own race.

Strange as it may seem, reformers wage warfare, stir up strife, and preach equality of the races. But if left alone by fanatics each race will find its own happiness in associating and fraternizing with that race, not trying to to mix colors or attempt to prove which is the superior race. Neither will they intermarry.

For each race has superior traits of character, let them be proud of this, and not try to envy other, not seek to become like the other race. Any white man is ill at ease with folks of other races, so is the yellow man if forced to be thrown closely with a white man or Negro. The Negro finds happiness only with his own. Why will people keep up the strife?

CHAPTER XXXI

In garish headlines the notice appeared in all the leading newspapers of the land, declaring at last the genuine Lucy Travis Barke had been produced. The long looked for woman had not been murdered by the Barkes, and her picture was shown on the front page of the papers.

Elsie Hamilton stared at that picture and blinked her eyes in amazement. "Someone has discovered my identity! Ben Hooper has betrayed my secret!" She said to herself in frenzied alarm. "I never dreamed he would stoop to such an act!" She wondered where he had gotten the photograph.

Trembling with fear and excitement she began to read, then she drew a breath of relief. "That picture deceived even me! She looks the world like me! Who can the impostor be?"

The story was a masterpiece. A Jonas Frency had found the woman and was claiming the award money. She was a New Jersey high school teacher in music. It was so near the truth, Elsie was alarmed and speedily sent Jerry a telegram.

"Son. Those imposters may succeed where others failed. We must not let them get away with their deception. Come at once. Mother"

Ben came barging into her cottage soon after seeing the headlines. "Miss Hamilton, why are you delaying? Why don't you make yourself known and end this torture for everybody," he demanded indignantly. "Haven't the Barkes suffered enough to satisfy you, even the old man?"

"The revelation rests with my son and his wife, Ben I just got through sending him a wire, asking him to come. I feel confident he will be here soon."

In a surprisingly short time Jerry and his family arrived. "Mother, I'm claiming that award money," he announced as soon as he alighted from the plane. "Besides, I'm getting what is coming to me from the trial. There should be plenty for both of us. I can find heaps of places for a bunch of money."

"I'm asking for nothing, Jerry. I signed away my rights twenty years ago."

"Yeah, and didn't you sign a statement that you would never reveal your identity?" The Barkes and Doc would be powerful happy to have you break that oath and if they had any dough left, they would gladly give it all to you to save their necks. Besides, Doc forced you to take that oath when you we sick and scared nearly to death."

When they reached her home Elsie said, "Take a look at this picture in the paper."

"We saw it on the plane. It surely is a striking likeness of you. But we will fix those impostors."

"How, Jerry?"

"Wait and see, my sweet mother."

Elsie assigned much of her work at the seminary to her assistants in order to attend the trial which had reopened. Lang Smith accompanied her, for she felt it best not to be seen with Jerry and his family.

The new evidence came out clear and decisive. Neither the woman claiming to be Lucy Travis Burke nor her witnesses could be tripped up. The newly found Mrs. Barke, the first, was beautiful, and dressed with exquisite taste. She answered all the questions in a low, distinct cultured voice, tinged with a tragic sadness. From the moment of her first appearance In the witness stand, she carried sympathy of the court-room.

She was saying, "I clutched my babe in my arms and ran away from the little Lawton Hotel for shame," she wiped her eyes pathetically. "I could not bear to let any one see me because I supposed I was a Negro. I hugged my child to my breast lest folks see it was a mulatto."

The court-room was all attention and frequently stole baleful glances at the three culprits who sat pale and grim.

"I found a colored boy and paid him to go for my baggage. The hotel manager did not see him as he brought my belongings to me, then he accompanied me to the lonely mountain.

"Because I was so weak and ill I dropped down on a flat rock to rest. The youth set down my grips and went back down the mountain promising to tell no one. The shadows began to fall and the air was cold on that high mountain. My child was hungry and and I had nothing to give it. What could I do?" The woman looked out over the tense crowd with tragic eyes.

"All night I sat on that rock hugging my child to keep warm. I too was hungry, for in my weakened condition after the birth of the twins and because my husband never came near me, I had eaten scarcely enough to keep me alive. My darling child wailed piteously for food and because he was cold.

"Three days passed, no food for the child who was so weak I could hardly hear his feeble moan. Because he was so weak, I feared I might drop him. The evening of the third day I heard footsteps coming up the mountain. I called but was too weak to be heard.

Then Mrs. Johnson came nearer searching for her cow. When she saw me she screamed, for maybe she took me for a ghost-I was so thin and white. She picked up the child and helped me stagger down the mountain path to her house.

"One week later," sobbed the heart-broken woman, "we made a small mound for my child. Hunger, exposure, and neglect had taken his frail life. I continued to make my home with this sweet Mrs. Johnson under the name of Tillie McCall-I feared to let the Barkes find me. Yes, I feared for my life."

"For ten years I lived with Mrs. Johnson, then I returned to college at Columbus, Ohio. Five years ago I received my degree and returned to my chosen profession of teaching music. I taught in Benson, New Jersey, for three years, and for the past two years I have been employed in the Carson, New Jersey high schools."

Mrs. Alice Johnson, an elderly common-looking woman, corroborated the woman's story. Cross-questioning could not change her testimony.

Jonas Bollman testified that he had heard the woman's story years before while visiting his brother Jim who lived down in the valley from Mrs. Johnson in Boonville, Alabama. At that time he had considered it just another strange story of the ignorant mountaineers.

He said he thought no more of the story, in fact forgot it until he read the Barke murder case which swept the nation. Every day as he read that story, in the back of his mind was the tale of the woman his brother had related so long before.

"I just couldn't get her story out of my mind and finally I said to myself, 'Maybe Tillie McCall is the missing woman. If she is it is wicked for me not to give the court the benefit of my knowledge, for the lives of several persons are at stake'.

"I visited my brother, Alice Johnson, and the mountain community. Finding Miss McCall gone I traced her to Carson, New Jersey. When I contronted her with the evidence that she was Lucy Travis Barke, at first she denied it but finally confessed to the truth, but was unwilling to revel her identity to the court."

"It took me a long time to make her see she was free from the guilt of tainted blood, that it was the Barkes, not she, who carried Negro blood. It was pathetic to hear her sob, 'but now I can see dear John. I've loved him all these years in spite of what he did to me. And to see my little Jeanette will give me such joy, for night after night I have cried myself to sleep for her.

The various witnesses were cross-examined, but they could not be veered from their stories either to the right or left. Each told a concise, logical story and each stuck to that story.

The woman purporting to be Lucy was brought back for questioning. "Why didn't you go back to your father after the death of your child? Your father needed you badly when your mother passed away. Why didn't you return home then?"

"I feared someone would ask me why my husband discarded me, besides I thought that maybe some of the neighbors knew I was part Negro, so I just wanted to get away, to hide my shame. When the report came that the detectives were looking for me, I was more afraid than ever."

When the woman cast her glance in the direction of John Barke, she lowered her long curling eyelashes and held a filmy bit of handkerchief to her face. Her lovely pathetic face was enough to melt a heart of stone. Of what was John thinking as he heard her testimony and looked at her charming face?

On one side of him sat his father and Dr. Cunningham, while Jeanette was on the other side. For the most part, he sat with bowed head, or with his hand shading his face, cutting off his haggard features from the woman on the witness stand.

The woman was saying, "When I saw my dear Jeanette, so much like I looked at her age, it seemed impossible for me to go on the the witness stand-" she broke down and could say no more.

The court-room wept with the heart-broken woman. Even the men stealthily sneaked out their handkerchiefs and blew their noses.

It was true that Jeanette did look enough like the woman to be her daughter. Their eyes, their features, and their figures were identical. The resemblance was most striking. Both had golden curls, the woman's showing a few strands of gray. Yes, that court-room believed Jeanette's mother had returned to claim her. How happy the girl should be, thought the people at the trial.

The investigations continued on for days. All of their stories were verified save one about the infant son dying. That was a bit hazy, but twenty years is a long time, neighbors could forget. Besides, Alice Johnson's log cabin stood alone on the mountain side, the nearest neighbor being a mile away.

Pictures of Jeanette Barke along side of her beautiful, long-lost mother look most dramatic in newspapers. The handsome John also found his picture near the charming returned-Lucy. Folks took the story in gulps.

Ben Hooper listened aghast-the evidence sounded authentic. "I can't believe Miss Hamilton has deceived me. She can't be an impostor! But if she is not, why does she sit here and take the story if it is false? I feel like forcing her hand and claiming the reward. But what would I do with the money?"

It seemed certain that Doc and the Barke men would be cleared of the murder charge. Miss Simpson was delighted even if she was suspicious of the woman. But Rose and Lucile acted strangely, their smiles were unnatural and they laughed even louder than ever.

Finally Elsie invited Ben over to meet Jerry, her long-lost son. At once the two young men struck u a strong liking for each other, this in spite of the fact that Ben was impatient for him and his mother to disclose their identity and expose the impostors.

Jerry gave Ben an inkling of the strategy he planned to employ to catch the false witnesses, although he did not take his mother entirely into his confidence. From this time on the boys were close friends, although they didn't deem it wise to be seen together in public. Neither did Ben tell Jeanette of his friendship for Jerry.

CHAPTER XXXII

When Ben Hooper saw Rose and her daughter talking to Jonas Bollman in a most confidential manner, he was surprised. At sight of Ben the trio stared in confusion and quickly separated. He immediately informed Elsie and Jerry, whereupon the boys decided to do some sleuthing on their own.

Late that night they followed Bollman and the alleged-Lucy Barke down one street, up another, then across in the other direction. "There they go into Rose Barke's apartment! Why would they call on her in her miserable quarters at this unearthly hour?" asked Ben.

"We better find out why," declared Jerry in a whisper, crouching behind some shrubbery. "If we could get close enough to hear what they say! Surely they won't stay all night."

After an hour's wait the door opened and the charming woman emerged accompanied by Alice Johnson and Jonas Bollman. All were laughing and chatting in subdued tones.

"Pretty late hour for poor old lady Johnson, whispered Jerry.

"Slick work! It was Jonas speaking with a chuckle. "But why should Rose claim half the award? Haven't I done the work, assisted by you two?

It was the soft tones of the younger woman. "If Rose is my cousin, I" have to admit she always managed to get the lion's share of everything since we were kids together. But of course Jonas, she did originate the whole scheme, knowing how much like Lucy I look." Then the conspirators passed on down the alley out of hearing.

In high spirits Jerry and Ben hurried to the hotel where Elsie and Marvel were eagerly awaiting them.

"So Rose plans to make a pot of gold as well as save her own neck," laughed Miss Hamilton.

As the trial dragged on with its questions and cross-examinations, Jeanette felt more uneasy each day, stead of rejoicing. She wondered why she could not believe the story and accept her as her longed-for-mother? Surely they were enough alike to be mother and daughter. Every one else, that is almost every one, accepted her. Why not she?

She wanted to feel grateful to her for saving her father's life, yes, and for sparing her grandfather too. Why not take her to her heart and love her as a mother? She could not understand herself.

The questioning ended. The judge instructed the jury. "The charge is murder. You must decide 'guilty or not guilty'."

The court-room was tense. This had been the most spectacular trial in the city for a half-century. Now the mystery was cleared up, and seemingly romance in the making. Now that Rose had divorced John Barke, would he take this charming creature to his heart again? She seemed more than willing. Surely he should be grateful to her for saving his neck.

Jeanette leaned over and whispered, Daddy, aren't you happy?"

"Sure pet, why do you ask?"

"You don't look one bit happy. Tell me the truth, have you decided yet I that woman is my mother?"

"She is not your mother," he said hoarsely, holding her hand tight. "She is an impostor!"

"Do grandpa and Doc know?"

"Doc can't decide. Dad doesn't care who saves him."

It was only ten minutes until the jury returned with the verdict, "Not guilty!"

The crowd cheered. People gathered about the shy pathetic figure of the newly-found Lucy Barke. A few well-wishers shook the hands with the three men whose fate seemed so dark but a short time before. Strange to say, neither Doc nor the Barkes were among the admiring group around the heroine of the court-room.

Jeanette stood and stared at the scene before her. She wondered why Ben had not sat by them as in the past. He seemed to have developed a great like for this new acquaintance of Miss Hamiton, and she wondered who the handsome young man could be. She had never heard her teacher mention him in the past.

"And who is that snowy-haired-distinguished appearing woman sitting with Miss Hamilton?" She asked herself. "I never saw that other lady either and I thought I knew all of her friends. Miss Hamilton seems very fond of that funny red-haired woman and her golden-haired baby." Did she have a twinge of jealousy.

She thought it strange her teacher had not come to congratulate her father, grandfather, and the doctor. Then she remembered she had been very distant to all three men since the trial. "Could it be because she now knows daddy is part Negro? She continued to philosophize and watch the milling, laughing crowd. She was glad Lang Smith was not one of those who neglected the rescued men, and that he was talking warmly to her father. He had been very friendly all through the court proceedings. "Why doesn't Miss Hamilton marry him?" she wondered.

Jerry, Miss Hamilton, and Ben went into a huddle, with the red-head trying to listen in, the crowd oblivious of their presence. Just behind them the two elderly women sat straight and dignified, seemingly disdainful of all transpiring about them.

As Jonas Bollman, accompanied by his two companions, made his way swiftly down the aisle, Jerry arose from his seat, towering above the crowd. The trio were whispering and he wanted to hear, but was unable to do so.

Jerry's long legs strode toward the desk of the judge, while Marvel's small fists clinched and she sat tensely on the edge of the seat, her baby in her arms.

Two bright spots shone on Elsie's cheeks as she clung to Ben's arm. "Steady, Miss Hamilton," he said for he felt the violent tremble of her hand on his arm.

Harriet Kieth and Maude Hardesty stared straight ahead of them, the corners of their mouths tucked firmly in. At Elsies's frantic call for them to be present at the closing days of the trial they had loudly protested but had responded. "We will come, but you are making the mistake of a lifetime," they had told her.

Jerry shouldered his way to the front of the room, then he shouted, "Bar the doors! Arrest Bollman and the imposture Lucy Barke. Grab Alice Johnson, Rose Barke and her daughter. The conspirators are on their way to claim the award! All have tried to defraud the court."

"Arrest the idiot! He is drunk" shouted one of the deputies, two of them running for Jerry, who stood calmly in that babbling crowd.

"What do you mean by this, young man?" demanded a deputy. The hubbub was deafening, everybody trying to talk at once.

"Grab Bollman! Shouted Jerry, trying to pull loose from the deputy. "He is trying to climb through the window! Catch him!" The man was half-way through the open window that was directly above the fire escape. "Silence in the court-room," shouted the judge, pounding with his gavel.

Then the attention of the deputies and the court were directed toward Jonas Bolman instead of Jerry. Half-through a burly deputy grabbed him and pulled him back and hand-cuffed him.

"Grab that women," yelled Jerry as he saw the imposter-Lucy running out of the door, followed closely by Rose and Lucile, Alice Johnson puffing and trying to keep up but making a poor showing. "They are headed for the train!"

The sheriff and the deputies started after the women, while the noise and confusion in the room began to quiet down. The judge leaned forward, looking over the top of his glasses? Please come up here and explain to the court." His manner showed only respect for the boy.

People craned their necks to see what was going on. John Barke and his father straightened up, trying to see. Doc stood and peered over the crowd. The room became so quiet the drop of a pin could be heard.

Rose and Lucile stood by the back door guarded by a deputy, their faces as white as milk, their eyes flashing like animals at bay.

Then the voice of the young man on the stand said, "I am Jerry Barke, the long-lost son!" J. B. Barke sat up as if some one had struck him. His eyes bulged as he was seeing himself as he looked fifty years before.

"Your honor," said Jerry calmly, "I claim the reward for myself and my mother." All eyes were riveted on the youth before the judge.

Down in the audience a stir was heard. The people turned to see what was the new excitement. A strikingly beautiful woman on the arm of a tall, handsome man was making her way down to the front of the room.

"Who is she?" whispered a girl to a friend. "She looks like the twin sister of the other woman claiming to be Lucy Bark.

"Don't you know?" She is Miss Hamilton, head of the music department department at the seminary. My daughter takes lessons from her. Can she be the missing woman?"

"Oh, daddy! Miss Hamilton and Ben. It is true! Of course it is true!" sank half-fainting into her father's arms.

"She is Lucy! Cried John. Oh, my darling wife!" Great drops of sweat stood as beads on his forehead.

The judge was asking, in a kindly voice, "Young man, what proof have you for your statement?"

As Elsie stepped beside him he placed an arm around her and said, "This is my mother, Lucy Barke, known as Elsie Hamilton, long time faculty member of the Boston Girls' Seminary."

"Oh, you have other-" the judge started to say.

Seemingly Jerry interrupted. "We have witnesses present and all of the legal proof to substantiate our identities."

The death-like silence was broken by an audible gasp from the audience. Scores of people there knew and recognized Miss Hamilton and had often seen her with Jeanette Barke.

Some persons in that audience even remembered how the teacher had nursed the girl back to health after the physicians had given her up to die. Yes, the audience knew that at last the genuine Lucy Barke had been found.

John covered his face with his hands to hide the hot tears that rolled down his cheeks. "Oh, Lucy to think you would sacrifice your fair name to save me after what I did to you."

Jeanette's breath came fast, her eyes were like stars, and her cheeks were flushed. "Won't the court ever end? I must see mother!"

Dr. Cunningham turned to the old banker. "Such thick-headed idiots as we have been. When Miss Hamilton snatched Jeanette from the jaws of death last year why didn't we know she was her mother?

"And, J. B.," said the physician with a peculiar grin, "that handsome buck is the discarded mulatto child."

"Yeah, and he is my very image at his age. Really, Doc, when he ran to the front and shouted that first command I thought I was seeing the ghost of my youth come back to me."

"He seems to be a fine young man," said the doctor.

"He has inherited my brains and fighting blood," the old banker said proudly. "Sh! Lucy is talking."

"Said the judge, a mist before his eyes, "Are you Lucy Barke, former wife of John Barke?"

"Yes, your Honor," replied Elsie tremulously, scarcely above a whisper. "And is this your son, Jerry?"

"Yes!" She answered clearly and proudly.

CHAPTER XXXIII

Not one of the conspirators escaped. All were placed under arrest. Rose and Lucile snarled and cried, making a great scene. John Barke wondered why he ever had been trapped by such a coarse, unscrupulous woman.

Court was recessed until the next day, that the new evidence in the case would be examined. It really seemed unnecessary, for not one soul in that court-room doubted that Miss Hamilton was the missing woman and Jerry her son. However, there would be other legal matters to attend to.

"Surely the building will tumble down," snapped Maude Hardesty to Miss Kieth. The crowd rocked the place with their deafening cheers. People rushed forward to grasp the hand of Jerry and his attractive mother.

Eager reporters surrounded the pair. Cameras clicked as Jeanette threw herself into her mother's arms, John shyly waiting for some recognition from Elsie. Jerry stood proudly aloof from his father.

"May I call you brother," asked Jeanette timidly of the tall Jerry.

"Sure, sis, just you don't get too uppity with your college-bred manners. Remember, your twin brother is only a rough cowboy," and he gave her his best bear-hug.

When red-headed Marvel planted her baby in Miss Hardesty's surprised arms and rushed to Jerry, kissing him soundly, crowd went wild. "Jerry, my prince," she cried proudly. "You were magnificent." and the cameras clicked sharply.

When at least he could get her attention, John Barke humbly offered his hand. "Words cannot express my gratitude, Lucy."

At the name she had scarcely heard for twenty year she gave an almost frightened start. She managed to take the proffered hand for an instant, murmured a few unintelligible words, and attempted to make her escape.

Harriet Kieth smoothed her fluffy white hair with one gloved hand and said, "Just as I told you, Aunt Maude. John Barke is right after Lucy. Now that Rose has divorced him, he will try his level best to win her back. Look at them now! And the photographers are focusing their cameras on them."

Jerry grabbed the little music teacher by the arm, "Come mother, we must go." He purposely ignored his father's outstretched hand and pleading eyes.

"Jerry, my son, won't you forgive your father?" John asked brokenly. With a hard eye and a grim face the young man made no reply as he attempted to lead his mother past his father.

Miss Hardesty said with a grim sigh, "Harriet, Lucy is blushing like a school girl, while John Barke devours her with his eyes. I fear you are right and she will welcome the man with open arms. It is difficult to understand people these days.

Doc and old J. B. Barke waited near the door. As Elsie came by Dr. Cunningham silently extended a trembling hand, saying not word. Remembering it was he who had helped save his daughter's life, she took his hand in a friendly grasp. But when the old banker stepped forward with a wide grin of assurance, she shrank back.

Jerry clinched his fist and demanded hotly, "How dare you offer to touch my angel mother's hand? You vile piece of humanity? Were you not my own flesh and blood, I'd sock you." He hurried his mother out of the room to join the group waiting for him.

Seemingly everybody in that court-room had welcomed Jerry Barke's revelation. But to Lang Smith, it was the death knell of all his fond hopes. He felt that it explained why Miss Hamilton had refused to marry him. Hadn't she said to him in the beginning of his courtship, "Lang, I have loved and lost. I can never love again."

"But, darling, how can I give you up," he thought to himself. "You deserve happiness and John has learned his lesson. He is a prince of a man and he loves you with all his heart-that is easy to see."

Lang had brought her to the trial that day, just as he had every day since her return, but now he felt he could not face her. "Ben," he said, "will you see that Miss Hamilton, I mean Mrs. Barke, gets home? She will no doubt want to be with her new-found family and won't need me."

The following day new evidence was heard in court. To all appearances the Boston Girls' Seminary tuned out in a body to witness the sensation. There was not standing room for all who wished to hear and see.

One of Lucile's old pals remarked, "Isn't Jeanette's twin brother handsome!"

"And to think that Lucile broadcast that Jeanette's brother was black. Too bad he has a wife already. I wonder how your pal and her mother like their new boarding place?"

"Don't you dare call Lucile my old pal. I never did care for her, and since she had that Nigger brat no one wants to be classed with her, especially after the youngin' didn't even have a name. You know that she and that so called count can not be considered legally married since he got married under an assumed name." However this particular pal was one of Lucile's staunchest friends and admirers when both were attending the seminary.

But such is life. A charming heiress is a very different individual from a cheap, loud girl, who has hitched-hiked across the United States, dresses poorly, works in a Dime Store, and is finally arrested for conspiracy to defraud. However, she may not have been too deeply involved in the latter case, for it had been the work of her mother.

Although the trial had run for many weeks, when the genuine evidence was presented, the case was soon brought to an end.

There was scarcely a dry eye in the court-room when Lucy told her story. The cross-examination was considerate and gentle. No one doubted the truth of her testimony. To look at her anguished face as she told of her feeling of sorrow and shame because she was discarded and when she parted with her infant was evidence enough.

The sympathy was just as sincere when Jerry related his experience and told of the persecution and abuse heaped on him because he was neither black or white.

Even the men shed tears when he said he had prayed for proof that he did not have Negro ancestors and now his sorrow and fear that his little daughter would some day have a child that would belong to another race.

"But continued the father with trembling lips, "no matter what may come, my daughter can never escape her fears. She will fear to marry lest her husband discard her as was my poor mother."

Lucy's heart bled for John, for her son was ruthlessly trying to turn the dagger in his heart. Jerry wanted the court-room to see John and the old banker as they appeared to him. Neither did he spare Dr. Cunningham.

Harriet Kieth, the attractive, snowy-haired teacher of Parkhurst College tersely gave her part of the drama. People gasped with astonishment at the cleverness and daring of the shrewd planning.

Lucy's sheltered home life with its culture and refinement was pictured as a haven from the evils of the world. Then her great love and trust in the man who had cast her from his door with their infant son in her arms, just to cover his disgrace.

When she described Lucy's shame and grief at becoming a fugitive, seemingly deserting her beloved infant to save him from future sorrow and embarrassment, the audience was almost ready to fall on the old doctor and the Barke men.

Miss Kieth knew how to show the cunning and the scheming of Rose Garner to capture John Barke. And she was ruthless in her condemnation of the woman as step-mother to the lovely daughter of Lucy.

In her testimony she did not spare the culprits when she told the death of Lucy's mother, a death caused by heart-break at the loss of her daughter and the child, for both she and the father felt that they had been murdered. Because Harriet realized Lucy had sacrificed herself to save the necks of the conspirators, she could say nothing too hard against them.

As she enlarged on Jerry's persecutions at the orphanages because his father had deserted his mother and him, John Barke turned as pale as death, while Marvel sobbed out loud.

Maude Hardesty, the heiress, grimly told of Lucy's coming to her in Florida, describing her pitiful condition. Her stern denunciation of the Barke's duplicity and cruelty added to the already-strong feeling in the court-room.

During this testimony Miss Babcock whispered to Margaret Sonne, "Do you suppose Miss Hamilton, I mean Mrs. Barke, will be soft enough to take back her husband.

"If she does, she should be taken to a psychiatrist. Most of the Barke money will be gone by the time that smart Jerry gets through with them. Riches seems to be all they ever had."

Miss Babcock snapped, "If she deserts Lang Smith after all his years of devotion, it would be a cruel shame, and she would deserve to be unhappy with John."

Miss Kieth presented authentic affidavits from the two orphanages and the farmer where Jerry had lived, and the court carefully examined them.

Lucy kept wondering what had become of Lang Smith, feeling sure he was not in the court-room. Yet she was more than thankful that he had not heard the account of her past life. She much preferred he think of her as she had been.

How would this knowledge affect him? It worried her to think that he might not forgive her for seemingly deceiving him. Yes, even her name was fictitious, besides she was the mother of two grown children. "Was that the reason he had run away and did not take me home yesterday? I can't blame him for being ashamed of all this publicity and scandal," she said to herself. And besides that I am a grandmother!"

The trial was ended. Jerry congratulated himself on his shrewdness in exposing the impostor and conspirators and his own good fortune. Since his mother would accept none of the award money he received it all. Besides, he had received a large sum of money awarded him by the court for damages done to him by the Barkes.

The judge had said, "The young man has suffered much at the hands of these men. He has not only the mental and physical anguish, but was denied home, parents, love, education, and culture." John Barke and his father received heavy fines, a well as the doctor. Lulu's light fine was paid by the Barkes. Having no money Rose was given a year in the reformatory for her part in the Barke case and for trying to win the award by defraud. The three other conspirators were fined and given time to get to the first train to be out of town, on the promise they would leave the state immediately thereafter.

Jerry moved his sister's belongings from the dormitory to his mother's cottage. "At last my dreams have come true," declared Jeanette. "Mother, dear your home has always seemed to me to be like heaven."

Jerry had impatiently awaited the ending of the court proceedings so he and his family might get home to their ranch and stock. But there was another reason, a bigger one why he was eager to get back to Wyoming.

"Marvell, do you know what we are going to do with our money? He asked.

"Buy a bank like your grandfather? Or maybe you are going to buy back his mansion for him," she teased.

"Not on your life! I wouldn't give that man a meal if he were hungry." he declared indignantly. We are buying the Gold-Bar Ranch. You remember how it lies right against our land on the east. Then we will be the biggest ranchers around Sheep Run, counting your father's place. "We'll buy sheep and all."

Marvel was dressing the baby and did not answer. "Say, honey, is it all right with you?" he asked anxiously. "I hadn't asked your advice yet?"

"Of course it is all right with me. You know best. Dad is sure to say you are using good judgment."

Turning to his mother he said, "Now, mom, we expect for you and Jeanette to spend vacations with us on the ranch. But let me tell you something, if you marry John Barke, you need not think we will speak to you again."

"Son, don't say such cruel things about him, he is your father."

"Yeah! Mother, don't you realize he is dying to get you back? From what everybody says, he never did love that Rose, but has loved you'll these year, but remember this, he let them kick you into the street! You are done with that man!"

"Jerry, you are only imagining a romance, and you must always be kind to your father. He too has suffered, you can see it in his face. Imagine living almost twenty years with Rose."

"Well, mom, I've told you how I feel about it!"

To Miss Kieth and Maude Hardesty he said, "Come and visit us any time, stay all summer." He had the typical western hospitality, besides he was eager to repay some of the kindness Harriet and shown him and his mother in their day of need.

"Jerry," said Lucy, "I wish you would take time to visit Grandpa Travis. If you do not have time to spare now, try to make him a visit sometime soon. I shall write him at once about the trial and invite him to live the rest of his days with me."

John decided to stay at the hotel in Boston. He had neither a home nor a business to return to. And except for Lucy and Jeanette not a soul cared what happened to him or what he did. While he hoped to find a job in the city in some bank, it was going to be difficult for it was still depression days. Then too, he wanted to be near his daughter and Lucy.

J. B. Barke and the doctor left for Iowa, taking Lulu with them. To the physician it seemed strange to be traveling on the bus. For no longer did he own a plane. Not only was he unable to keep it, it had gone to pay for the fines and attorney fees. He and the nurse went direct to his office in Jamestown. His business had suffered, and besides his heath was failing, yet he felt like a young man again, thankful to face life anew. For hadn't he all but tasted prison fare and looked through cold iron bars? To him the sun never had looked so bright or the air smelled so fresh.

The old banker went to the country to see his wife. "Minnie, how is she?"

"Quite poorly. I have only been waiting for you to come to send for the doctor. You better have Dr. Cunningham come at once and check her heart.

"You didn't let her get wind of the trial in Boston, did you?" he asked sharply.

"Of course not. You know me, Mr. Barke." Minnie didn't mention the entire country had been breathlessly discussing his case in court in Boston.

Then she wondered to herself if some one had told Mrs. Barke; if that was the reason for her sudden pains in her heart. She remembered that two weeks before she had gone to town, and upon her return found Lilly Mansen there. Seeing Minnie leave, the neighbor had sneaked in at the back door. That very night Mrs. Barke became very ill. She dared not let the banker know about what had happened.

CHAPTER XXXIV

"Doc, is there no hope for her?" asked J. B. Barke brokenly.

"Her heart is extremely bad. There seems to be little hope of her pulling through. You see she is delirious. Perhaps it would be more accurate to say she is having hallucinations. See if you can catch what she is saying." The old doctor was gradually losing his sense of hearing, although he did not want to admit it to himself.

"Oh, Jerry, come and see me before I go. I am so glad you are alive, for I have loved and grieved for you all these years. I love you even if you are a Negro, you are my son. Lucy, let me see your dear face before I die. Pa, how could you deceive me-to think you would discard your poor Lucy—when it was you who carried tainted blood-"

"Doc, she is not delirious or having hallucinations. Well, anyway she knows something of what she is saying. Some one told her about the trial!"

"Minnie, you wench!" he said, running to find the woman. "Why did you tell her?" He grabbed the cowering old woman and shook her as a dog shakes a rat.

"Stop!" she screamed. "I did not tell her! Help! Lil Manson sneaked in and told her-stop! You are killing me!"

"J. B. Barke, let go of her! You beast, let loose of her," yelled Dr. Cunningham. He finally got the woman loose, then tried to reason with the enraged man. Seeing it was useless he said, "Run for your life, Minnie. Call the sheriff. He has gone mad."

Minnie ran to the telephone but before he could call the old banker broke the cord, then started for her again.

"Run for your life!" said the doctor, trying to hold the old man.

"The woman escaped through a side door and screamed for help. Two men in a near-by field came to the rescue. With their aid Doc tied the hands of the banker. "Carry him to that room farthest from his wife where she can not hear him. We better strap him down to the bed. I will give him a sedative to try to quiet him. He has high blood pressure that may cause a stroke any minute.

"Send out the sheriff and have the telephone company repair the telephone cord he broke. And please take this telegram to the office, for his son must get here as fast as he can."

Turning to Minnie the doctor said, "J. B.'s blood pressure has been high for years, and now since the trouble about Lucile's kid in California and with the trial, it has gone sky-high."

The man in the bed gave a diabolical laugh. "Ha, ha! I outsmarted them. Not one soul knows I am part Nigger. Kept it from my wife and all the world for nigh to fifty years. Yep, I got brains. Made way with Lucy and her brat."

Then his jarring laugh turned to terror and anger. "Minnie, did you tell her? You wench! I'll get you! My wife must not know!" With horrible shrieks of horror and fear he yelled, "I'm a Nigger! Why did my father marry a Nigger? Why couldn't I have pure blood like other boys?" Again his mood changed. "I'm a blue blood! Ha!"

John stood beside his bed, and asked, "Doc, will father ever be any better?"

"I doubt it, son. He is old and his blood pressure is very high, besides he never would be calm or try to save himself, but was always flying off the handle as you know so well. Now it seems that his mind is gone, and he seems to be violent all of the time, and chafes more than the ordinary patient at being restrained."

When poor little Mrs. Barke heard her husband raving, she became worse and that night quietly fell asleep never to awaken till the judgment day. She was laid to rest in the Jamestown cemetery in the grave once marked "Lucy Barke, Wife of John Barke."

Ben and Jeanette came home for the funeral, and most of of the people of Novinger turned out to pay their respect to the kind little woman they loved only from the distance. They knew she had died suddenly and surmised that her death was caused by the shock she received from the trial.

It was not long before the powerful and proud bank president of the Citizens' Bank of Novinger lay screaming in the psychopathic ward in the state hospital of Iowa. Where else could he be cared for? For there was no money to pay for a private institution.

After the funeral of grandma Barke, It was Ben's car that took Doc, John and Jeanette through Novinger to look at the old homes that had formerly belonged to the Barkes. They could scarcely believe their eyes. How could such a change be brought about in but a few short months?

The old man's home had fared the worst. The front lawn that had been the joy of the town as well as the joy of the Barkes was now filled with children's rubble. A playhouse graced the south side where once the pretty lawn chairs sat. Swings hung from three of the cedar trees, a tree-house was built in a tall cypress, while broken bicycles, rusty tin cans, a trike, a scooter, an old wheel-barrel, an old ladder, and a broken down glider filled the space in front of the big white house.

The lovely lawn north of the house had become a ball-diamond. Not one flower remained in the beds; the flowering shrubbery was broken down, and not a blade of grass was to be seen any place on either the front or the back yard, Most of the lawn furniture lay in broken heaps in the back.

Being so close to the ball diamond, many window panes were broken, while rags filled the space. The bright green shutters had been roughly used, some of them hanging by a single hinge. The railing of the front veranda was broken, and all of the paint gone from the front porch. A basket-ball basket was nailed to the west side of the house.

To Jeanette, the grief at seeing the beautiful house so abused was almost as great as the loss of her grandmother. John averted his eyes and said, "Ben, drive on. I can't stand to see any more. Maybe my house is still on the foundation. Please drive over there let us see."

Uncle Ted had done his best to keep the house and premises in good condition, but that was not easy with a dozen nieces and nephews visiting him many times each day to remind him their dad had given him the place. It wasn't that the children were any different from children of any race who had been brought up as these Barke children had.

In their slum home there had been little they could damage when they played, besides every child that had been old enough to work had done just that. Now the children had nothing to do, and with their mother to remind them that they they had bushels of money, they didn't feel the need of being careful, if they thought anything about it. This family is an example of what happens sometimes when someone gets rich quick. The money came too fast.

When their father tried to caution them to take care of the property, his wife interfered by saying, "Now Jerry let the kids have fun. They hain't had nothin' before. If somethin' gets busted, we can get it fixed or buy another."

John had a nice visit with Uncle Ted. "I'm glad to know you John," Uncle Ted said. "And I hope you will forgive me for bringing all this trouble on you and your family. When I wrote Jerry, my nephew, I hoped to bring only happiness, instead I brought a curse. To my brother, the banker, I caused insanity and to his wife death. John, you and Jeanette have suffered shame. But worst of all, the money has been a double curse to Jerry and his family. In the slums they were happy.

"I am miserable because I don't know what to do with myself without work. Jerry K. wants work, honest work so much he can't sleep nights thinking about it. Mayme hates the town and everybody in it because the white folk don't associate with her. Novinger hates us for squatting down in their midst, as they call it, while Mayme pushes them off the sidewalk and calls them 'Pore white trash' to their faces."

At this point in the conversation, Mayme's daughter Belle interrupted by saying, "Mr. Doctor, ma wants you all to come over for dinner. It's pretty nigh ready, chicken, biscuits, pie, and all kinds of awful good things to eat."

Courteously the doctor said, "Thank you dear, but I am with Ben, John, and Jeanette and Ben's family have already invited me to have dinner with them. Perhaps some time later we can accept your invitation."

"I would starve before I would eat in that dirty wench's kitchen, even if it is father's house," John said indignantly as they drove away.

At the dinner table, Mr. Hooper said, "Folks, I tell you this town has just had about enough of these darkies and is about to egg them out of town. The only reason we don't is because of our respect for Uncle Ted and Jerry K- they are both fine men, just as good and honorable as any white man. No better citizens can be found anywhere."

"It's not just a matter of living near a colored person, but the problem is Mayme and those children, and she is to blame for the way that they perform. They won't keep their place or leave us alone. They act as if they own the village. When we chance to meet that fat old gal on the sidewalk, we politely step aside and give her the right away or she will push us off. Usually most of us give her the entire walk, for the sake of safety. Give her an inch and she takes a mile."

"But you don't know the horrible part," put in Mrs. Hooper. "Mayme is trying to induce her husband to sell off the land behind the mansion to a bunch of darkies, friends of theirs. Won't it look nice to see a row of shanties surrounding the lovely house? Most of us have our homes for sale, for we are sick of the entire situation.

It was with a sad heart that John and Jeanette took a long, last look at their homes, the bank, and the little town of Novinger. As they drove back to Jamestown to take a bus to Boston, accompanied by Ben, they felt that life could be very cruel.

"Surely life is a mystery," remarked John. "A kind providence hides the future from our eyes. Had any one told me twenty years ago my life would be such a tragedy, I would have laughed in his face. Now what does the future hold for us?"

But as Ben Hooper looked into the eyes of Jeanette, he hoped he had found the answer. Youth can usually find a solution, if they are not too hasty or impatient. So now while John mourned for the past and dreaded the future, the two young people looked fearlessly to their future.

Upon their return to Boston, John went dismally to his hotel, while Jeanette went to her mother's arms at the cozy cottage. Ben reentered school and again life began to slip back into the routine after so many weeks of turmoil and upheaval.

As Lucy awoke awoke each morning to see her daughter lying peacefully by her side, she wondered if she were dreaming or awake. Surely this could not be happening to her after so many long years of loneliness and heartbreak.

CHAPTER XXXV

One evening not long after Jeanette's return from the funeral of her grandmother she asked, "Mother, could we have daddy here for dinner tonight? He is so lonely at his hotel. He has not found a position yet, and with nothing to occupy his time, all he does is sit and brood over his troubles."

"Y-e-s, daughter," she replied, trying to sound natural. "Tell Maggie to plan for one more, please. Should we count on Ben, too?"

"I had hoped you would say that, for he is sure to show up around meal time."

"Jeanette, you must feel free to invite your company here at any time, for this is your home. As you know I am busy at school, having lost so much time at the trial, so maybe I cannot always be here but make your plans and tell Maggie what you want and she will do your bidding."

That first dinner was an embarrassing one for both John and Lucy. But Ben and Jeanette were so engrossed in conversation they did not seem to notice the strained relations. After they had finished the meal John proposed that they all go to the theater, but Lucy explained she had a faculty meeting and would they excuse her.

John tried to hide his disappointment, for he was living just for one thing: a reconciliation with Lucy.

Almost every evening Ben dropped in, spending the entire time with Jeanette. Lucy was pleased to see him making progress with her daughter. He had waited long enough, and she was sure the girl loved him, only because she had know him all her life, it didn't seem the romantic love she expected.

One evening when Ben called to see Jeanette, Lucy said, "Where is Lang? I haven't seen him or heard a word from him since the day I revealed my identity at the trial."

"How strange! I see him quite often around the university. The last time I talked to him he thought that he might go to Palm Beach, Florida, for the winter. He mentioned he was not feeling too well and the winters in New England hurt him, and he did look a bit under the weather."

That night Lucy lay staring into the darkness, unable to sleep. She wondered if he would say good-by before leaving. He she offended him? Why did he treat her so?

The next evening Ben called as usual. In the midst of a conversation he said abruptly, "Mrs. Barke, I almost forgot to tell you. Lang asked me to say he had suddenly been called to Baltimore and he regretted he could not see you before leaving."

Lucy felt icy fingers clutching her heart. For years she had taken Lang for granted. He was here for all time. Had he found a younger woman? Maybe he had decided to marry a young girl. He was attractive enough to catch one. "Now that he knows I am a grass widow with two grown children, maybe he no longer is interested in me."

While she was mulling this over in her mind John Barke called and asked to take them all to the opera. "Ben, you and Jeanette would like to go wouldn't you?" he asked, yet not looking at them but Lucy.

When Jeanette saw that her mother was preparing to decline the invitation she said, "Please, mom, it will do you good to get out tonight," and she planted a kiss on her mother's cheek.

Lucy knew she had no plausible excuse for staying at home, so decided to go with them. However, before the evening was half spent she regretted her decision. John's eyes haunted her, they were so beseeching.

Upon their return while Ben lingered on with Jeanette in the yard, she was left alone with John for a moment on the front porch. "Lucy," he began, taking her trembling hand in his, "can you forgive the past?"

What could she say? She wished Ben and Jeanette would come on to the porch and prevent further embarrassing questioning. But she replied, "Yes, John, I forgave you when we watched together by the side of our sick daughter two years ago. Until then I was bitter, but I saw that you too had suffered."

"Lucy," he said, still holding her hand, "I've never known any peace since I lost you. I have never loved anyone but you–"

Just then Ben and Jeanette stepped on the porch. She had been so sure he never could touch her again, but she was more shaken than she cared to admit to herself.

After the the two men left she thought to herself, "I'm just a sentimental old fool. Lang is gone, and when another man comes along and says he loves me, I am flattered. My pride is hurt because I fear Lang has fallen in love with a younger woman. Tonight John was merely a salve for my wounded vanity." Was this true?

But Jeanette came dancing into the room, interrupting her thoughts. "Mother, oh mother. I'm so happy I could fly!" Gaily she whirled her mother about the room until both were dizzy.

"What now, my giddy daughter?

"Look mother!" She held up her left hand. The sparkling beauty told its own story. "Until tonight I never realized it was only Ben, for I never loved Howard as I now know I care for Ben."

Later John Barke too pronounced his blessing on the happy lovers. However, he was thinking more of his own interrupted words with Lucy.

"Mother," said Jeanette said that night, "If I dropped my teaching could I graduate this year? Ben insists we be married as soon as he graduates from the seminary in June."

"Yes, if you stop teaching immediately you could finish this June, too. Besides, you no longer need to work, for now I have a right to pay your school expenses."

"Father can pay my school expenses for he feels soon that he will land a job."

The next morning Lucy took the mail from the box. When she saw Lang's handwriting on a card her heart skipped a beat and her hand trembled. Then because it was only a card telling her he had arrived in Palm Beach and was sorry not to have seen her before leaving, she felt very sad. "Only a card, Lang, dear!" She said to herself.

She tried to reason to herself that they did have much in common with their daughter's approaching marriage. But reasoning could not settle her nerves or quiet her pulse.

John had not called to discuss plans for their daughter's wedding. This was an opportunity he dare not let pass by. He did not hesitate but said at once, "Lucy, you know what I would say. You have read my heart, and have nothing to offer but my love. Darling, do I dare hope?"

"Please John, I can meet you as a friend and as Jeanette's father, nothing more. Maybe you have guessed the truth-"

"You mean because I carry tainted blood? He bowed his head in shame.

"Oh, no John, not that! Is is because, er-I-"

"Of course no sane woman would marry a pauper."

"John, why are you so blind? So stupid? Can't you see that I love some one else?" Her cheeks were blazed and her eyes were downcast."

"You mean Lang Smith?" His face went white.

"Y-e-s," She faltered.

"Jeanette told me once that Lang had begged and begged for you to marry him for years. From that I decided you did not care for him, did not love him, otherwise I never would have asked you to come back to me."

"Because I supposed I carried tainted blood, I refused to marry Lang. Now that I now know the truth, I am ready to accept him. B-u-t-he-has-deserted me!"

"Deserted you? What do you mean?"

"He went away, perhaps for the winter, without even coming to see me or bid me good-by. Neither have I seen him once since the day at the trial when I made myself known. You see I had never told him my true name or that I had been married, because I had deceived him; he must have found someone else, some young woman, and oh, I love him so!"

"Don't worry Lucy, he will come back. I know he will. Since you can never care for me again, can't we at least be friends for the sake of our daughter whom we both worship."

"Yes, John. Please forget what I said about Lang."

The very next day Jeanette came home with the question, "Mother did you know that father went to Florida? He had never even mentioned to me that he was thinking about going on a trip. He left by plane with one of Ben's classmates this morning."

"Well, John Barke, when did you get here?" asked Lang Smith, grasping and extended hand in a warm embrace. "How is everyone at the Seminary?

Seems to me as if I have been gone a year instead of just two weeks. Guess I am no globe trotter. Home is the best place after all." He didn't look as if the beach had done his ailment much good.

"Lang, everything appeared to be much as usual around the college when I left yesterday. You probably know that Jeanette moved in with her mother, but did Ben tell you that he and she are to be married in June as soon as he graduates. It makes me feel old to have married children, and to be grandpa."

Lang Smith made no reply, his thoughts were too busy, he just gazed off in space.

John continued his bantering tone, "What's this about the dashing young widow or was it a gal you visited in Baltimore on the way down?"

"What do you mean Barke? I don't know any women in Baltimore. In all my life never have I had anything to do with but one woman. Guess I'm a one woman man. I loved and I lost. I can never love another," he said, quoting the very words Elsie had spoken to him years before."

"But, you, John. How come you are down here on the beach alone?"

"What do you mean?"

"Why, er, old man, aren't congratulations in order?" Lang tried to speak lightly, but he didn't feel that way."

"Smith, what are you driving at? Can you be referring to Lucy, my former wife?"

"John, I could not help but read your face when she made herself known that day in court. You once made a mistake, but have paid dearly for it. You are a good man and should be able to make her very happy. Lucy deserves happiness and so do you. With all my heart, I wish the very best for you both."

As he grasped his hand John replied, "Lang, if only your supposition were true!" he said huskily. "I too have loved only one woman, whom I foolishly cast aside, trampled on her heart. I would give my life to have her back. She kept avoiding me, finally when I pushed her in a corner, she made it plain. That is why I ran away, for I can not bear to be near her, knowing she never will be mine again."

Lang took a step nearer, looking keenly at the man before him. "John are you sure? Women sometimes love to play with men's hearts."

"You know Lucy would never trifle with any man's affections."

"Forgive me Barke. I merely said that to test you, and I am indeed sorry for you, old man. But say that reminds me that I have an important business engagement. Please excuse me. Be seeing you." His long legs made for the elevator.

He rushed into his room, grabbed the telephone and yelled, "Operator, Operator! Give me the airport! Hello! When can I get a plane to Boston? Not till eleven o'clock tonight? That's five hours. What's the matter with you?"

Lang set his steamer trunk in the middle of the room, opened the lid, and began pitching his clothes toward it. "Why did I bring all this junk anyway? Imagine me spending a winter any place but home. I can't wait to get out of here!"

He ordered his luggage sent to the airport, bought his ticket, and bolted a light dinner. Then he ordered a taxi to drive him to the loneliest stretch beach to be found. There he started walking and he must have traveled many miles, slushing through the mushy sand.

Finally he dropped down on a rock to rest, thankful that not a soul was to be seen as far as his eyes could reach. He took out his watch, and stared at it belligerently. "It must have stopped." But when he put it to his ear he learned it was ticking off regularly."

"Why haven't I bought myself a plane?" he growled to himself. "Prevent these disgusting waits."

In a surprisingly short time he resumed his patrol of the white sandy beach. Far down the coast he noticed the shadow of a lone figure sitting dejectedly upon a projecting rock. Curiously he walked in that direction, maybe because 'Misery loves company' he said.

John Barke turned with a start as Lang sat down next to him. "You too watch the stars come out, I see," said Lang with a hearty laugh. "Doesn't the moon look beautiful rising out of the watery horizon?"

"Yes, very pretty," John replied without enthusiasm. To himself he thought, "Well enough for Lang to rave about stars and moonshine. Such days have passed out of my life forever."

"By the way, Barke, I forgot to mention that I am leaving for Boston on the eleven o'clock plane. Sorry to desert you just as you got here, but pressing business. Word just reached me but a short time ago."

"Pressing business alright," John said bitterly to himself as he watched Lang's tall, erect figure make its way rapidly over the warm sand to the waiting taxi. He sat lost in thought, the past twenty years rising up before him like an ugly ghost."

He tossed a pebble into the roaring surf and said aloud, "At least I did one honorable deed to my credit. Why should I permit Lucy to cry out her eyes waiting while Lang Smith sat eating out his heart here at the beach?"

Once on the plane Lang wondered why the time was passing so slowly, and why the plane could not go faster. He said to himself, "I have urgent business to take care of in Boston!"

The stewardess looked curiously at Lang, noticing he was so restless. She had seen him before on the plane and he had always seemed so calm. She thought to herself, "Maybe this gentleman has sickness in his family."

With all of his impatience to get to Boston he spent a lot of time thinking about what he should wear and how he could look good. When he landed, he set out to execute that important piece of business.

When Lucy saw him coming, striding up the front walk, she knew she had never see such an attractive man, despite his unusual pallor and thinness. To the blushing, palpitating woman, hurriedly looking in the mirror to see if she looked all right, she walked toward her modern Romeo at the door.

She wished that Jeanette or the maid was there to answer the door-bell.

However, when he saw her standing there in the open door before him, all he could say was, "Lucy," and held out his arms. A few breathless moments later he managed to say, "Darling, I thought you were waiting for John Barke."

"You foolish man! Didn't you know that I stopped loving him long ago! Why couldn't you see and understand how much I wanted and needed you?"

"I guess I have been a stupid fool, dear. But I could not think of standing in the way of your happiness. To think that we have lost all this time grieving over our supposed loss. Let's forget it and settle down to the big and all important question; when shall it be darling?"

Lucy blushed and her dimple played havoc with Lang's poor foolish heart; then she became serious and said, "Mr. Smith, I am a widow, a grass widow, the mother of two grown children. Besides you do not want to marry a grandmother!"

"That is about enough, young lady," and he pressed his hard cheek against her soft curls. Remember this, you are one year, seven moths, two weeks younger than me."

"And there is something else, Lang. Do you forgive me for seeming to deceive you? Under oath, I had sworn never to divulge the past, and I could not break that oath even to you. When you ran off to Florida, I thought you had deserted me because I deceived you and had not told you my real name and all about my past, and I thought you would never forgive me."

"I forgive you for everything that you have told me and have not told me, and for every wicked deed you commit in the future except putting me off longer."

"Lang, don't you understand why I could not marry you years ago?"

"No, Lucy, that is what I can't understand, for I had supposed you still loved John."

"Can't you see, Lang, that I felt I could not marry you or any man because I thought I might have tainted blood."

"O-h! I see! Well, honey, I don't believe it would have made any difference, but I really don't know for sure. That is a difficult test, one I'd never want placed before me. But, Lucy- I just can't get used to calling you anything but Elsie-you still haven't answered that vital question."

"Oh, you mean-"

"Yes, you know what I mean, when will you be mine?"

"What do you think, Lang? When would you like me to dutifully say, 'I will'?"

"Christmas day, my sweet."

"Why Lang Smith, that is almost here! And with all my work at the college!"

"That is another thing, Mrs. Barke- I'm glad I won't have to use that name much longer-I am going to tell you something. I Lang Smith, President of the Board of Regents of the Boston Girl's Seminary, do hereby demand the resignation of Lucy Barke as instructor of the college for reasons best known to myself."

"Lang, we must talk that over. You mean you don't want me to continue teaching after we get married?"

"Of course not, my precious. I can not have my wife working! Couldn't you be content to take care of yours truly and boss the servants-my house has thirty rooms-I can not remember how many helpers I possess without counting them."

"I-I don't know, Lang. I had just taken it for granted I would keep on teaching-well, at least until I became too old and they wouldn't want me any longer."

"And as for the time of the wedding, it would be nice for Jeanette and me to have a double ceremony. Don't you think so? That would be about the first of June, when she will graduate."

"It would be most romantic for you to have double wedding, and I can't blame you for wanting it that way, but, honey, seems I have waited for you half-a-century. It is so long until June."

"I know, Lang, you have had to wait too long, but it could not possibly be at Christmas time. Besides, we need to think over and decide about me continuing to teach. It is all so sudden, for I didn't expect to see you until next spring and here you are trying to rush me into a marriage in almost no time."

"It perhaps is a bit sudden after all these years. And as for me taking time to decide when I want the wedding, I have definitely settled that to my entire satisfaction, also the question of your teaching after we are married. Still, Lucy, you have the right to be given a little time to come around to my way of thinking."

Then Jeanette proposed a solution. "Mama, why don't you meet him half way? There is no question about the date of the wedding-you and I are being married at the same time, and that has to be in June. "I'll tell Lang so too. And of course as the wife of that great man, you cannot continue teaching. If you give in and quit working when you marry, he will let you wait until my wedding date." And he did.

But Jeanette and her mother were not the only women who were considering wedding bells. For Lucile visited her mother in the Massachusetts Women's Reformatory for the express purpose of divulging her secret.

Unashamed and unabashed Lucile tripped up to the door and asked to see Rose. Greeting the woman decked in her fashionable prison garb, she said, "Mother, a few more months and you will be out of your iron cage."

And she quoted blithely, "Only a bird in a gilded cage and a beautiful sight to see." Then flippantly she announced, "Sorry you can't be turned loose in time for my wedding."

"Oh, darling, has he proposed already?" asked the woman, always excited over her daughter's romances, no matter what the character.

"Yep, he's scared war will break out and he might be drafted."

"Can't you wait until your poor mother gets her freedom again? I want to see my baby married."

"Jake is quitting his job as janitor of the Dime Store tonight and we will be married at the court house Friday, then we are going on the farm he has rented. I have already quit my job. We figure that if he is a farmer and has a wife to support, he will be deferred when the government begins drafting men."

"But Lucile you have only known Jake a month."

"So what? Wasn't that the length of time I knew the Count before I married him? Or perhaps it was a little longer and you were pushing us hard."

"Yes, and see what we got."

"Well, the store manager has known Jake since he started working there six months ago. He doesn't know his folks, and I did hear that his brother is in the penitentiary, but so is my darling mama. So with you a convicted criminal and me with Nigger blood, I can't be choosy. If he won't ask about my folks, I will be satisfied not to delve into his past or that of his people. He never reads the paper. He doesn't know a thing about my ancestry or supposed marriage, or anything about my exciting and colorful past.

"Mom, sometimes when I hear him reeling off his low-brow speech, with its horrible grammar I laugh to myself. Should I tell him I was once an heiress to the Barke millions and married a Count, he would lock me up in a psychopathic ward. Really, I doubt if he completed the sixth grade! And I? I am an accomplished pianist, having attended the Boston Girls' exclusive seminary, finishing two years! But he thinks me as a numb skull like himself because I can use slang and work in a Dime Store, besides, I can drink just as much as he and smoke, too.

"I don't feel happy about you marrying such a man, neither do I like for you to be tied to such a low, uncultured fellow."

"My grief is that I can't have a wedding like Jeanette. I hear it is to be a magnificent affair. And Lucy has turned down poor John Barke, my loving dad, to wed the rich and influential Lang Smith. Mother, they are to have a double wedding, and all of the seminary will be there, and I can't attend. Think of it mom, my own sister hasn't invited me to attend her wedding and I won't be permitted to step inside the church.

"And, mother, the Lang mansion is even more grand than the Everett home, and he has twice as much money. Surely this is an unjust world. Jeanette and her mother have everything and you and I have absolutely nothing.

"But I must be going, for I have plenty to do to finish my wedding dress and get the rest of my cheap finery ready. Perhaps we will be too rushed for me to see you again before the wedding at your lovely location. Yet, you shouldn't be lonesome with so many fine pals. Bye. When you get your walking papers, come visit us on the farm."

CHAPTER XXXVI

"Jeanette, we have not decided yet where we are to live after we are married next June," said Ben Hooper. "It is not too long until school is out and summer is here again."

"I have been thinking about that and talking with mother. Of course she wants me here near Boston, but were it not for the Jerry K. Barkes there is no place for me like dear old Novinger, Iowa."

"You know how I feel. City life here bores me to death, in fact I hate it. It may not be too bad for students and an occasional vacation just to see the bright lights and strange sights. But once seen what is there to life in a metropolis except high prices and noise? But, oh, just a few more months and you will be mine-"

"Children," began Lucy, joining the young couple on the front porch, I have a bit of news that might interest you. Maybe I told you I took over another Negro family in the slums after the elevation of the Hokes. This family regularly hear from Mayme. Guess what my new people told me today?"

"Has Mayme built a city hall in which to entertain her friends?" queried Ben.

"My guess that she has sold off part of the grounds of the mansion and have begun to put up shanties for a lot of her colored friends," was Jeanette's prediction.

"One more guess for me," Ben said. "They have knocked out the foundation of the big house."

"You are a mile wrong, for the family hate Novinger, even Mayme and the kids. Uncle Ted insists he will never be happy again until he gets back to his two-room shack in the Canadian woods to his trappings. For there he is considered a respectable, hard-working colored man. While in Novinger he is looked upon as a lazy, shiftless, good-for-nothing Nigger.

"Besides," continued Lucy, "the woman has squandered her money, sowing it like the autumn leaves. "She has handed out gifts right and left to folks back in Boston, put on house parties that cost enormous amounts, especially because she often kept guests for days in her home. Now they have about wrecked their finances."

Ben said, "Now that is just what I have been preaching for years. If the wealth of the people were divided equally among the people soon everybody would be back to where they started, given enough time. Give the pauper wealth and mansions, and soon his house is in shambles and his money gone to the winds. Now, probably this would not apply to Uncle Ted and Jerry K. who are poor because of circumstances, but Mayme holds the purse strings, does the managing, as she calls it, and that's why their finances are ruined.

"But I failed to tell you the most important news of all. All the Barkes, even Mayme and the children are eager to sell out and get back to Boston.

In fact, they are practically forced to sell. But because she despises the folks of the village, they have not let their straits be known and are seeking buyers elsewhere. Now, children, I was just thinking-" Lucy was not permitted to finish.

For Ben Hooper grabbed his hat and said, "Thanks, Mrs. Barke, for telling me. Good-by darling. I'm on my way to the telegraph office to authorize dad to cinch both of those places for me immediately. Even if the houses are almost demolished, they will be ours. I shall catch the next plane to Novinger. Hurrah, won't the folks in town be glad to get those darkies out of their midst?"

"Do hurry, Ben," cried Jeanette. "Some one else may grab the places."

"But no one in that community except dad and I can swing such a big deal, no outsider would care to settle down in Novinger, especially in such dilapidated houses. However, no grass shall grow under my feet on this deal."

"Oh, Ben you are an angel! Which house shall we live in?"

"That's for you to decide, but this is what popped into my head, just now. We can live in the mansion and your father can have his own house. When we want to entertain our Boston and Wyoming friends, your grandparent's house would be exactly what we need. You know when the

Lang Smiths call on us, we will want to put on the style, and with that house rebuilt, I'm hoping it may not be too bad."

"Ben, you sound like Mayme with her house parties," said Lucy, laughing and blushing.

"Your father could have his home, Jeanette, find a housekeeper, and I know I can get him in the bank again as a cashier, for dad and I owe most of the shares. John Barke would never be happy to work in any place but the bank. Then too, he will want to be near you."

"Benjamin Hooper, you are going to be the best husband I ever expect to possess! Won't father be delighted. I wish he were here. Now, mother dear, if you and Lang and Jerry and Marvel and the baby would only come and live in Novinger, Iowa it would be simply Paradise."

"Lang would never be satisfied to live any place but in Boston. I know I am going to miss teaching, but it will be nice to have time to do many things there never was time before. We will have our own plane-"

"Didn't I tell you? Lange is buying his own plane, so you see we will be practically your next-door neighbor. Why we can even get to your place for breakfast if we start early enough. Then when we want to visit Jerry we can pick you up and take you along to Wyoming."

After Ben left Jeanette said, "Mama, don't feel puffed up over your new plane. Did you never hear of the flying farmers of the Middle-West? While we may live in town, like people of ancient times, we still will be farmers, for Ben has hundreds of acres to look after. Well, he plans to buy a plane within the coming year, maybe as soon as we make the house livable."

Then school was drawing to a close, with Ben and Jeanette receiving their long looked for sheep-skins. It had been a hurry-gurdy time with the girl having to give her recital, and she and her mother shopping for their trousseau s. Although they never discussed it, both women remembered another such preparation two years before. To both it seemed a lifetime, so much had taken place since that memorable day, Now they were blissfully happy, with no sinister cloud hanging over their heads.

Seemingly all skeletons had been dragged from their closets, carefully examined under the microscope, and disposed of. No longer did Lucy fear some ghost would rear its head to embarrass or frighten her. Even Jeanette faced the future with its mysteries and uncertainties with clear, confident eyes. With Ben by her side, what could trouble her world?

The wedding was to take place in Boston early in June, soon after the closing of school. Both students and faculty members had been given a most cordial invitation and were eager to attend to show honor to their teacher and lovely daughter, although they were disappointed that Lucy would not be their instructor again.

Lucy and Jeanette also had to make preparations for their house guests; Jerry and family, grandfather Travis, Maude Hardesty, and Harriet Kieth.

However, Father Travis changed his mind at the last minute.

"Daughter dear, he wrote, "I'd love to come and attend your wedding, and especially to see you and my grandchildren, but I am too old to venture forth. You could never induce me to fly in one of those new-fangled contraptions. Lucy, I haven't long to live and I prefer to play it safe.

"Thank you for inviting me to live with you and your new husband, but you know I would soon die all penned up in a city. Come visit me, but I'm staying in my own little house."

Jerry and Marvel and the baby arrived. "Mother, it is a good thing you are marrying Lang Smith instead of John Barke. How did you manage it?"

One of the prettiest church weddings ever witnessed by the Boston Girls Seminary was that of the double-wedding of Lucy and Jeanette Barke. The guests could not decide which was the more attractive, the mother or the daughter. Each groom knew his bride was the prettiest. All agreed that it was the happiest wedding ever looked upon.

THE END

Printed in the United States
By Bookmasters